Ultimate
AIRCRAFT

BRITISH AEROSPACE/
AÉROSPATIALE CONCORDE

GRUMMAN F8F
BEARCAT

Ultimate
AIRCRAFT

PHILIP JARRETT

A Dorling Kindersley Book

Dorling DK Kindersley

LONDON, NEW YORK, SYDNEY, DELHI,
PARIS, MUNICH, and JOHANNESBURG

Project Art Editor Jamie Hanson
Project Editor David Tombesi-Walton
US Editors Chuck Wills, Gary Werner
Assistant Designer Nigel Morris
DTP Designer Jason Little
Production Elizabeth Cherry, Silvia La Greca
Picture Researcher Anna Grapes
Photographer Gary Ombler

Managing Art Editor Nigel Duffield
Senior Managing Editor Jonathan Metcalf

Additional editorial assistance
Reg Grant, Frank Ritter
at Grant Laing Partnership

Published in the United States by Dorling Kindersley Publishing, Inc.,
95 Madison Avenue, New York, New York 10016

First American Edition, 2000

2 4 6 8 10 9 7 5 3 1

Library of Congress Cataloging-in-Publication Data

Jarrett, Philip.
    Ultimate aircraft / Philip Jarrett.
        p. cm.
    Includes index.
    ISBN 0-7894-5961-2
    1. Airplanes--History. 2. Airplanes--Pictorial works. I. Title.

TL670.3 .J37 2000
629.133'34'09--dc21
                                                        00-025755

Color reproduction by GRB Editrice, Verona, Italy
Printed and bound by L. Rex Printing Company Ltd., China

see our complete catalog at
www.dk.com

LOCKHEED T-33

GRUMMAN F7F TIGERCAT

CONTENTS

PART ONE
THE HISTORY OF AIRCRAFT 6–17

PART TWO
GALLERY OF AIRCRAFT 18–141

WESTLAND DRAGONFLY

INTERIOR OF VICKERS VISCOUNT

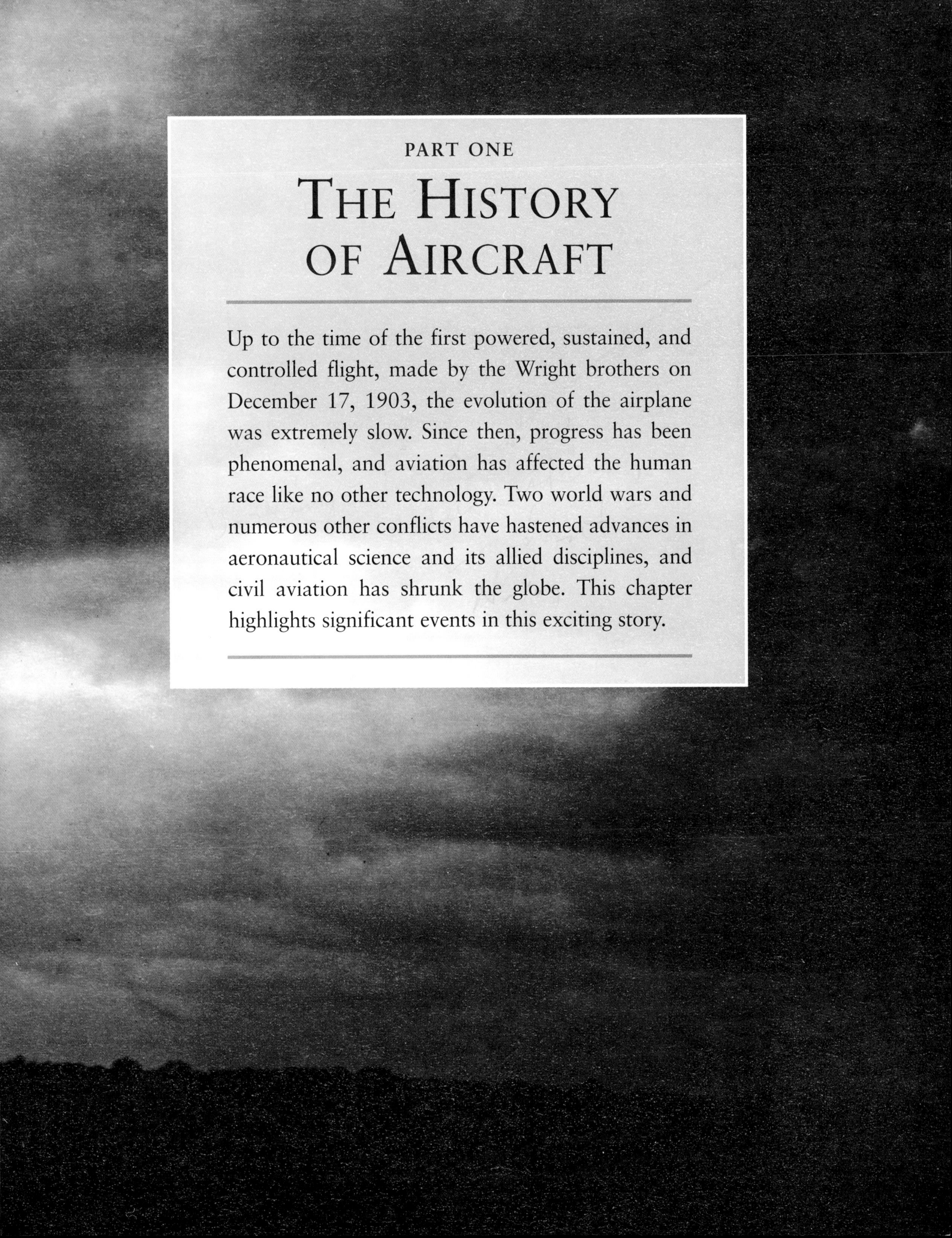

THE HISTORY OF AIRCRAFT

Up to the time of the first powered, sustained, and controlled flight, made by the Wright brothers on December 17, 1903, the evolution of the airplane was extremely slow. Since then, progress has been phenomenal, and aviation has affected the human race like no other technology. Two world wars and numerous other conflicts have hastened advances in aeronautical science and its allied disciplines, and civil aviation has shrunk the globe. This chapter highlights significant events in this exciting story.

The HISTORY of AIRCRAFT

The success of aviation in the twentieth century has made it easy to forget how remarkable an achievement flight is. The first powered airplanes were the end product of almost 100 years of courageous experimentation. The rapid development of aircraft since that time has been the result of numerous triumphs of invention and applied science.

FANTASY FLIGHT

Engravings of English inventor W.S. Henson's "Aerial Steam Carriage" flying over exotic regions of the world were widely published in the early 1840s despite the fact that a full-size version of the aircraft was never even built. Henson's design was a monoplane with twin pusher propellers, fabric-covered wooden wings, a tricycle undercarriage, and an enclosed nacelle for the pilot and passengers.

The human desire to fly like the birds can be traced back to the earliest days of recorded history. The legends of ancient peoples often contain colorful accounts of flights, perhaps most famously in the Greek myth of Daedalus and his son Icarus, who used wings of feathers embedded in wax to escape imprisonment on the island of Crete – with tragic consequences for Icarus, who plummeted to his death after flying too close to the sun.

Probably the first person to give serious thought to human flight was the great artist and scientist Leonardo da Vinci (1452–1519), whose manuscripts, tragically hidden from public view for centuries, contain copious observations on bird- and batflight and descriptions and drawings of human-powered flying machines – mostly ornithopters (flapping-wing devices), but also including a type of helicopter.

BALLOONS AND GLIDERS

When humans really took to the air for the first time, however, it was beneath a balloon. François Pilâtre de Rozier became the first aeronaut when he made a tethered ascent in a Montgolfier balloon at the French court at Versailles on October 15, 1783. With the Marquis d'Arlandes, de Rozier made the first untethered balloon flight the following month. For many years after, aeronauts in balloons had no control over the direction of their flight. The first powered flight in a dirigible, or steerable, balloon was made by Frenchman Henri Giffard on September 24, 1852. This line of development eventually led to the airships produced by the German Count Zeppelin from 1900 onward.

Heavier-than-air aviation traces its origins back to the early nineteenth century, when Sir George Cayley, a baronet from Yorkshire, England, took

up the study of flight. In 1804 he made the first proper model airplane, a glider 5 ft (1.6 m) long. By 1809 he had built a full-sized glider which was successfully flown uncrewed, and in 1809–10 he published a three-part paper, entitled *On Aerial Navigation*, in which he laid the foundations of the modern science of aerodynamics.

In 1842, English lacemaker William Samuel Henson developed a remarkable design for an "Aerial Steam Carriage." The following year he patented it and set up the Aerial Transit Company in an effort to form what we would now call an airline to operate worldwide services. Helped by John Stringfellow, who devised light steam engines, Henson built and tested a model with a 20-ft (6-m) wingspan during 1844–47, but it achieved only slowly descending powered glides.

Henson's experiments stirred Cayley into action again, and in 1849 he built a full-size triplane with a flapper propulsion system. In this machine a ten-year-old boy made both free and towed flights, reportedly of "several yards." This boy was the first person to fly in a heavier-than-air aircraft. In 1853 Cayley built another machine, in which his reluctant coachman made an unpiloted gliding flight across a dale on Cayley's Brompton estate. The coachman then tendered his notice to his employer, saying: "I was hired to drive, and not to fly."

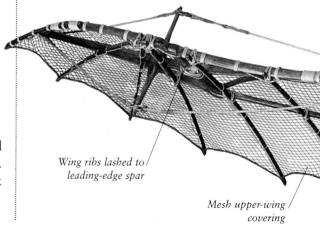

Wing ribs lashed to leading-edge spar

Mesh upper-wing covering

Streamlined envelope containing lifting gas

Experiments with heavier-than-air flight also took place in France, and French naval officer Félix du Temple de la Croix built the first powered airplane able to sustain itself in the air. A monoplane with swept-forward wings, a retractable undercarriage, and a hot-air engine driving a tractor propeller, it took off briefly after a downhill run in 1874.

STEAM MACHINES

The last two decades of the nineteenth century saw a flurry of experiments with ambitious steam-powered airplanes. In Russia in 1884 Aleksandr Fedorovich Mozhaiskii's large monoplane, powered by two steam engines, with a mechanic at the helm, was launched down a ramp but crashed after a short hop. French electrical engineer Clément Ader came to the fore in 1890 when he tested his bat-winged *Éole*, a monoplane powered by a 20-hp steam engine, at Armainvilliers. Although ungainly and unpractical, it did leave the ground for about 165 ft (50 m), but it lacked an adequate control system. In England, expatriate American inventor Sir Hiram Maxim spent nearly £20,000 building an enormous multiplane "test rig" powered by a pair of ingenious 180-hp steam engines. The machine underwent its main trial in July 1894, but the inadequately controlled apparatus was damaged and further tests were abandoned.

Meanwhile, another group of brave pioneers had decided to take an alternative approach, starting with small, primitive hang gliders in which they launched themselves into the air. Foremost among these was the German engineer Otto Lilienthal, who, starting in 1891, built and flew a series of 12 biplane and monoplane gliders until his death, as the result of a crash, in 1896. Photographs of Lilienthal soaring over spectators' heads were widely published, and he sold several examples of his most successful glider, the No. 11 of 1894, to fellow experimenters.

By the 1890s the gasoline engine had emerged as an alternative to the steam engine. In 1899 Lilienthal's greatest disciple, Englishman Percy Pilcher, was preparing to fit a gasoline motor to a newly completed triplane when he was killed in a gliding accident. In 1901, Samuel Pierpont Langley, the eminent American astronomer, flew a quarter-size model powered by a gasoline engine – the first gas-powered airplane to fly. Langley completed a full-size machine two years later. Powered by a remarkable radial engine, it was twice launched by catapult from a houseboat on the Potomac River, Washington, D.C., in October and December 1903, but on both occasions it suffered structural failure and plunged into the water.

THE WRIGHT STUFF

Only nine days after the second of Langley's spectacular failures, the world's first powered, sustained, and controlled flights took place in obscurity, in a remote part of North Carolina.

MUSCLE POWER

This modern reproduction is based on Leonardo da Vinci's designs of the late 1490s for an ornithopter, or flapping-wing aircraft. The fabric wing covering was arranged as a series of flaps that closed against the netting upper surface on the downstroke to form a lifting surface, but opened on the upstroke to let the air pass through.

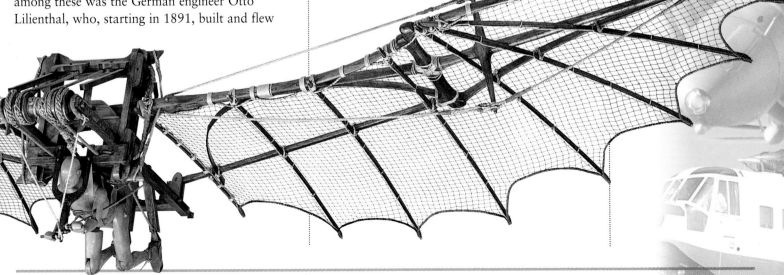

HISTORIC IMAGE

Without doubt the most famous photograph in aviation history, this image captures the Wright brothers' first *Flyer* as it takes to the air on the world's first powered, sustained, and controlled flight, at Kitty Hawk, North Carolina, at 10.35 a.m. on December 17, 1903. Orville Wright was at the controls. Three more flights were made that day, the brothers taking turns to fly their creation.

FLYING PUZZLE

Louis Blériot's epoch-making cross-Channel flight from Les Baraques, near Calais, France, to Northfall Meadow near Dover Castle, England, on July 25, 1909, formed the subject of all manner of souvenirs, including this jigsaw puzzle. Blériot won a £1,000 prize from the *Daily Mail*, and his No. XI monoplane became a best seller, remaining in production until 1914.

Spurred into action by the news of Lilienthal's death in 1896, two brothers, Wilbur and Orville Wright, who ran a bicycle business in Dayton, Ohio, studied the work both of earlier pioneers and of their contemporaries and then, from 1899, embarked on an unprecedented series of trials and experiments. As well as flight-testing their own gliders, they conducted windtunnel tests, and devised the first effective three-axis control system, with a rudder to control yaw (side-to-side movement), a forward elevator for pitch (up and down), and a means of applying a helical twist to the wings – "wing warping" – for lateral (roll) control.

Having tested the system in a series of gliders from 1900 to 1902, they then designed and built a powered airplane, also designing and building its 12-hp gasoline engine, which drove twin pusher propellers. Their efforts were rewarded at Kitty Hawk, North Carolina, on December 17, 1903, when the *Flyer* made four flights from level ground into a wind of 20–27 mph (32–43 km/h), the fourth and best covering 852 ft (260 m) in 59 seconds. The machine's airspeed was about 30 mph (48 km/h).

Over the next two years the Wright brothers perfected the design, and their *Flyer III* of 1905 was the world's first practical powered airplane, capable of long, fully controlled flights.

Instead of revealing their creation to the world, the Wrights now stopped flying and set about selling it. They realized its potential as a military scouting machine, but were loathe to reveal too many details in case their ideas were stolen. Although they stated that any contract would be null and void if the airplane failed to perform as required by the customer, the public failures of eminent scientists such as Ader and Langley, and the pretentious claims made by charlatans and speculators, had made governments wary. Selling the *Flyers* proved even harder than creating them.

FLYING FRENZY

Meanwhile there had been a reawakening of flight experiments in Europe. Stirred into frenzied action by news and pictures of the Wright gliders, several French pioneers, including Captain Ferdinand Ferber, Robert Esnault-Pelterie, and Gabriel Voisin, began experimenting with crude copies. In Germany Karl Jatho had begun making tentative flights in 1903; in Denmark Jacob Ellehammer achieved some success with monoplanes, biplanes, and then triplanes during 1906–08; and in England Alliott

FRENCH ELEGANCE

Antoinette monoplanes designed by Léon Levavasseur competed successfully in many early flying meetings. This version of the Antoinette IV of 1908–09 has ailerons; others had wing warping.

Sprung outrigger balancing wheel

Verdon Roe and expatriate American Samuel Franklin Cody (born Cowdery) were slowly working toward powered flight.

Paris-domiciled Brazilian airship pioneer Alberto Santos-Dumont made the first officially recognized powered flight in Europe in 1906 in his 14*bis*, a cumbersome tail-first biplane. The flight, on 23 October, covered only 197 ft (60 m), but another flight on November 12 covered 722 ft (220 m).

Things really began to stir in 1908. In France the Voisin brothers were developing a box-kite biplane displaying the influence of both the Wrights and the boxkite invented by Lawrence Hargrave in Australia. Using modified Voisin biplanes, Henry Farman and Léon Delagrange began to make creditable if somewhat precarious flights. The forebears of the successful Antoinette and Blériot monoplane families also appeared. Then, in August and September 1908, Wilbur Wright gave a series of demonstration flights in France that made the Europeans realize how far ahead the Wrights were. Orville, meanwhile, was undertaking military

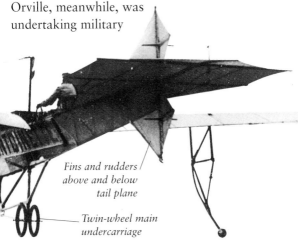

Fins and rudders
above and below
tail plane

Twin-wheel main
undercarriage

trials at Fort Meyer, Washington, D.C. Tragically, his passenger, Lt. T.E. Selfridge, was killed on September 17 when the airplane crashed following a structural failure. In 1909, however, a replacement machine was to pass the US Signal Corps trials and become the world's first military airplane.

Another significant event, late in 1908, was the appearance of the first of the Gnome rotary engines, developed by the Seguin brothers in France. These remarkable engines, in which the cylinders and propeller revolved around the stationary crankshaft and were therefore self-cooling, doing away with the added burden of a water-filled radiator, played a prominent part in aviation's early days, through to the end of World War I and even beyond.

Thus was heralded the true dawn of heavier-than-air flight in 1909. Two major events in that year stand out above all others: Louis Blériot's momentous flight across the English Channel on July 25 in his No. XI monoplane, and the first airplane meeting in history, the Reims aviation week in France, which took place in August. Although the American Glenn Curtiss won the speed contest at Reims, at 43.38 mph (69.8 km/h), the US was now set to lose its lead in the new technology to mainland Europe.

STEADY PROGRESS

In the period between 1910 and 1914 aviation technology progressed steadily. Three principal configurations – the pusher and tractor biplane and the tractor monoplane – became established. The most popular types were Farman biplanes and Blériot monoplanes, both of which were widely exported and copied.

For their structure, most airplanes used a frame of wood with a covering of fabric. Among the most notable exceptions to this rule were the Deperdussin racing monoplanes of 1912–13, which had beautifully streamlined monocoque fuselages of molded plywood. One Deperdussin machine attained a world record speed of 126.6 mph (203.8 km/h) in 1913.

Practical seaplanes and flying boats were pioneered by Glenn Curtiss in the US and the Short brothers in Britain. Between 1910 and 1912 the first takeoffs from ships, both at anchor and under way, were accomplished. The Schneider Trophy seaplane contest was initiated at Monaco in 1913.

As flights carrying small cargoes and air mail began to explore the peaceful potential of the airplane, the major powers started to look into

AIRCRAFT ARTWORK

People flocked in their thousands to the popular aviation venues of the pioneer era. One of the greatest was the London Aerodrome at Hendon, established by pilot and entrepreneur Claude Grahame-White in 1910. The proximity of two mainline railway stations made it accessible, but visitors could also take the underground railway (as advertised in this period poster) to Golders Green and then continue by bus.

WAR GREETINGS

Designed by artist and Royal Flying Corps pilot Flt. Cdr. Roderic Hill, this Christmas card from the Western Front shows the Nieuport 17 scouts of 60 Squadron. The nearest aircraft is the one flown by Albert Ball, Britain's first recognized air hero.

CIERVA AUTOGIRO

its military uses, experimenting with gun-carrying and bomb-dropping, as well as aerial reconnaissance. Airplanes were first used in warfare by the Italians, during a war against the Turks in Tripolitania, North Africa, in 1911–12.

When World War I broke out in August 1914 the major European powers were equipped with assorted airplane types, many unsuited to operation in the field. On November 21, three Avro 504s of the RNAS (Royal Naval Air Service) flew from Belfort to bomb the Zeppelin works at Friedrichshafen, and on January 19, 1915, the first Zeppelin raid on the English mainland was launched, bombs being dropped on the coast of East Anglia. By the time the German airship raids reached their peak in 1916, the defensive airplanes were gaining the upper hand. The decisive antiairship weapons were tracer and incendiary or explosive ammunition, introduced in mid-1916.

WARTIME INNOVATIONS

The first bombsight appeared in 1915, the year that also saw the introduction of the first successful machine-gun interrupter gear. This allowed a machine gun to be fired directly forward through the arc of a revolving propeller. Developed by Fokker engineers in Germany and fitted to the company's Eindecker single-seat scout monoplanes, it caused serious Allied losses until effective pusher scouts such as the Airco D.H.2 and Royal Aircraft Factory F.E.8, and Nieuport biplanes with guns mounted on their upper wing center sections, started to restore the balance. For artillery

COMBATIVE CAMEL

One of World War I's greatest fighters was the Sopwith F.1 Camel, which claimed more enemy aircraft than any other Allied fighter. Tricky to fly because of the forward concentration of weight and the torque of its rotary engine, it was extremely agile in the hands of an experienced pilot.

Twin Vickers .303-in machine guns on nose

B6291

Bungee-sprung undercarriage

observation and reconnaissance, reversal of the pilot's and observer's positions, placing the pilot in front, enabled the observer to put up a better defense against fighters, using a movable gun or guns mounted on a ring encircling the rear cockpit.

Bombers grew steadily in size through the war and night-time raids became routine, speeding the development of nightfighter operations. The Gotha G.V, one of Germany's greatest long-range bombers, could carry six 110-lb (50-kg) bombs in raids on England in 1917. By the war's end the RAF (Royal Air Force) was operating the Handley Page O/400, which could carry up to 2,000 lb (900 kg) of bombs, and Germany had developed a range of giant aircraft such as the four-engined Staaken R.VI, which had a maximum bomb load of 4,400 lb (2,000 kg).

The best German fighter at the war's end was the Mercedes- or BMW-engined Fokker D.VII. Britain had the Sopwith Camel, powered by a Clerget, Le Rhône, or Gnome Monosoupape rotary engine, and the Royal Aircraft Factory S.E.5a. France had the Hispano-Suiza-engined SPAD S.XIII. The RNAS used the Felixstowe F.2A twin-engined flying boat effectively for antisubmarine patrols, and the first true aircraft carrier, HMS *Argus*, equipped with Sopwith Cuckoo torpedo bombers, joined Britain's Grand Fleet in October 1918.

AERODROME DU BOURGET

Service régulier Paris-Londres. "l'Aérobus Goliath" de la C⁴ des Grands Express Aériens

CHANNEL HOPPER

On September 18, 1928, this Cierva C.8L Autogiro became the first rotating-wing aircraft to fly across the English Channel; the pilot was its inventor, Spaniard Juan de la Cierva. This photograph was taken in 1926.

FROM WAR TO PEACE

After the war ended in 1918, aircraft industries and air arms were allowed to run down. Nations went on using World War I airplanes for military duties and also converted them to fulfill civilian roles. In France, the Farman Goliath bomber was turned into an airliner. In Britain, the Vickers Vimy – used for the first nonstop transatlantic flight and the first England–Australia flight in 1919 – evolved into the Vimy Commercial, and the Handley Page bombers began to metamorphose into a family of airliners. Through the 1920s, pioneering long-distance and route-surveying flights began to prepare air links between the world's cities, but air transportation grew only slowly, remaining overwhelmingly the preserve of the wealthy and powerful.

Most airplanes in the postwar period still used the traditional wire-braced wood-and-fabric structure, though Fokker's airliners had welded steel tube fuselages and Junkers' products were all-metal, with corrugated skinning. The decade saw an important episode in the evolution

of the helicopter: Spaniard Juan de la Cierva's development of the Autogiro. This machine had a passive rotor that windmilled as the aircraft went along, but Cierva developed the articulated rotorhead – allowing the individual blades to move in the vertical and horizontal planes – that would eventually enable a practical helicopter to be built.

Private flying began to develop as a sport and pleasure for the wealthy. Small single- and two-seaters, such as the de Havilland D.H.60 Moth, and cabin biplanes and monoplanes for touring, were produced in all of the industrialized nations. Some of their owners used them to make impressive record-breaking long-distance flights that drew much attention in the media.

The Schneider Trophy contests – which ended in 1931 when the trophy was won outright by Britain – did much to encourage the development of powerful engines and streamlined airframes. By the late 1920s and early 1930s, metal increasingly began to replace wood in airframe structures, although these were still largely fabric-covered.

During the 1930s the US resumed a leading role in aviation. The appearance of the twin-engined, ten-seat Boeing Model 247 airliner in 1933 heralded a radical change. An all-metal low-wing monoplane with a retractable undercarriage, the 247 was nearly twice as fast as its European

GENTLE GIANT

Begun as a bomber late in World War I, the Farman F.60 Goliath emerged as one of the most important early passenger transports. Powered by Salmson nine-cylinder radial engines, it carried eight passengers in the rear cabin and four in the front, with the raised open cockpit for the crew of two in between.

POPULAR MOTH

The de Havilland D.H.60 Moth family of light aircraft was popular for recreational flying and long-distance record attempts in the interwar years. Built in 1928, this D.H.60X was powered by a 105-hp Hermes II four-cylinder engine.

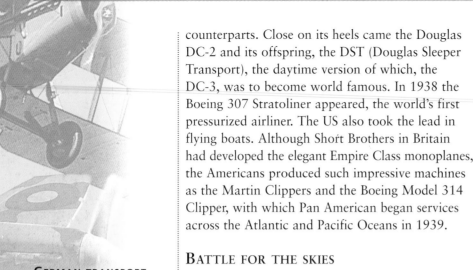

counterparts. Close on its heels came the Douglas DC-2 and its offspring, the DST (Douglas Sleeper Transport), the daytime version of which, the DC-3, was to become world famous. In 1938 the Boeing 307 Stratoliner appeared, the world's first pressurized airliner. The US also took the lead in flying boats. Although Short Brothers in Britain had developed the elegant Empire Class monoplanes, the Americans produced such impressive machines as the Martin Clippers and the Boeing Model 314 Clipper, with which Pan American began services across the Atlantic and Pacific Oceans in 1939.

BATTLE FOR THE SKIES

Military aviation also changed in the 1930s. All-metal monoplanes began to appear, such as Boeing's P-26 and, in France, Dewoitine's D.500 series. In 1936 Soviet designer Nikolai Polikarpov's I-16 saw service in the Spanish Civil War. It was the world's first single-seat, low-wing cantilever monoplane fighter with a retractable undercarriage. One of its opponents in Spain was Willy Messerschmitt's even more advanced Bf 109, which had a stressed-skin monocoque fuselage. Britain's Hawker Hurricane still made extensive use of wood and fabric, but the Supermarine Spitfire, which entered RAF service in 1938, was all-metal and proved to have great development potential. Britain was also slow in

introducing all-metal bombers. Russia, with Tupolev's ANT-6 and SB series, Germany with its Heinkel He 111 and Dornier Do 17, and the US with the Martin B-10 and Boeing B-17 were in the lead.

The fighters deployed by the combatants in World War II (1939–45) had reflector gunsights, armor protection, air-to-air and air-to-ground radio, electrical generator circuits to operate equipment, and hydraulic systems. In the 1940 Battle of Britain, the RAF's Hurricanes and Spitfires denied the Luftwaffe control of the skies, forming part of a co-ordinated defensive system based on the "Chain Home" radar stations. In the course of the war, radar systems became lighter and were fitted to aircraft; nightfighter crews no longer relied on their eyesight to find targets.

Britain's four-engined heavy bombers – the Avro Lancaster, Handley Page Halifax, and Short Stirling – took the war to Germany. They were joined by the US's Boeing B-17 and Consolidated B-24 day

GERMAN TRANSPORT

One of the world's greatest transport aircraft, the Junkers Ju 52/3m trimotor first appeared in 1932. Built in large numbers, it served as a commercial transport and also with the Luftwaffe and other military air arms, often as a paratroop transport. Many continued in commercial service well after World War II. This rare color photograph shows a Lufthansa aircraft at Croydon Airport, England, in the late 1930s.

Direction-finding loop antenna

Airframe covered with corrugated duralumin

Thick-section, all-metal wing

MASS PRODUCTION

The USSR's Ilyushin Il-2/10 Shturmovik armored ground-attack and anti-tank aircraft of World War II holds the record for being produced in larger numbers than any other single airplane type in history. At least 40,492 of these aircraft were produced.

bombers. Boeing's B-29 Superfortress, which dropped the atomic bombs on Hiroshima and Nagasaki in 1945, was the first production aircraft to have remotely controlled defensive armament.

Probably the war's most versatile aircraft was the RAF's de Havilland Mosquito. It began as a high-speed bomber, but proved equally effective in the fighter, nightfighter, photoreconnaissance, and ground-attack roles. Outstanding fighters included Germany's Focke-Wulf Fw 190, Russia's Yakovlev Yak-9, and the US's North American Mustang and Republic Thunderbolt. In the bitterly fought war in the Pacific, carrier-based US Navy fighters such as the Chance-Vought F4U Corsair and Grumman F6 Hellcat, and USAAF (US Army Air Force) Lockheed P-38 Lightnings and Curtiss P-40s, came up against Japan's Mitsubishi A6M Reisen (Zero) and J2M Raiden fighters.

The first jet-propelled airplane to go into action was the rocket-powered Messerschmitt

Long-span slotted ailerons (Junkers "double-wing")

Me 163 Komet, used to intercept Allied bombers from May 1944. The RAF's Gloster Meteor I began intercepting V1 flying bombs in August of the same year, and the twin-engined Messerschmitt Me 262 was deployed in December.

The first practical helicopters had begun to appear in the late 1930s, and Germany and the US used some operationally during the war. The most prolific transport airplanes were the Junkers Ju 52 and Douglas C-47, though the DC-4 and Lockheed Constellation both served as military aircraft.

AIRLINERS TAKE OFF

The return of peace after 1945 saw the DC-4 and Constellation adopt their intended roles as airliners, and grow into successful families. Britain initially had to make do with modified bombers, the Avro York and Lancastrian, until new civil designs were ready. Although flying boats had given valuable service in the war, the widespread building of airfields during the conflict rendered them obsolete. Coming up fast, however, were the first turboprop and jet airliners: Britain's Vickers Viscount and de Havilland Comet respectively. The Comet first flew in July 1949 and entered service in 1952. In 1955 the USSR flew the Tupolev Tu-104, a derivative of the Tu-16 bomber, and France the smaller Sud-Aviation Caravelle. While the turboprop enjoyed only a brief spell on center

EARLY SIKORSKY

One of the outstanding early practical helicopters was Igor Sikorsky's two-seat R-4, here fitted with pontoons during shipboard trials in 1943. Its seven-cylinder 185-hp Warner R-550-1 radial engine gave it a cruising speed of 65 mph (105 km/h).

BRITISH FIRST

Depicted here on the cover of a contemporary manufacturer's brochure, the de Havilland D.H.106 Comet was the world's first turbojet commercial airliner. It started regular operations in May 1952.

THE DE HAVILLAND
COMET
The modern airliner of universal application

stage, the jet airliner soon consigned its piston-engined forebears to the past. Unfortunately for Britain, after a promising start, major structural problems caused the Comet to lose its lead to the Boeing 707, which entered service in 1958.

SUPERSONIC WARRIORS

Jet aircraft also became preeminent in military aviation, as the Cold War confrontation between the US and the USSR initiated an arms race that bred a wide and constantly improving range of fighters and bombers. The problems posed by supersonic flight were overcome and swept-wing fighters appeared. The first combats between swept-wing jets occurred during the Korean War (1950–53), when North American F-86 Sabres met Soviet-built MiG-15s.

In the 1950s, while the US developed its "Century series" fighters, including the North American F-100 Super Sabre, Lockheed F-104 Starfighter, and Convair F-106 Delta Dart, the USSR produced the MiG-17, the MiG-19, and the outstanding MiG-21, of which 12,000 were built. Britain had its Hawker Hunter, Gloster Javelin, and English Electric Lightning, while in France Dassault produced its Super Mystère. Their 1960s successors included the Dassault Mirage and McDonnell F-4

In the 1960s reconnaissance, previously assigned to special variants of fighters or bombers, became the job of a dedicated design with the advent of the Lockheed U-2. Its successor, the SR-71, embodied a new concept, being the first Mach 3 airplane to enter service with the USAF, in 1966.

Two innovations introduced into service use in the second half of the 1960s were the swing-wing (variable-geometry) aircraft and vertical take-off and landing (VTOL). Variable geometry was subsequently incorporated in designs on both sides of the Iron Curtain,

Paired jet engines in underwing pod

Nacelle for piston engine driving pusher propeller

BIGGEST BOMBER

When Convair's massive B-36 strategic bomber entered service with the USAF (United States Air Force) in 1947 it had six Pratt & Whitney R-4360 piston engines. These were augmented in later models by four podded General Electric J47 jets. With its 230-ft (70-m) wingspan, the B-36 is the biggest bomber ever to have served in the USAF.

Phantom II; both were built in large numbers. Bombers progressed from the huge Convair B-36, eventually powered by six piston engines and four jets, through the Boeing B-47 to the eight-jet B-52 Stratofortress and the Convair B-58 Hustler, the first supersonic bomber to go into service, in 1959. Parallel development took place in the USSR, which fielded the twin-jet Tupolev Tu-16, the four-turboprop Tu-95, and the four-jet Myasishchyev 3M.

The great potential of helicopters was first realized during the Korean War, when types such as the Bell 47 proved invaluable for casualty evacuation. Helicopters were soon being used for tasks such as firefighting, police work, and cropspraying. They later also found a role as gunships, with helicopters such as the US Bell AH-1S Cobra and Soviet Mil Mi-24 "Hind" providing formidable opposition to tanks and other armored vehicles.

including the General
Dynamics F-111,
Panavia Tornado,
Sukhoi Su-24,
MiG-23 and -27,
the Rockwell B-1
and Tupolev Tu-160 bombers, and the
outstanding Grumman F-14 Tomcat carrier-
based multirole fighter. The Tomcat was
the world's first production aircraft
to have look-down, shoot-down
capability and track-while-
scan, its radar enabling it to track over
20 targets and launch Phoenix missiles against the
six most threatening. The long struggle to devise a
practical VTOL aircraft culminated in the brilliant
British Aerospace Harrier ground-attack aircraft,
later developed as the McDonnell Douglas AV-8B.

On the civil side, conventional airliners such as
the de Havilland D.H.121 Trident, Vickers VC10,
and Boeing 727 were joined in 1969 by the mighty
400-seat Boeing 747, as well as by the supersonic
Concorde and Tupolev Tu-144. In addition, the
advent of the high-bypass turbofan engine, which
offered greater power and efficiency, led to the
appearance of smaller "widebodies" such as the
Lockheed TriStar and McDonnell Douglas DC-10.
In December 1970 Europe's Airbus Industrie was

*Retractable canard
surfaces added to improve
takeoff and landing*

established to challenge Boeing's predominance in
the airliner market. Its first product, the A300B,
took to the air in October 1972, and a second
widebody twin, the A310, was on offer by the late
1970s, while Boeing was developing its 757/767
family. The biggest success, however, was Boeing's
737 of 1968, which became the world's most
successful jet design, with over 4,000 sales. The

Airbus A320, appearing in the late 1980s,
introduced digital fly-by-wire controls and the
advanced "glass" cockpit. Boeing's first fly-by-wire
design, the 777, entered service in 1995. Ultralarge
airliners, seating more than 500 passengers, are
planned for early in the twenty-first century.

CUTTING EDGE

Private flying has burgeoned since World War II,
with a great variety of light aircraft coming on the
market, as well as corporate jets for executives who
prefer to fly when they want rather than when
airline timetables dictate. According to his or her
income, the private owner can now possess
anything from a veteran airplane to a small
"homebuilt" assembled from a kit, or even an
ultralight or powered parasail. The next symbol
of ultimate wealth may be a supersonic business jet.

In military aviation, the greatest impact recently
has been made by the new technology that reduces
an airplane's radar signature to an absolute
minimum. This "stealth" technology is epitomized
by the Lockheed F-117A and Northrop B-2 bombers,
and by the latest fighters, such as the Lockheed
Martin/Boeing F-22 Raptor, which is due to enter
USAF service in 2005.

TROUBLED TUPOLEV

Although it was the first
supersonic transport
aircraft to fly, in December
1968, and the first to
exceed Mach 2, the USSR's
Tupolev Tu-144 had a
troubled existence and
was never really successful.

FUTURE SHOCK

The Lockheed F-117A
Nighthawk stealth bomber
points the way to future
developments in military
aviation. Its angular design
incorporates many devices
to deflect and deceive
enemy radar and infrared
sensors, rendering it
almost invisible in
hostile airspace.

*Swivelling ruddervators
operate both as rudders
and elevators*

*Wing has three-spar
torsion box structure*

PART TWO

GALLERY OF AIRCRAFT

Throughout aviation's history, certain companies, aircraft types, and achievements have marked the path to the future. Although flight itself seemed something of a miracle in the early days, the quest to fly faster, higher, farther, and safer has challenged scientists, designers, and pilots ever since. In this chapter we look at the aircraft that, for various reasons, have played leading roles in the story, either by representing the peak of achievement in their respective classes, or by showing the way ahead.

THE EARLY YEARS

THIS WAS THE PERIOD when conquest of the air started to become a reality, although the early pioneers were often targets of ridicule. Their unsuccessful efforts frequently left them desperate for financial backing, since those investors who had already lost money to charlatans and hare-brained inventors were slow to fund others. Consequently, many pioneers struggled on small incomes, sustained by their convictions and devoted enthusiasm. When earnest experimenters did at last begin to make extended flights, the excitement was extreme; the early meetings attracted thousands of spectators. Any aviator making an emergency descent in a remote field would be quickly surrounded by a swarm of curious locals. The first great airplane and engine manufacturers emerged during this period, as well as famous pilots.

MUSICAL WINGS

In its exciting pioneer years before World War I, aviation inspired all kinds of popular entertainment and ephemera. This cover design for a piece of sheet music features a Blériot XII monoplane.

RACE WINNER

Typical of biplane designs in this period, the US-designed 1910 Curtiss pusher was fast for its day and won many prizes at flying meetings.

1890·1913 GLIDER PIONEERS

THE FIRST HEAVIER-THAN-AIR aircraft to fly were hang gliders, quite similar to those flown for sport today. The greatest pioneer in this field was Otto Lilienthal, a German engineer, who built his first glider in 1891 and went on to produce a dozen different designs, both monoplanes and biplanes. He had made more than 1,000 flights by the time of his death in a flying accident in 1896. Those inspired by Lilienthal's example included Orville and Wilbur Wright. The Wright brothers' work in turn inspired French pioneers in the early 1900s.

Hinged tail plane

"Fences" attached to upper surface maintain wing curvature

LILIENTHAL'S BIPLANE

Otto Lilienthal built his large biplane in 1895. Here he is seen flying it from his "Fliegeberg," an artificial hill he had built in Lichterfelde, a Berlin suburb. His gliders had radial ribs of willow, and were covered with English cotton shirting material.

Pilot controls glider by swinging his body from side to side and fore and aft

PILCHER'S HAWK

English pioneer Percy Pilcher built five gliders, the most successful of which was the Hawk. In 1896–97 he made many flights under tow, using a line stretched from one low hill to another. Pilcher lost his life in September 1899 when the Hawk glider crashed due to a structural failure during a demonstration flight.

Cambered wing can fold back for easier ground handling

Hollow bamboo leg contains spiral spring to absorb impact of landing

Wing structure kept rigid by struts and wire cross-bracing

Primitive front elevator controls pitch of glider

CRUDE IMITATION

French pioneer Ferdinand Ferber built this Wright-inspired glider in 1902. Unfortunately it was very crudely constructed, and Ferber had no comprehension of the control system that the Wright brothers had devised. As a result, the glider's performance was poor. However, Ferber's efforts spurred a new burst of activity in France.

Tensioned bracing wires

BRITISH BAT

Percy Pilcher developed this Lilienthal-inspired glider, the Bat, in 1895, and tested it in Scotland with some success. Here he lets it float on the breeze for the benefit of the photographer, simply by holding the front ends of the "fuselage" members. Pine and bamboo were used, and over 100 bracing wires maintained the wing's curvature.

Circular fin bisects circular tail plane

Single-surface wing with small number of ribs

AMERICAN DEVELOPMENT

Octave Chanute and Augustus Herring created this elegant biplane, which made many safe glides in the Indiana sand dunes in 1896–97. Chanute, a railroad engineer, used a cross-bracing system based on the bridge-builder's Pratt truss, which has formed the basis of most multiplane bracing systems ever since.

Spar to which ribs are attached

Cruciform tail surfaces keep glider on straight course

Upper tail boom is attached to spring device to dampen effects of wind gusts

Supported in frame beneath lower wing, pilot controls glider by body movements

1890·1913 FIRST POWERED AIRPLANES

ATTEMPTS AT BUILDING powered, human-carrying airplanes date back to the late 1800s, when the lack of a suitable power plant posed an insurmountable problem. Most experimenters sought the solution in light steam engines, but these were relatively inefficient for their weight, and required large quantities of fuel and water. Such problems did not deter a number of would-be aviators from spending enormous sums of money on their endeavors.

Gasoline-powered cycle engine drives wing-flapping mechanism

Wings contain hundreds of custom-made silk feathers

Test frame for ground experiments only

COPYING THE BIRDS

Edward P. Frost of Cambridgeshire, England, believed the solution to flight lay in ornithopters, or flapping-wing machines, that emulated birds. This test rig, built in 1906, had elaborate 20-ft (6-m) span wings made of hundreds of artificial feathers, driven by a 3-hp BAT gasoline engine.

SHIP OF THE AIR

Russian sea captain Aleksandr Mozhaiskii began building his large monoplane, powered by two English-designed and -built steam engines, in St. Petersburg in 1876. It was launched down a ramp on the military campsite at Krasnoe Selo in 1884, but crashed after a short hop.

Stiffening rib of main wing

Cone-shaped fuel tank in front of engine

TETHERED TRIALS

Jacob Christian Ellehammer of Copenhagen, Denmark, made a tentative tethered flight of 138 ft (42 m) around a circular track in this Ellehammer II semi-biplane on September 12, 1906. It was driven by an 18-hp three-cylinder motor, which Ellehammer built, but had no control system.

STEAM-POWERED BAT

In France, distinguished electrical engineer Clément Ader completed two steam-powered bat-winged aircraft. His first, the *Éole*, managed a brief hop on October 9, 1890. The second, the *Avion III* (*left*), powered by two 20-hp steam engines, was tested twice on a circular track at Satory on October 12 and 14, 1897, but failed to fly.

Two sets of monoplane wings in tandem

Single-surfaced wings based on those of a bat

AIRCRAFT CARRIER

On October 7 and December 8, 1903, US astronomer Samuel Pierpont Langley twice attempted to launch this 52-hp "Aerodrome" by catapulting it from the roof of a houseboat on the Potomac River. On both occasions it suffered a structural failure and deposited its pilot, C.M. Manly, in the river.

Swept-forward wings braced above and below

Catapult launch mechanism

Additional loose "sail-wing" above main wing

Triangular tailplane

FIRST OFF THE GROUND

This prophetic monoplane with its swept-forward wings and hot-air or steam engine was created by French naval officer Félix du Temple. Tested about 1874, with a sailor as its pilot, it took off briefly after a run down a ramp, becoming the first full-size powered airplane to leave the ground.

Rudder for steering

Thin single spar of main wing

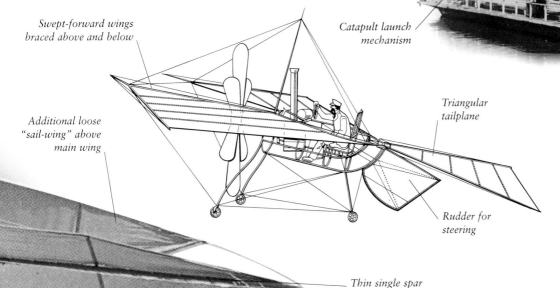

Movable elevators carried on booms extending fore and aft

Two-bladed propellers with fan-type blades

AMBITIOUS BIPLANE

American-born inventor Hiram Maxim built this gigantic test rig at Baldwyns Park, Kent, England, in the 1890s. Powered by two 180-hp steam engines driving 17¾-ft (5.4-m) diameter propellers, it lifted from its rails on July 31, 1894. However, it fouled and broke the upper restraining rails and was badly damaged. Its control system was inadequate.

1890-1913 THE WRIGHT BROTHERS

BY DEVISING A PRACTICAL CONTROL SYSTEM and proving it on gliders before building and testing their first powered aircraft, Wilbur and Orville Wright of Dayton, Ohio, were able to make the world's first powered, sustained, and controlled flights in December 1903. During the process of development the brothers conducted wind-tunnel tests on several different wing sections, designed and built their own engines and propellers, and carried out all of their own test flying. Unfortunately, they continued to adhere to their original twin-pusher propeller layout while their contemporaries progressed to more advanced designs.

UNSTABLE BUT RESPONSIVE

In their No. 3 glider of 1902 the Wrights mastered control. A movable rear rudder worked with wing warping to counter the drag caused by the downwarped wingtip and facilitated smooth banked turns. They made their machines unstable to increase their response to the controls.

Biplane elevators ahead of wings

Twin rudders carried on booms

THE ARISTOCRAT'S CHOICE

The Wright Type A of 1909 was a fully practical airplane capable of making repeated long flights, and was the choice of several prominent pilots, including French nobleman Comte Charles de Lambert. He is shown here at the Reims meeting in August 1909, where he covered 72 miles (116 km) in under two hours.

EARLY CONVERSION

The Wright Model B (*above*) of 1911 did away with the forward biplane elevator, favoring instead a monoplane elevator behind the twin rear rudders. In 1912 floats were made available to convert the aircraft into a seaplane, as seen here. The wing warping can be seen in action.

THE WRIGHTS' RACING BABY

Seen here at Hendon Aerodrome, England, is a Baby Wright racer dating from 1910. Also known as the Model R or Roadster, this small single-seater was designed for use in speed and altitude competitions. The pilot sat close beside the engine, with his left arm around the nearest strut to hold one of the two control levers.

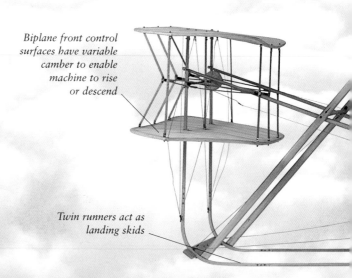

Biplane front control surfaces have variable camber to enable machine to rise or descend

Twin runners act as landing skids

COMPANY HIGHLIGHTS

1899 Wrights flight-test first glider.
1903 The brothers accomplish world's first powered, sustained, and controlled flight.
1905 Wright Flyer III is first practical airplane.
1908 Wilbur demonstrates Wright biplane in Europe.
1909 US Army Signal Corps accepts Wright Flyer for military use. Wright Company formed in November.
1912 Wilbur Wright dies of typhoid.
1915 Company sold to a syndicate.
1948 Orville Wright dies.

SOARING SUCCESS

In 1911 Orville Wright returned to Kill Devil Hill, North Carolina, the site of the brothers' initial flights, to fly a new glider with English pioneer Alec Ogilvie. Many successful soaring flights were made; and on October 24, with a flight of 9 minutes 45 seconds, he set a new world record that stood for a decade.

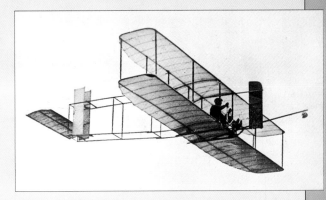

OUTMODED BIPLANE

When it appeared in 1914, the Wright Model H was a distinctly antiquated design. A 60-hp Wright engine in its enclosed fuselage had the traditional chain-and-shaft drive to twin pusher propellers, and it retained wing warping for lateral control. This example was tested at the Royal Aircraft Factory, Farnborough, England, in 1915.

THE WRIGHT STUFF

The famous 1903 Wright Flyer, the brothers' first powered aircraft, made only four flights, all on December 17, 1903. Its best was the last one, covering 852 ft (260 m) over the ground in 59 seconds. It was powered by a 12-hp four-cylinder water-cooled engine driving two pusher propellers through chains and shafts, and took off from a wooden monorail.

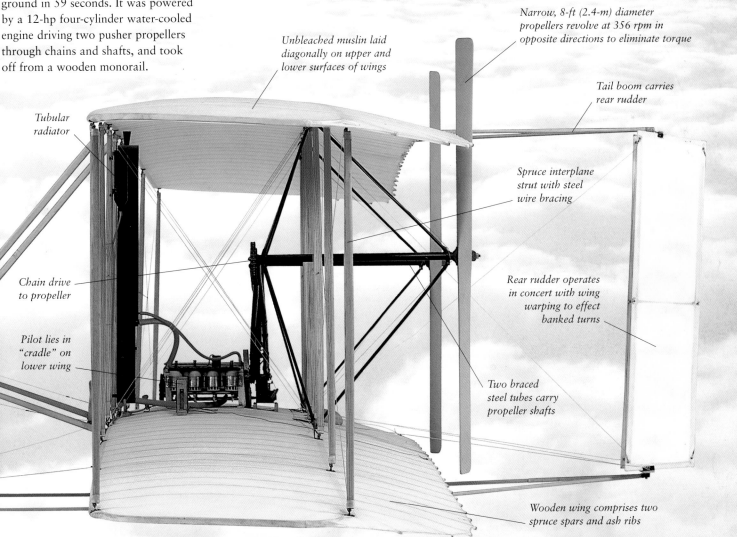

Unbleached muslin laid diagonally on upper and lower surfaces of wings

Narrow, 8-ft (2.4-m) diameter propellers revolve at 356 rpm in opposite directions to eliminate torque

Tail boom carries rear rudder

Tubular radiator

Spruce interplane strut with steel wire bracing

Chain drive to propeller

Rear rudder operates in concert with wing warping to effect banked turns

Pilot lies in "cradle" on lower wing

Two braced steel tubes carry propeller shafts

Wooden wing comprises two spruce spars and ash ribs

1890·1913 FRENCH PIONEERS

IN THE EARLY 1900S France was the scene of intense aviation activity, and a place where many flying machines were produced. A number of the manufacturers that arose at this time built outstanding airplanes. The Deperdussin company, for example, became famous for its racers, while the twin-boom Caudrons evolved into training machines. As manufacturers gained experience and pilots developed their skills, the records for speed, altitude, and endurance were broken with incredible regularity.

A SHORT HOP

Before Wright's demonstration of a practical airplane in France in 1908, even brief "hops" were acclaimed. Brazilian Alberto Santos-Dumont was credited with the first powered flights in Europe in this box-kite biplane known as the 14*bis*. However, the longest it stayed aloft was 21.2 seconds, traveling 720 ft (220 m), in 1906.

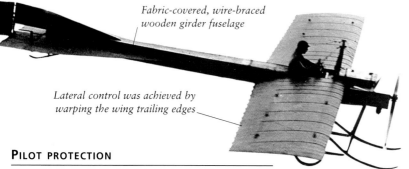

Fabric-covered, wire-braced wooden girder fuselage

Lateral control was achieved by warping the wing trailing edges

PILOT PROTECTION

With their enclosed fuselage, Deperdussins were, for their time, elegant, clean designs. The 1911 Type C had its 70-hp Gnome rotary engine partly cowled, reducing the spray of castor oil inflicted on the pilot by the "total loss" engine lubrication system.

Double layer of fabric along wing leading edge

Deeply arched wing ribs

TWIN-BOOM BIPLANE

This early machine, like most of René Caudron's output, is a tractor biplane with twin booms carrying a tail plane on which twin fins and rudders are mounted. The powerplant would have been either an Anzani radial engine or a Gnome rotary.

Wing warping provides lateral control

Pylon carries wing bracing wires

Lower booms double as landing skids

SHAPELY SAULNIER DESIGN

Between 1910 and 1914, Gabriel Borel designed a series of monoplanes, seaplanes, and flying boats. The monoplanes, such as this 1912 model, despite their sleeker shape, displayed a distinct Blériot influence. This is because Raymond Saulnier worked for both Borel and Blériot. This aircraft has a Gnome rotary engine.

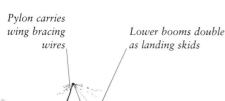

Lower booms act as skids

Large spinner streamlines aircraft nose

RECORD-BREAKING SPEED

Powered by a 160-hp two-row Gnome rotary, this sleek 1913 Deperdussin monoplane with its wooden monocoque fuselage won that year's Gordon Bennett race at Reims, France, on September 29. On winning the race, pilot Maurice Prévost also set a new world speed record of 126.6 mph (203.8 km/h).

THE BIPLANE BROTHERS

This *c.*1909 biplane was one of a series of bulky box kites built by Gabriel and Charles Voisin using interplane "side curtains" for lateral stability. Initially these machines had no ailerons for lateral control and the pilot had to make cautious turns on the rudder alone to avoid sideslips.

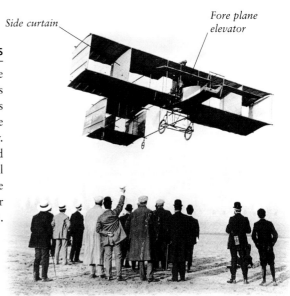

Side curtain

Fore plane elevator

Wings wider at tips than at roots

EARLY CAUDRON

This early version of René Caudron's distinctive biplane has the pilot's seat in the lower wing, while the Anzani radial engine is set between the innermost pairs of struts. In later versions the engine was mounted on the front of a nacelle, providing the pilot with some protection.

Struts fitted in socket castings

Fuel tank

Anzani radial engine

Wooden interplane strut

Skids project forward to prevent nosing over

1890·1913 BLÉRIOT XI MONOPLANE

ON JULY 25, 1909, Louis Blériot took off from Les Baraques, near Calais, France, and flew across the English Channel to Dover. He landed near Dover Castle after 36½ minutes, winning the £1,000 prize offered by the *Daily Mail* for the first cross-Channel flight. His mount was a Blériot XI monoplane much like this one, equipped with flotation bags in the rear fuselage in case of ditching. With its front-mounted "tractor" engine, tricycle undercarriage, wings at the front, and the tail plane, elevators, and rudder grouped at the rear, the Blériot XI established the principal configuration for monoplanes for generations to come.

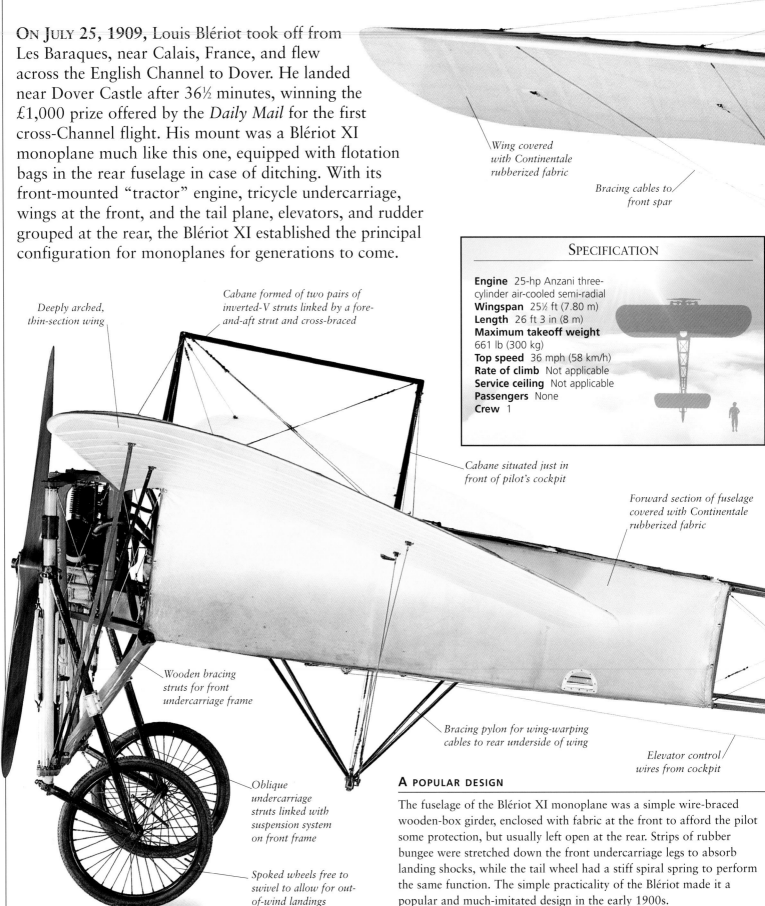

Wing covered with Continentale rubberized fabric

Bracing cables to front spar

Deeply arched, thin-section wing

Cabane formed of two pairs of inverted-V struts linked by a fore-and-aft strut and cross-braced

Cabane situated just in front of pilot's cockpit

Forward section of fuselage covered with Continentale rubberized fabric

Wooden bracing struts for front undercarriage frame

Bracing pylon for wing-warping cables to rear underside of wing

Elevator control wires from cockpit

Oblique undercarriage struts linked with suspension system on front frame

Spoked wheels free to swivel to allow for out-of-wind landings

SPECIFICATION

Engine 25-hp Anzani three-cylinder air-cooled semi-radial
Wingspan 25½ ft (7.80 m)
Length 26 ft 3 in (8 m)
Maximum takeoff weight 661 lb (300 kg)
Top speed 36 mph (58 km/h)
Rate of climb Not applicable
Service ceiling Not applicable
Passengers None
Crew 1

A POPULAR DESIGN

The fuselage of the Blériot XI monoplane was a simple wire-braced wooden-box girder, enclosed with fabric at the front to afford the pilot some protection, but usually left open at the rear. Strips of rubber bungee were stretched down the front undercarriage legs to absorb landing shocks, while the tail wheel had a stiff spiral spring to perform the same function. The simple practicality of the Blériot made it a popular and much-imitated design in the early 1900s.

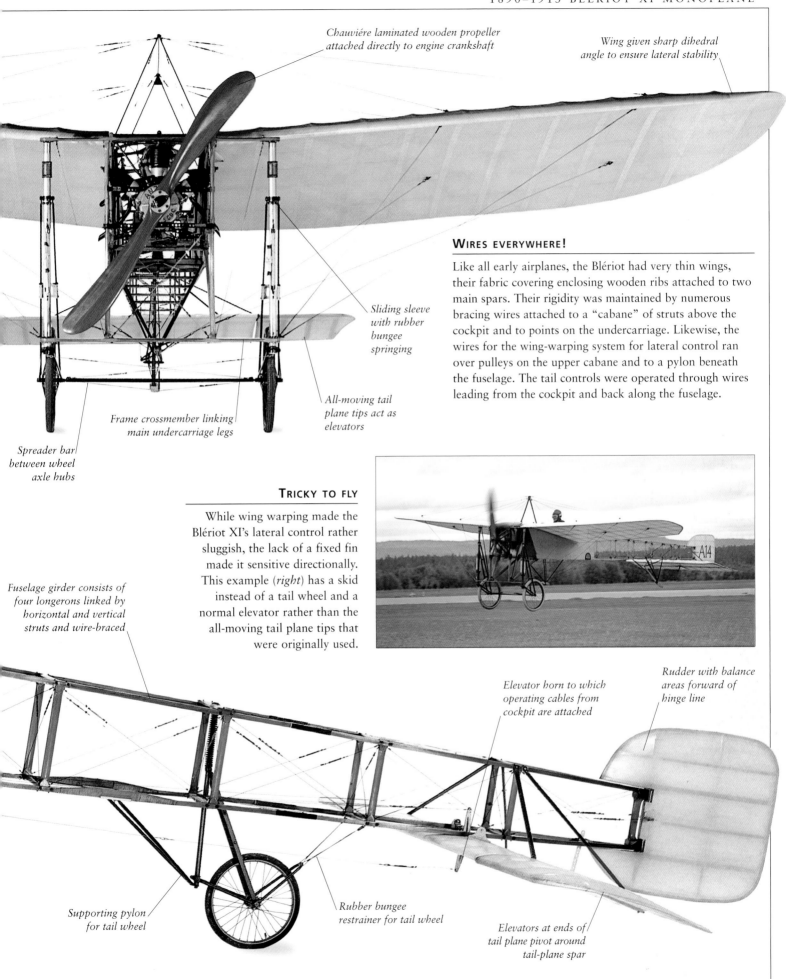

Chauviére laminated wooden propeller attached directly to engine crankshaft

Wing given sharp dihedral angle to ensure lateral stability

Sliding sleeve with rubber bungee springing

All-moving tail plane tips act as elevators

Frame crossmember linking main undercarriage legs

Spreader bar between wheel axle hubs

WIRES EVERYWHERE!

Like all early airplanes, the Blériot had very thin wings, their fabric covering enclosing wooden ribs attached to two main spars. Their rigidity was maintained by numerous bracing wires attached to a "cabane" of struts above the cockpit and to points on the undercarriage. Likewise, the wires for the wing-warping system for lateral control ran over pulleys on the upper cabane and to a pylon beneath the fuselage. The tail controls were operated through wires leading from the cockpit and back along the fuselage.

TRICKY TO FLY

While wing warping made the Blériot XI's lateral control rather sluggish, the lack of a fixed fin made it sensitive directionally. This example (*right*) has a skid instead of a tail wheel and a normal elevator rather than the all-moving tail plane tips that were originally used.

Fuselage girder consists of four longerons linked by horizontal and vertical struts and wire-braced

Elevator horn to which operating cables from cockpit are attached

Rudder with balance areas forward of hinge line

Supporting pylon for tail wheel

Rubber bungee restrainer for tail wheel

Elevators at ends of tail plane pivot around tail-plane spar

1890·1913 EARLY DESIGNS

FROM 1910 AVIATION DEVELOPED RAPIDLY in both Europe and the US, as a growing number of small companies originated a great assortment of designs. Many of these companies were to disappear without a trace, but others, such as Avro, Blackburn, and Handley Page in Great Britain, Curtiss and Martin in the US, and Sikorsky in Russia were destined to grow into great manufacturing enterprises employing thousands of people. Initially, however, their founders often had to strive against great difficulties before achieving recognition or success.

LIKE A BIRD ON THE WING

The elegant Taube ("Dove") monoplane design – seen here in a 1911/12 version built by Edmund Rumpler – was developed in Germany by Igo Etrich, but adopted by various manufacturers. The aircraft was so-named because its wing planform resembled that of the bird. In this illustration, the Taube's complex wing bracing system can be seen clearly.

Fabric-covered
wooden fuselage

EARLY MONOPLANE MAKER

Inspired by Wilbur Wright's first flights in Europe in 1908, Robert Blackburn of Yorkshire, England, built his first airplane in 1909, and in 1910 set up his own business. Blackburn's first products were a range of Antoinette-type monoplanes. This one, built for a private customer in 1912, is still flying today on the power of its 50-hp Gnome engine.

Wings wire-
braced above
and below

Circular cowling
contains oil
splashing from
engine

Pairs of wheels
attached to skids
with bungee cord

SUCCESSFUL SOVIET

Russian Igor Sikorsky built the world's first successful large airplanes. Starting with the Bolshoi Baltiskiy, or Grand, in 1913, he then built a series of Il'ya Mouromets biplanes powered by four 100-hp Argus engines. This non-flying reproduction of one of the latter types was built for movie use in the 1980s.

BLACKBURN ON THE BEACH

Robert Blackburn's Mercury II of 1911 was powered by a 50-hp Gnome engine, which gave the 32-ft (9.75-m) span monoplane a top speed of 70 mph (113 km/h). Blackburn monoplanes were often flown from the beach at Filey, Yorkshire. This picture shows a Mercury II at that location attracting the locals' admiring gazes.

MAGNIFICENT FLYING MACHINE

The Farman-inspired Bristol Box Kite of 1910–11, produced by the British and Colonial Aeroplane Company (later Bristol), met with great success, and was bought by the British and Russian governments. A total of 78 were built, powered by the ubiquitous 50-hp Gnome rotary engine. This reproduction, made for the movie *Those Magnificent Men in Their Flying Machines*, still flies on calm days.

SUCCESSFUL SPORTSTER

From 1911, the Morane-Borel-Saulnier company produced a series of sporting monoplanes, such as this one (*right*), that enjoyed many successes in races, both as landplanes and seaplanes. They had no fixed tail plane, only elevators, which made the pitch control rather sensitive. The wing-warping mechanism on these monoplanes was very sluggish.

Pylon for warp control wires

Leaf spring between wheels

Spiral-tube radiators for water cooling

WINNING FORMULA

A sharp two-seater, the Type E (*left*), powered by a 60-hp ENV water-cooled engine, was the first in a line of successful aircraft for the Avro company founded by Alliott Verdon Roe. It was soon followed by the company's 500, and, later, the 504, of which a great many were produced.

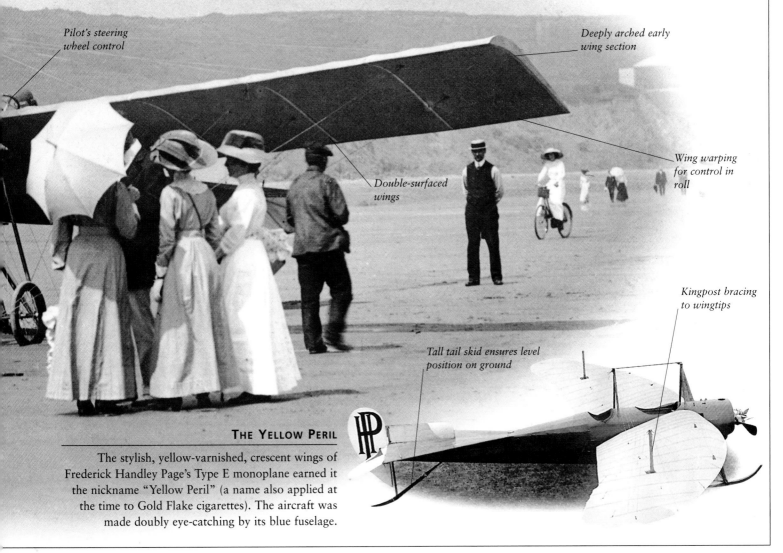

Pilot's steering wheel control

Deeply arched early wing section

Double-surfaced wings

Wing warping for control in roll

Kingpost bracing to wingtips

Tall tail skid ensures level position on ground

THE YELLOW PERIL

The stylish, yellow-varnished, crescent wings of Frederick Handley Page's Type E monoplane earned it the nickname "Yellow Peril" (a name also applied at the time to Gold Flake cigarettes). The aircraft was made doubly eye-catching by its blue fuselage.

1890·1913 THE FARMAN LINE

THE BROTHERS HENRY and Maurice Farman, French-domiciled children of English parents, both created successful families of aircraft before setting up their joint company in 1912. Henry began by buying a Voisin box-kite biplane in 1907 and progressively modifying it until he had a practical machine. By 1909 he was building his own designs. His classic HF III biplane was copied worldwide. Maurice began building his own machines in 1909, and evolved the MF.7 and 11, which became standard military trainers.

PROVEN WARHORSE

Appearing in the summer of 1912, the Henry Farman HF.20 military three-seater was powered by either a Gnome or Le Rhône 80-hp rotary engine. It served throughout World War I, latterly mainly as a trainer.

BIPLANE TO TRIPLANE

In November 1907 Henry Farman modified his Voisin biplane into triplane form by adding a short-span third upper surface. Known in this form as the Farman 1*bis*, it had a 50-hp Antoinette engine and was equipped with ailerons for lateral control, though it retained the Voisin's quaint side-curtains between the wings.

Upper-wing aileron

Lower-wing aileron

FAVORED STEED

The classic pre-World War I Farman biplane, the Henry Farman HF III was sold around the world. Usually powered by the 50-hp Gnome rotary engine, it was the choice of many famous pilots. This one has extensions to its upper wing to increase lift and reduce landing speeds.

Twin rudders behind biplane tail plane

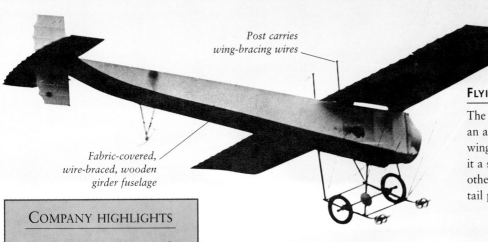

Post carries wing-bracing wires

Straight wing

Fabric-covered, wire-braced, wooden girder fuselage

FLYING PLANK

The rather flimsy-looking Henry Farman Monoplane, an angular two-seater with a 33-ft (10-m) planklike wing, appeared in 1911. Its Gnome rotary engine gave it a speed of 62–68 mph (100–110 km/h). Like some other designs of the period, it lacked a fixed fin and tail plane, having only a movable rudder and elevator.

COMPANY HIGHLIGHTS

1907 Henry Farman achieves the first 0.6-mile (1-km) closed-circuit flight in Europe.

1908 Henry Farman makes first cross-country flight in Europe.

1909 HF III biplane introduced.

1909 Maurice Farman's first design appears.

1912 Joint factory, Avions Henri et Maurice Farman, opens in January. Becomes France's largest aircraft factory.

1912 Advent of the MF.7 "Longhorn."

1936 Company nationalized; the brothers retire.

STAGGERED SEAPLANE

The Maurice Farman MF.2 seaplane, with its exaggerated wing-stagger, took part in the hydroairplane meeting at Monaco in 1912. A pusher biplane, it had a water-cooled Renault engine and distinctive curved booms that extended forward to carry an elevator, at that time becoming a trademark feature of this family of aircraft.

PRECURSOR OF THE "LONGHORN"

Seen here in its developed form, the Maurice Farman Type Coupe Michelin first flew in 1910, powered by a 50-hp Renault engine. It introduced the forward elevator mounted on curved booms, and foreshadowed the appearance in 1913 of the MF.7, a ubiquitous military trainer nicknamed the "Longhorn," for obvious reasons. It originally had equal-span upper and lower wings with side-curtains near their tips.

All-moving forward elevator

Fabric-covered nacelle for pilot and passenger

Extended-span upper wing

Sprung main undercarriage

AIR-SUPPORTED AILERONS

Powered by a 50-hp Gnome rotary engine, the Henry Farman 2/2 parasol-winged monoplane appeared in mid-1910. Easily visible in the photograph are its "single-acting" ailerons, which hung down when the machine was on the ground but were supported by the airflow in flight. The ailerons moved downward only, manipulated via cables from the pilot's control column.

1890-1913 WEIRD & WONDERFUL

STRANGE AND ECCENTRIC designs have appeared throughout the course of aviation's development, but during the pioneer years they were evident in abundance. Many ambitious inventors, full of faith and optimism but often having little knowledge of aerodynamics and structures, built machines incorporating their pet theories, hoping for fame and fortune. Sadly, quite a number of their ingenious machines had no real hope of success, even if they did manage to get off the ground.

FLYING FORK

Called Diapason – French for the tuning fork that it resembled – this aircraft had its wings swept back in a wide curve. Built by Louis Schreck and powered by a 50-hp Gnome rotary engine, it did actually fly in 1911.

ASSISTED TAKEOFF

In France in 1910 a Belgian named César built a cumbersome short-span tandem biplane with a four-wheel undercarriage, powered by a 50-hp Prini-Berthaud engine driving a pusher propeller. In a vain effort to help it into the air he added a sausage-shaped balloon envelope, in which new form his futile contraption was described as a "biplan mixte."

Gas balloon was intended to augment dynamic lift generated by aircraft's wings

Twin rear rudders for directional control

Frontal elevators for control in pitch

HUMBLE BEGINNING

Built in 1909, the Breguet-Richet No. 3 was renamed Breguet No. 1, and as such was the first airplane built by this soon-to-be-famous company. It made short flights under the power of its 50-hp Renault engine until it crashed at the 1909 Reims meeting.

Interplane struts link front spars only

Nacelle carries pilot and engine

Wingtip stabilizing wheels augment single main wheel at center

NO-HOPER

Grandly called the Hércolite Phénomenon, Victor Thuau's crude monoplane of 1910 had short-span, sail-type wings and a deeply arched tail plane. Installing a more powerful engine and changing propellers could not induce it to fly.

MARINE PIONEER

Despite its quaint appearance, Henri Fabre's hydroairplane, later named Hydravion, was the world's first aircraft to make a powered takeoff from water, on March 28, 1910. It was powered by a 50-hp Gnome Omega rotary engine. Sadly, the design lacked development potential.

Engine mounted in nose of fuselage

Ailerons at tips of upper and middle wings

ARMORED ASTRA

Spanning over 42 ft 6 in (13 m), the ungainly armor-plated Astra Triplane of 1911 was built under the sponsorship of Henri Deutsch de la Meurthe. Its four huge main wheels were centered on the leading edge of the lower wing, and it carried a crew of two on its 75-hp Renault engine. Only one was built.

Engine and propeller mounted at extreme rear of aircraft

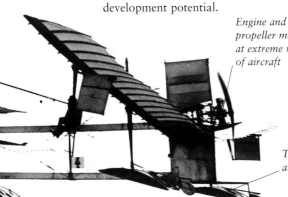

Twin floats at rear

Concentric circular wings connected by vanes

Fuel tank at rear of triangular-girder fuselage

FLAP OR FLOP

The Marquis Picat du Breuil sponsored the construction of three monoplanes with steel-tube wing leading edges supporting loose fabric wings set at an acute angle. Although the machines had rudders and elevators, there seems to have been no provision for lateral control.

FLYING IN CIRCLES

Claude Givaudan built this curious machine, with its tandem concentric-circle wings, in 1911. Each wing unit could pivot, the front for control in pitch and the rear for directional control. Unfortunately, its 40-hp Vermorel engine could not persuade it to fly.

1914·1918

WAR IN THE AIR

ALTHOUGH SOME ATTENTION had been given to its military potential during the early years, World War I saw the airplane mature from a frail, unreliable machine into a sturdy workhorse. Aerial reconnaissance, bombing, and liaison provided valuable support to the armies on the ground; and the need to either prevent these duties from being carried out, or to protect the aircraft performing them, led to the development of the "scout," or fighter. Bombers grew in size and complexity and took the war to the cities and towns of the combatant nations. This, in turn, led to the creation of national defense forces and nightfighters. At sea, the operation of airplanes from ships became routine, while the flying boat became a useful weapon against the submarine. In parallel with these developments, structures, weapons, and equipment steadily improved.

A NEW BEGINNING
This late-World War I poster encouraged men to join Britain's new Royal Air Force, which came into being on April 1, 1918, when the Royal Flying Corps and Royal Naval Air Service were combined.

GERMAN WARBIRD
The Albatros D.V of 1917/18 was one of Germany's foremost World War I fighters, and had elegant, curvaceous lines.

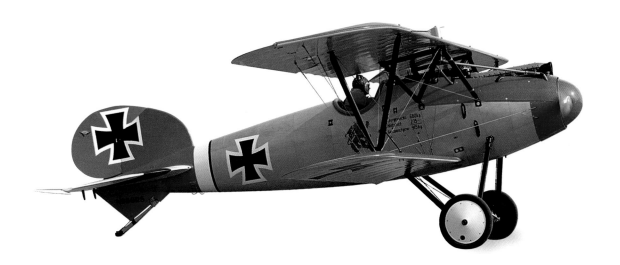

1914·1918 WORLD WAR I FIGHTERS

WORLD WAR I SAW FIGHTER airplanes (or "scouts" as they were known at the time) develop from relatively frail and primitively-armed machines, intended primarily to protect reconnaissance and bomber aircraft, into maneuverable single-seaters. The later machines could be deployed in roles that were much more aggressive than their established ones. Crucially, the perfection of gun-synchronization devices eventually enabled the fighters' guns to be fired through the arc of the revolving propellers, the pilot simply having to aim his aircraft at his opponent and press the trigger.

PFALZ FIGHTER

The 1917 Pfalz D.III was armed with twin Spandau machine guns and powered by a 160-hp Mercedes inline watercooled engine. Top speed was 103 mph (165 km/h).

MOUNT OF ACES

Along with the Sopwith Camel, the Royal Aircraft Factory S.E.5a of 1917–18 was the finest British fighter of the war. Powered by a Hispano-Suiza or Wolseley Viper inline engine, it had a Vickers gun on the fuselage and a Lewis gun above the upper wing. Top speed was 138 mph (222 km/h).

Unsynchronized Lewis gun above upper wing

Large, curved rudder with no fixed fin surface

Faired pilot's headrest behind cockpit

"V" interplane strut arrangement

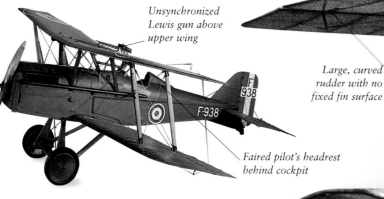

GERMANY'S BEST

The German Fokker D.VII entered service in 1918 and quickly proved itself in combat, being sensitive, highly maneuverable, and delightful to fly. Its 185-hp BMW inline engine gave it a top speed of 124 mph (200 km/h). It was armed with twin Spandau machine guns.

Flat frontal radiator

GALLIC STYLE

The elegant French Nieuport fighters, represented here by the Nieuport 17 of 1916, were small and agile, powered by Le Rhône rotary engines. A Lewis machine gun was often mounted on the upper wing, firing above the propeller arc.

Wings free of wire bracing

All-wooden semi-monocoque fuselage

Large domed spinner over propeller hub

AGGRESSIVE ALBATROS

The mount of many German aces, the Albatros DV had an elegantly streamlined monocoque fuselage with a neatly installed 180/200-hp Mercedes water-cooled engine. It was an excellent combat aircraft, but in a prolonged dive could break up, owing to faulty design of the smaller lower wing.

FAST FRENCHMAN

The Morane Type N of 1916, known as the Bullet because of its 90 mph (144 km/h) top speed, had wing-warping for lateral control, and elevators but no fixed tail plane. There was no gun interrupter gear as yet, so steel wedges were fitted to the backs of the propeller blades to deflect any mistimed bullets.

Wing warping provides lateral control

Fabric-covered fuselage faired to circular cross-section

Pilot's cockpit between fuel tank/engine and gunner's position

Movable .303-in Lewis machine gun on spigot mounting

POTENT PUSHER

Before gun synchronization, one way of overcoming the forward-firing gun problem was to have a pusher engine and a gunner in front of the pilot. The Vickers F.B.5 Gunbus of 1914–15 used this layout successfully, although the drag of the extra tail bracing and struttery imposed heavy performance penalties.

Hoops protect wingtips during ground maneuvering, takeoff, and landing

POPULAR MOUNT

A fine French fighter, the Spad XIII of 1917–18 had a 235-hp water-cooled Hispano-Suiza engine and was armed with twin .303-in Vickers machine guns. Nearly 8,500 were built, equipping many Allied squadrons.

Long exhaust pipes along fuselage sides

Bungee-sprung wheels with fabric covers over wire spokes

Skids project forward to prevent aircraft nosing over on landing

1914·1918 BRISTOL F.2B FIGHTER

DESIGNED BY CAPTAIN Frank Sowter Barnwell of the British and Colonial Aeroplane Co., the Bristol Fighter first flew, as the Bristol F.2A, on September 9, 1916. When it first entered service with Britain's Royal Flying Corps in 1917 it was flown as a reconnaissance airplane; but once the correct strategy for formations of four or five two-seat fighters was worked out it became a popular and effective fighting machine.

LONG SERVICE HISTORY

By the end of October 1918 a total of 1,754 Bristol Fighters had been delivered, and 1,583 remained in RAF (Royal Air Force) service. They served well into the interwar years, notably in India and the Middle East. The last Mk IVs were withdrawn from service in 1931–32.

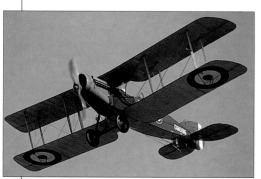

BEAST OF BURDEN

The F.2B Mk 1 could carry up to a dozen 25-lb (11-kg) Cooper high-explosive bombs on racks under its fuselage and lower wing. The post-World War I Mk IV flown by the RAF could carry four Cooper bombs or two 112-lb (50-kg) bombs and a camera gun on the lower wing center-section. An aerial-reconnaissance camera, a radio, and heating equipment could also be attached.

9½-ft (3-m) diameter propeller is geared down to improve efficiency

Fixed Vickers .303-in machine gun under cowling

Metal engine cowling

Fabric-covered wire-spoked wheels

Cable links ailerons on upper and lower wings

SPECIFICATION

Engine 275-hp Rolls-Royce Falcon III water-cooled V12
Wingspan 39 ft 3 in (11.96 m)
Length 25 ft 10 in (7.87 m)
Height 9 ft 9 in (2.97 m)
Loaded weight 2,848 lb (1,292 kg)
Top speed 123 mph (198 km/h)
Rate of climb 838 ft (255 m) per min
Service ceiling 20,000 ft (6,096 m)
Armament Two .303-in machine guns; up to twelve 25-lb (11-kg) Cooper bombs on underwing racks
Crew 2

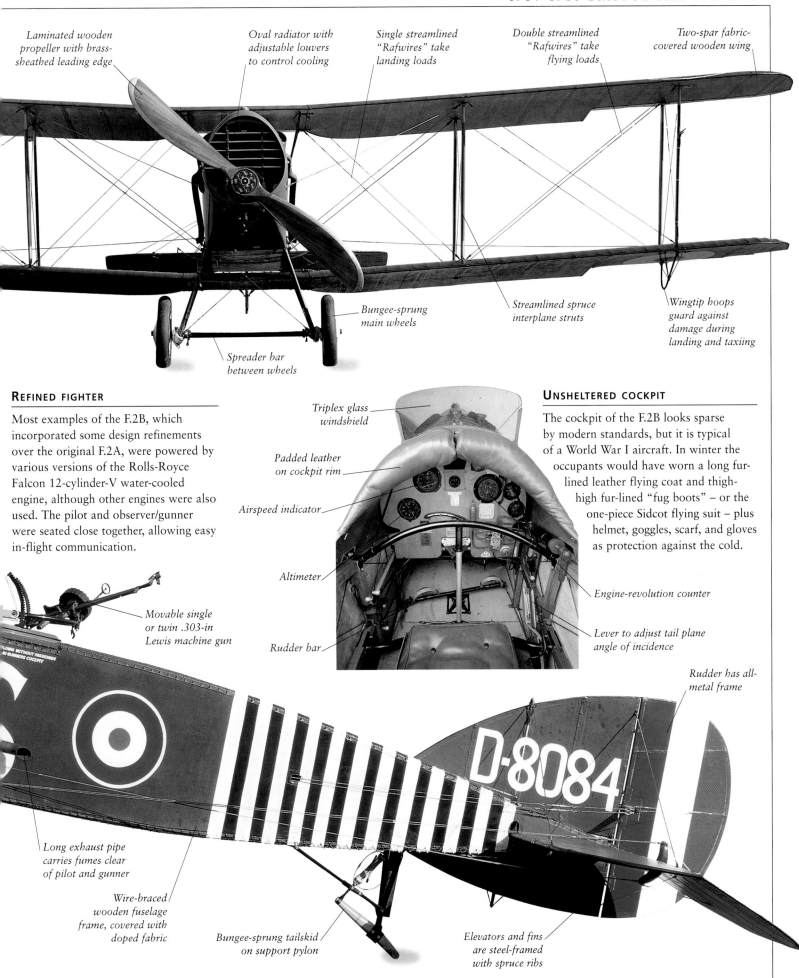

Laminated wooden propeller with brass-sheathed leading edge

Oval radiator with adjustable louvers to control cooling

Single streamlined "Rafwires" take landing loads

Double streamlined "Rafwires" take flying loads

Two-spar fabric-covered wooden wing

Streamlined spruce interplane struts

Wingtip hoops guard against damage during landing and taxiing

Bungee-sprung main wheels

Spreader bar between wheels

REFINED FIGHTER

Most examples of the F.2B, which incorporated some design refinements over the original F.2A, were powered by various versions of the Rolls-Royce Falcon 12-cylinder-V water-cooled engine, although other engines were also used. The pilot and observer/gunner were seated close together, allowing easy in-flight communication.

Triplex glass windshield

Padded leather on cockpit rim

Airspeed indicator

Altimeter

Rudder bar

Movable single or twin .303-in Lewis machine gun

UNSHELTERED COCKPIT

The cockpit of the F.2B looks sparse by modern standards, but it is typical of a World War I aircraft. In winter the occupants would have worn a long fur-lined leather flying coat and thigh-high fur-lined "fug boots" – or the one-piece Sidcot flying suit – plus helmet, goggles, scarf, and gloves as protection against the cold.

Engine-revolution counter

Lever to adjust tail plane angle of incidence

Rudder has all-metal frame

D-8084

Long exhaust pipe carries fumes clear of pilot and gunner

Wire-braced wooden fuselage frame, covered with doped fabric

Bungee-sprung tailskid on support pylon

Elevators and fins are steel-framed with spruce ribs

1914·1918 THE FOKKER LINE

IN 1910, 20-YEAR-OLD Dutchman Anthony
Fokker built the first of his Spin ("Spider")
monoplanes, and just two years later he
formed the Fokker Aviation Company. During World
War I Fokker's products included such famous fighters
as the eindecker (monoplane) scouts, the Dr.1 triplane,
and the D.VII, while the interwar years saw the
development of a series of successful airliners and
military aircraft. After a hiatus during World War II,
the company continued with production from 1945
until 1996, when it went bankrupt.

LATERALLY STABLE SPIN

Anthony Fokker's Spin designs were all low-wing
monoplanes with a sharp dihedral angle to their
wings for lateral stability. The M series of two-
seat military trainers followed this format.
The airplane pictured here is a 1913
variant of the M.I.

360-hp
Rolls-Royce
Eagle VIII
engine

Pilot seated
on port side

FIVE-SEAT AIRLINER

Designed in 1920, the F.III airliner accommodated five
passengers in its cabin. It had a cantilevered wooden wing
and a welded-steel-tube fuselage, and in the earliest versions
the pilot had to endure the discomfort of an open cockpit.
The first customer for this type was Dutch airline KLM. The
type of engine fitted was chosen by the purchaser.

Fabric-covered
wings

Engine cowling houses
modern radial engine in
this replica aircraft

MILITARY DISCHARGE

Following the style set by the Spin series, the M.III of 1913
was designed by a Mr. Palm under Fokker's instructions. It
had a slab-sided fuselage and a distinctive streamlined
rudder, but no fin. Powered by a 100-hp Mercedes or 70-hp
Renault engine – giving it a top speed of 60 mph (96 km/h) –
it proved unsuitable for army use and production was halted.
Palm was fired when his next design, the M.IV, also failed.

Lower portion of engine
exposed for cooling and
emission of lubricant

Fairing covers
spreader bar
between wheels

Single
interplane
struts link
wing spars

COMPANY HIGHLIGHTS

1912 Fokker Aviation Company Limited is formed on Feb 22.

1915 The E.I eindecker scout appears.

1917 The prototype Dr.1 flies, and the triplane goes into production.

1919 The V.45, prototype of the F.II, makes its maiden flight in Oct.

1925 The forerunner of the F.VIIb-3m, the F.VII-3m, flies on Sept 4.

1936 The D.XXI fighter flies. Foreign licenses to build Fokkers granted.

1939 Anthony Fokker dies on Dec 23.

1955 F.27 Friendship first flown.

1996 Fokker files for bankruptcy.

THE SHAPE OF WINGS TO COME

The D.VIII, a sleek, parasol-winged monoplane, was the last Fokker fighter to enter service in World War I. Its welded-steel-tube fuselage and wooden wing later formed the basis of the company's postwar transport aircraft. Like the Dr.1, the D.VIII had a rotary engine and a pair of fixed, forward-firing machine guns above the engine.

POINT 'N' SHOOT

Fokker's E.III eindecker of 1915/16, based on the French Morane-Saulnier designs, had an interrupter gear fitted to its machine-gun armament. The pilot merely aimed his aircraft at an enemy fighter and pressed the trigger. Allied casualties were heavy until countermeasures were taken.

Interrupter gear allows gun to fire between revolving propeller blades

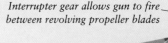

Bungee-sprung main undercarriage

Horn-balanced ailerons on top wing only

RED BARON'S MOUNT

Fokker based his highly maneuverable rotary-engined 1917 Dr.1 triplane fighter on the Sopwith Triplane. Armed with two forward-firing machine guns, it gained fame as the mount of aces such as Baron Manfred von Richthofen, who claimed a record 80 victories.

TURBOPROP SUCCESS

One of the most successful "DC-3 replacements," Fokker's F.27 Friendship was the world's bestselling turboprop-powered commercial transport. Flown for the first time in November 1955, it was powered by a pair of Rolls-Royce Darts and had a pressurized passenger cabin. The aircraft was built under license by Fairchild in the US as the F-27 and FH-227.

Fillet increases fin area

Undercarriage retracts into rear of nacelle

Each nacelle houses a Roll-Royce Tay turbofan

MULTIPLE-CHOICE JET

First flown in November 1986, the Fokker 100 short-to-medium-range airliner carries 107 passengers in its standard configuration, and is powered by two Rolls-Royce Tay turbofans. A corporate and VIP version, the Executive Jet 100, was also available in an Extended Range model with increased fuel capacity. A shorter variant, the Fokker 70, was launched in 1993.

Tail plane bracing strut

Bungee-sprung tail skid

Wingtip skids ̷event damage ̷uring landing

1914·1918 FOKKER D.VII

THE D.VII PROTOTYPE, the V.II of 1917, won a German competition for single-seat fighting scouts in January 1918, and the design was soon put into production, reaching operational units in April. By the autumn over 40 Jastas (fighter squadrons) had received D.VIIs, and it gained a reputation as the best German fighter of World War I. By the time of the Armistice almost 4,000 D.VIIs had been ordered from Fokker and other builders. It was the only aircraft specified in the Armistice agreement among items of military equipment to be handed over to the Allies.

THE FOKKER WAY

The D.VII's fabric-covered fuselage used the welded steel tube box-girder that had become common in Fokker aircraft. The system of struts between the two wings eliminated the need for drag-inducing bracing wires.

CHOICE OF COLORS

One of the many notable fighter pilots to fly the D.VII was Hermann Goering, who commanded Jagdgeschwader I. Like many German fighter pilots he had his airplane painted to his personal taste, choosing the overall white finish seen here. Although the D.VII initially had a 160-hp Mercedes engine, later models were equipped with a 185-hp BMW.

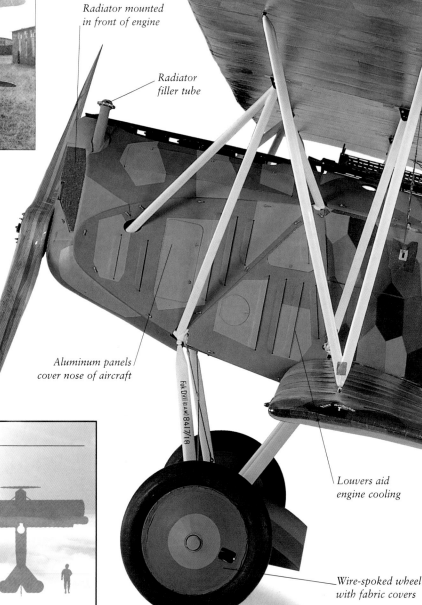

Radiator mounted in front of engine

Radiator filler tube

Aluminum panels cover nose of aircraft

Louvers aid engine cooling

Wire-spoked wheel with fabric covers

SPECIFICATION

Engine 185-hp BMW III six-cylinder in-line water-cooled
Wingspan 29 ft 3 in (8.9 m)
Length 23 ft (7 m)
Height 9 ft 2 in (2.75 m)
Loaded weight 1,870 lb (850 kg)
Top speed 116.6 mph (186.5 km/h)
Rate of climb 3,280 ft (1,000 m) in 2½ mins
Ceiling 22,900 ft (6,980 m)
Armament Two fixed forward-firing Spandau machine guns
Crew 1

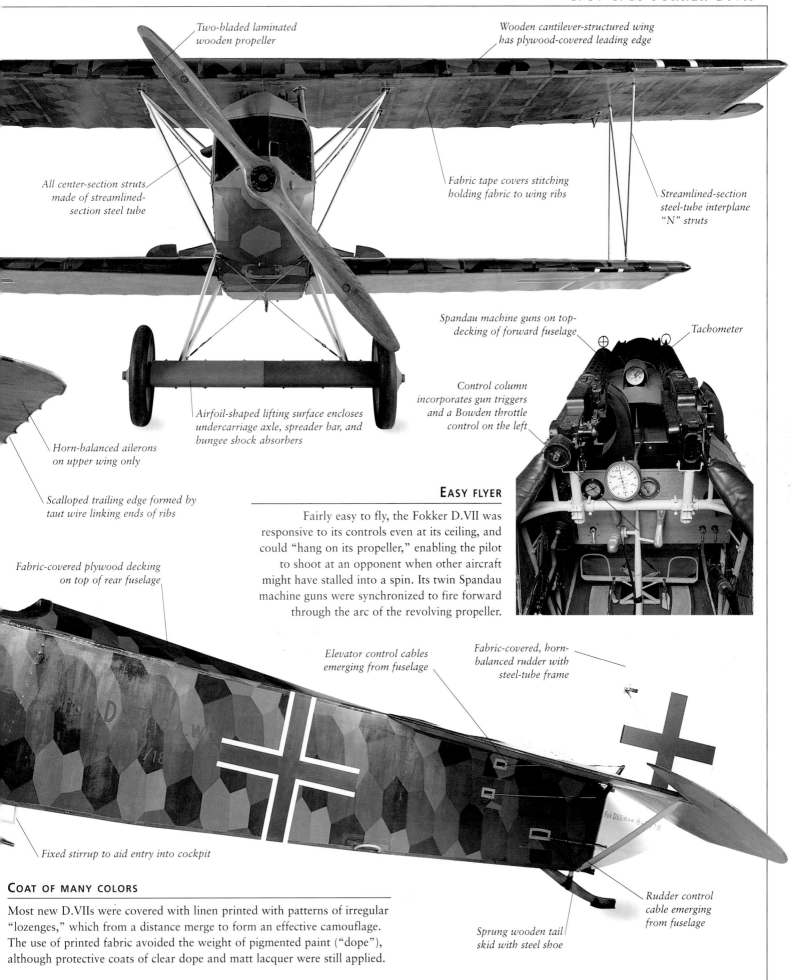

Two-bladed laminated wooden propeller

Wooden cantilever-structured wing has plywood-covered leading edge

All center-section struts made of streamlined-section steel tube

Fabric tape covers stitching holding fabric to wing ribs

Streamlined-section steel-tube interplane "N" struts

Spandau machine guns on top-decking of forward fuselage

Tachometer

Control column incorporates gun triggers and a Bowden throttle control on the left

Airfoil-shaped lifting surface encloses undercarriage axle, spreader bar, and bungee shock absorbers

Horn-balanced ailerons on upper wing only

Scalloped trailing edge formed by taut wire linking ends of ribs

EASY FLYER

Fairly easy to fly, the Fokker D.VII was responsive to its controls even at its ceiling, and could "hang on its propeller," enabling the pilot to shoot at an opponent when other aircraft might have stalled into a spin. Its twin Spandau machine guns were synchronized to fire forward through the arc of the revolving propeller.

Fabric-covered plywood decking on top of rear fuselage

Elevator control cables emerging from fuselage

Fabric-covered, horn-balanced rudder with steel-tube frame

Fixed stirrup to aid entry into cockpit

Rudder control cable emerging from fuselage

Sprung wooden tail skid with steel shoe

COAT OF MANY COLORS

Most new D.VIIs were covered with linen printed with patterns of irregular "lozenges," which from a distance merge to form an effective camouflage. The use of printed fabric avoided the weight of pigmented paint ("dope"), although protective coats of clear dope and matt lacquer were still applied.

1914·1918 THE SOPWITH LINE

Sopwith

ALTHOUGH IT EXISTED for only eight years, the Sopwith Aviation Company produced a rich variety of aircraft types, of which more than 18,000 were built by the parent company and subcontractors. Founded by Thomas Octave Murdoch Sopwith at Kingston-on-Thames, England, in 1912, the company first attained prominence when its Tabloid seaplane won the 1914 Schneider Trophy contest. It went on to build some of the greatest airplanes of World War I, including the Pup and Camel single-seat fighters; and Sopwith aircraft were used by both the military and naval air arms of the Allied forces.

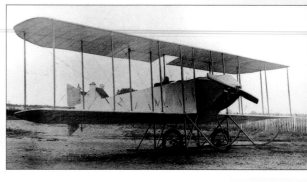

SLOW START

The first Sopwith airplane, this two-seat Sopwith-Wright hybrid appeared in July 1912. Its new fuselage was paired with wings based on those of a Wright-type pusher biplane. Before being replaced with an 80-hp version, its 70-hp Gnome rotary engine gave it a speed of 55 mph (88.5 km/h), slow even in those days. Only two were built.

WATER WINGS

The first successful British flying boat, the Bat Boat appeared in 1913. The wheel-equipped version seen here, powered by a 100-hp engine, won the £500 Mortimer Singer prize for amphibious aircraft on July 8 of that year. Several other variants were built.

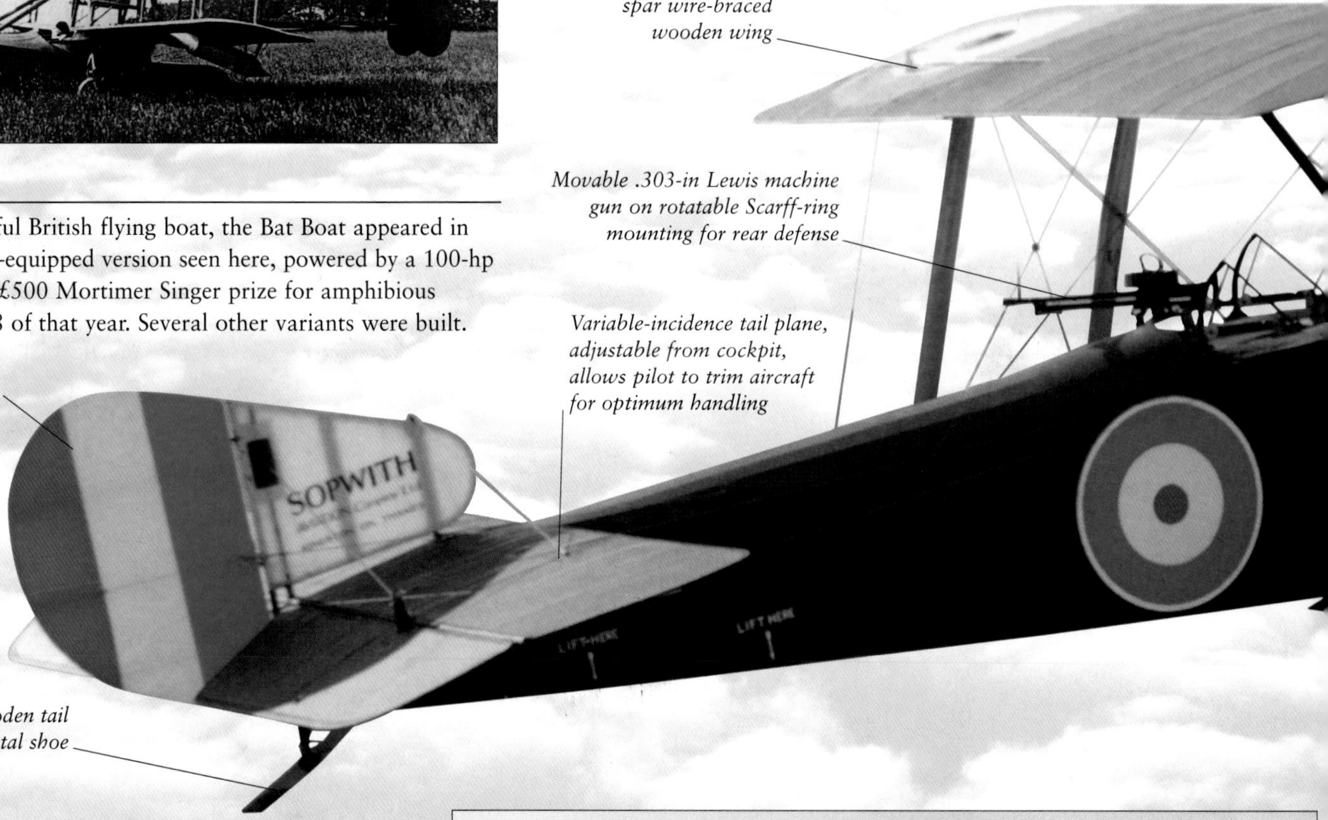

Fabric-covered two-spar wire-braced wooden wing

Movable .303-in Lewis machine gun on rotatable Scarff-ring mounting for rear defense

Variable-incidence tail plane, adjustable from cockpit, allows pilot to trim aircraft for optimum handling

Fabric-covered, unbalanced rudder with steel-tube frame

Sprung wooden tail skid with metal shoe

HEROIC FAILURE

In 1919 Sopwith produced the 360-hp Rolls-Royce Eagle-engined Atlantic for an attempt at the *Daily Mail*'s £10,000 prize for the first nonstop transatlantic flight. Pilot Harry Hawker and navigator Lt. Cdr. K.K. Mackenzie-Grieve left St. Johns, Newfoundland, on May 18, 1919, but incorrect operation of the radiator cooling louvers forced Hawker to ditch. Both men were successfully rescued.

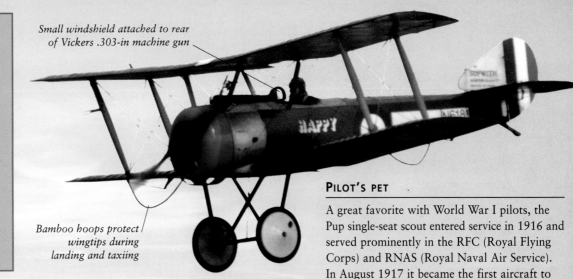

COMPANY HIGHLIGHTS

1912 Sopwith Aviation Company founded.

1914 Tabloid seaplane wins Schneider Trophy contest at Monaco.

1915 Prototype 1½ Strutter appears.

1916 Sopwith Pup makes first flight, as does F.1 Camel.

1917 Sopwith Cuckoo, first landplane torpedo carrier capable of carrier operation, appears.

1919 Harry Hawker attempts non-stop transatlantic flight.

1920 Large tax bill causes Sopwith to liquidate company; he forms H.G. Hawker Engineering.

Small windshield attached to rear of Vickers .303-in machine gun

Bamboo hoops protect wingtips during landing and taxiing

PILOT'S PET

A great favorite with World War I pilots, the Pup single-seat scout entered service in 1916 and served prominently in the RFC (Royal Flying Corps) and RNAS (Royal Naval Air Service). In August 1917 it became the first aircraft to land on the deck of an aircraft carrier.

Two upper wing panels, joined at center

Single forward-firing .303-in Vickers machine gun, synchronized to fire through propeller arc

DEADLY DOLPHIN

A single-seat fighter, the 5F.1 Dolphin first entered service with the RFC late in 1917 and proved to be an excellent fighter. Its 200-hp engine gave it a top speed of 128 mph (206 km/h), and it was armed with two fixed Vickers .303-in machine guns and one or two movable Lewis guns.

Ailerons on upper and lower wings, linked by cable

TWO-SEAT PIONEER

Named after the unusual arrangement of its interplane struts, the 1½ Strutter was a compact two-seat fighter reconnaissance aircraft. It pioneered the concept that led to the Bristol Fighter, and was the first Allied aircraft to go into combat with a synchronized forward-firing gun. It also served as a shipboard fighter.

TRIPLE TROUBLE

The Sopwith Triplane of 1916 succeeded the Pup, but was used operationally only by the RNAS. A very agile combat aircraft, this single-seat fighter was designed to allow its pilot the best possible field of view and ensure maneuverability.

1914·1918 WORLD WAR I BOMBERS

WHEN WAR BROKE OUT in 1914 most airplanes could carry only small bombs, which were dropped over the side of the observer's cockpit. Soon, however, purpose-designed bombers appeared, with their deadly cargoes either carried on racks beneath the fuselage and wings or housed within a special bay in the fuselage. These were released by a mechanism operated by the pilot or bomb-aimer. Bombing raids on civilian populations and industrial targets became an accepted practice.

Two-spar wooden wing with fabric covering

Four-bladed wooden propeller with fabric-covered tips

Parabellum machine gun on rear mounting for tail defense

DAY AND NIGHT BOMBER

Introduced into service towards the end of 1916, the German AEG G.IV lacked the range and lifting power of the Gothas but was built in large numbers and served until the war's end, performing day and night raids on Allied targets behind the lines. It carried an 880-lb (400-kg) bomb load.

Tail surfaces carried on twin boom extensions of engine nacelles

Nacelle for Mercedes engine mounted on lower wing

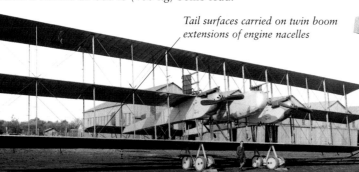

ITALIAN TRIPLANE

In Italy, Caproni produced a range of bombers, including the Ca 4 series of triplanes, such as this 98-ft (30-m) span Ca 42. Up to 26 small bombs were carried in a special streamlined bomb carrier attached to the bottom wing.

DAYLIGHT RAIDER

Germany's Gotha bombers were widely used for daylight raids on London and southern England in the later war years. The Gotha G.III seen here had two 260-hp engines driving pusher propellers, and introduced a rear-fuselage tunnel enabling a defending gunner to fire downward beneath its tail.

Large horn-balanced rudder

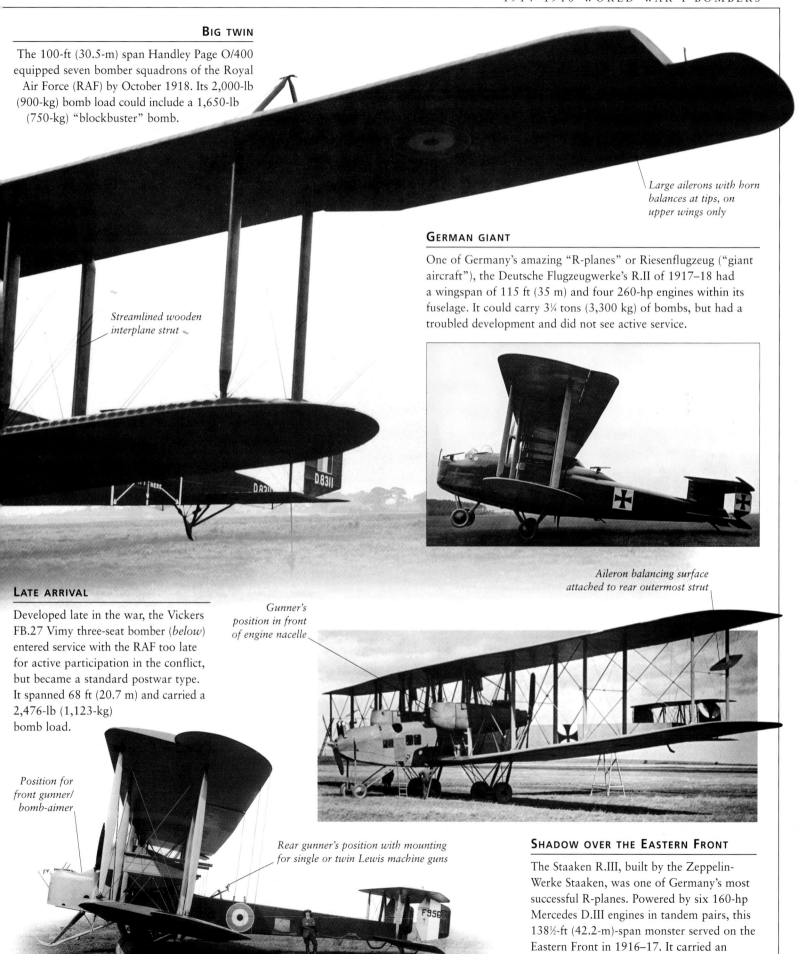

BIG TWIN

The 100-ft (30.5-m) span Handley Page O/400 equipped seven bomber squadrons of the Royal Air Force (RAF) by October 1918. Its 2,000-lb (900-kg) bomb load could include a 1,650-lb (750-kg) "blockbuster" bomb.

Large ailerons with horn balances at tips, on upper wings only

Streamlined wooden interplane strut

GERMAN GIANT

One of Germany's amazing "R-planes" or Riesenflugzeug ("giant aircraft"), the Deutsche Flugzeugwerke's R.II of 1917–18 had a wingspan of 115 ft (35 m) and four 260-hp engines within its fuselage. It could carry 3¼ tons (3,300 kg) of bombs, but had a troubled development and did not see active service.

Aileron balancing surface attached to rear outermost strut

LATE ARRIVAL

Developed late in the war, the Vickers FB.27 Vimy three-seat bomber (*below*) entered service with the RAF too late for active participation in the conflict, but became a standard postwar type. It spanned 68 ft (20.7 m) and carried a 2,476-lb (1,123-kg) bomb load.

Gunner's position in front of engine nacelle

Position for front gunner/ bomb-aimer

Rear gunner's position with mounting for single or twin Lewis machine guns

SHADOW OVER THE EASTERN FRONT

The Staaken R.III, built by the Zeppelin-Werke Staaken, was one of Germany's most successful R-planes. Powered by six 160-hp Mercedes D.III engines in tandem pairs, this 138½-ft (42.2-m)-span monster served on the Eastern Front in 1916–17. It carried an 882–1,764-lb (400–800-kg) bomb load.

1919·1938

THE GOLDEN ERA

WORLD WAR I HAD BOOSTED airplane production to unsustainably high levels, and with its end air forces were downsized and orders canceled. Manufacturers found that the military could not afford new aircraft, and the market for custom-designed civil aircraft was tiny, many airlines using crudely converted bombers. As the 1930s approached, things slowly improved. Helped by pioneering long-distance and survey flights, the larger airlines began to stretch their networks across and between continents, and record-breaking flights pushed the technology steadily forward. This period saw radical developments in both military and civil aircraft, with the advent of sleek all-metal monoplanes with enclosed crew and passenger accommodation, retractable undercarriages, autopilots, and devices to improve low-speed handling and safety.

LEGEND REVIVED

This 1930s poster, advertising Dutch airline KLM, relates modern technology to the legend of the Flying Dutchman. The aircraft depicted is a Fokker F.VIII.

LONG-SERVER

Although it entered service as early as 1936, and was obsolescent by the outbreak of World War II, the Fairey Swordfish torpedo bomber served valiantly with Britain's Fleet Air Arm throughout the entire conflict.

1919·1938 AIRSHIPS

ONCE FRENCHMAN HENRI GIFFARD had flown in his steam-powered airship in 1852 and demonstrated that such a craft could be controlled, the airship developed steadily. There are three basic types: nonrigid, in which the envelope's shape is maintained by the pressure of the gas and air ballonets therein; semi-rigid, which has a rigid keel to help maintain the envelope's form and to support the loads; and rigid, in which a framework gives the airship its shape. Although airships are still with us, they have never regained the prominence they attained in the early years of the 20th century.

"Fusiform" (tapering) envelope reduces resistance of vessel in forward flight

FRENCH AIRSHIP

This French semi-rigid airship, the Lebaudy *Patrie*, was built by Pierre and Paul Lebaudy in 1906. Over 200 ft (61 m) long, it had a 60-hp engine and a speed of 28 mph (45 km/h). It was lost in 1907 when carried out to sea by a stray wind.

A GIANT'S TRAGIC END

Launched in 1936, Zeppelin LZ 129 *Hindenburg* was the largest airship conceived up to that time, with a length of 804 ft (245 m). Of its 63 flights, 37 were ocean crossings. It was lost while approaching its mooring at Lakehurst, New Jersey, on May 6, 1937, when it burst into flames. Although 35 crew and passengers died in the disaster, 62 were saved.

Hull encloses 17 separate gas containers plus 17 fuel tanks

Control gondola and passenger section

Forward engine car on each side with a 530-hp Maybach engine

Wide fabric belts carry cables from which framework and car are suspended

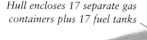

SECOND TO NONE?

Developed and built at Farnborough, England, in 1907 under Col. John Capper and S.F. Cody, Army Dirigible No. 1, *Nulli Secundus*, was Britain's first military airship. A 120-ft (36.6-m) long semi-rigid, it could fly at only 16 mph (26 km/h). Its performance was even worse when "improved" in a 1908 reconstruction.

Small forward control surfaces in framework beneath envelope

FLIGHT TO DISASTER

In the 1920s a scheme for airship services linking the various parts of the British Empire resulted in the construction of two large rigid airships, one of which was the government-built R 101. After a troubled development, it set off on its inaugural flight to India on October 4, 1930. The next day it crashed in France, taking 48 lives.

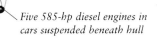

Small, swept tail surfaces

Streamlined hull

Five 585-hp diesel engines in cars suspended beneath hull

Large fins and tail planes in cruciform arrangement

LOST AT SEA

One of America's last two large rigid airships, the Goodyear-Zeppelin USS *Macon* first flew on April 21, 1933, a few weeks after its sister ship, USS *Akron*, was wrecked at sea. Built for the US Navy, it had a top speed of 84 mph (135 km/h) and could carry four Curtiss Sparrowhawk single-seat fighters, which could be launched and retrieved while the airship was in flight. Suffering a structural failure on February 12, 1935, *Macon* came down in open sea.

Wire-braced and fabric-covered hull built from duralumin girders

SUPERSTAR OF THE SKIES

Representing the acme of Zeppelin design, and benefiting from the company's unmatched airship experience before and during World War I, the *Graf Zeppelin* first flew on September 18, 1928. It was over 776 ft (236 m) long, had a volume of 3,708,040 cu ft (105,000 cu m), and could fly at 79.5 mph (128 km/h). By the time it was broken up in March 1940 it had become the most famous and most successful airship ever built, having made 590 flights.

AIRSHIP ADVERTISING

Goodyear produced for the US Navy a series of nonrigid airships, which proved very effective in an antisubmarine role during World War II. More familiar now are the company's smaller public-relations airships, such as the *Columbia IV* of 1974, with illuminated advertising on their sides.

1919·1938 THE FIRST AIRLINERS

WHEN COMMERCIAL AIR transportation began to get off the ground after World War I, many of the aircraft used were hastily converted military bomber and reconnaissance machines. In some cases the intrepid passengers needed to be quite hardy to endure the discomfort of basic seating, minimal facilities, and exposure to considerable cold. Airlines soon realized that better conditions would have to be provided if they were to attract fare-paying customers in any numbers – even if the pilots were still expected to sit in open cockpits.

Auxiliary fuel tanks beneath upper wing

BOMBER NO LONGER

The Breguet 14T*bis* of 1921 was a fairly basic conversion of the company's reconnaissance/day-bomber biplane. The fuselage was deepened to incorporate a two-seat cabin with windows in its sides. This cabin unfortunately obstructed the pilot's forward view during landing. A 300-hp Renault engine was commonly used.

CHANNEL HOPPER

The Blériot 165 appeared in 1926. The aircraft was powered by a pair of 420-hp Gnome Rhône Jupiter air-cooled radial engines, could attain speed of 112 mph (180 km/h), and carried 15–16 passengers. There were only two examples built and both saw service with the French airline Air Union, operating on its Paris–London route.

Wide-track undercarriage provides stability when landing and taxiing

Baggage compartment in nose, in front of cockpit

CONVERSION OF A CLASSIC

Vickers produced the Vimy Commercial (*left*) by combining the flying surfaces of its Rolls-Royce Eagle-engined Vimy bomber with a new oval-section fuselage, which had a monocoque front section incorporating a 10-passenger cabin. First flown in April 1919, it had a stately cruising speed of 84 mph (135 km/h).

Horn-balanced rudder

NEW USE FOR FLYING EYE

At the smaller end of the scale were conversions of military two-seat reconnaissance aircraft, adapted to carry two passengers. This German AEG N.I was a development of the J II two-seater, with a cabin in front of the pilot's cockpit. Used on Frankfurt–Berlin services in 1920, it survived to serve with Lufthansa in 1926. It had a 200-hp Benz engine.

Two passengers carried in open bow cockpit, with pilot's cockpit behind

BOW PASSENGERS

The Handley Page O/11 of 1920 was a converted O/400 bomber operated by Handley Page Transport Ltd. It carried two passengers in the bow cockpit and three in a cabin in the rear fuselage, plus freight in a hold amidships. Two 360-hp Rolls-Royce Eagle engines gave these beasts a maximum speed of 97.5 mph (157 km/h). Another version, the O/10, carried 12 passengers.

Biplane tail plane with central fin and twin outer rudders

SPORTY MODEL

A more racy design than most was the Blériot Spad 33 with a Salmson radial engine, first flown in December 1920. Its four passengers were accommodated in a wooden monocoque fuselage, three circular windows usually being provided in the cabin. Two side-by-side open cockpits were sited behind this cabin for the pilot and a fifth passenger.

ROOM FOR NINE INSIDE

First flown in 1922, de Havilland's D.H.34 accommodated nine passengers seated in wicker chairs inside its plywood-covered fuselage. Powered by a 450-hp Napier Lion water-cooled engine, it cruised at 105 mph (170 km/h) and was used on services from London's Croydon Airport to Le Bourget, Paris.

Engine-cooling water radiator on center section of upper wing

Ailerons on upper and lower wings, linked by pushrod

Two passengers in forward compartment

1919-1938 THE TRAILBLAZERS

As soon as World War I ended, a number of intrepid pilots prepared to attempt long-distance intercontinental flights to win large money prizes. These were the first of many interwar flights that opened up the commercial air routes linking the world's major cities. Many of the pilots, like Charles Lindbergh and Alcock and Brown, became household names, as did some of their aircraft.

Fabric-covered, wire-braced wooden biplane wing structure

SURVEYING AFRICA

In this Short Singapore I flying boat, powered by two 650-hp Rolls-Royce Condor water-cooled engines, Sir Alan Cobham made a 23,000-mile (37,000-km) survey flight around Africa on behalf of Imperial Airways during 1927–28. He reported on more than 50 possible seaplane bases in and around Africa, making some 90 takeoffs and landings in 330 hours of flying.

Skid to prevent aircraft nosing over on landing

AUSTRALIAN SUCCESS

In December 1919 Australian brothers Capt. Ross Smith and Lt. Keith Smith, with two crew members, completed the first flight from Britain to Australia in this Vickers Vimy bomber (*above*). Flying 11,294 miles (18,183 km) in 135 hours, 55 minutes, they won knighthoods and £10,000 from the Australian government.

Radiators on front of engine nacelles for water-cooled engines

One-piece wooden wing has two main box spars, plywood ribs, and plywood covering

Welded-steel-tube fuselage structure with fabric covering

FIRST AROUND-THE-WORLD FLIGHT

On April 6, 1924, four US Air Service Douglas World Cruisers set off from Seattle, Washington, to attempt the first around-the-world flight. Lt. Lowell H. Smith and Lt. Erik Nelson, piloting *Chicago* and *New Orleans* respectively, completed the 27,553-mile (44,340-km) trip 175 days later, on September 28. The total flying time was 371 hours, 11 minutes.

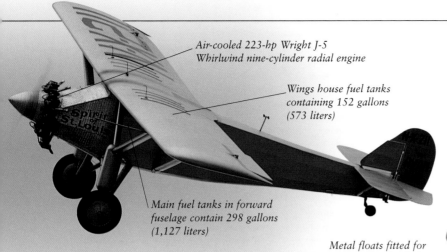

Air-cooled 223-hp Wright J-5 Whirlwind nine-cylinder radial engine

Wings house fuel tanks containing 152 gallons (573 liters)

Main fuel tanks in forward fuselage contain 298 gallons (1,127 liters)

FROM NEW YORK TO PARIS

The first solo nonstop flight across the North Atlantic was made by American Captain Charles Lindbergh in his Ryan NYP monoplane *Spirit of St. Louis* during May 20–21, 1927. Lindbergh took off from Long Island, New York, and landed at Le Bourget, Paris, after flying 3,610 miles (5,810 km) in 33 hours, 39 minutes. His average flying speed was 107.5 mph (173 km/h).

Cabin for passengers and crew, in front of pilot's open cockpit

Metal floats fitted for Australia flight

NONSTOP TRANSATLANTIC FLYERS

Pilot Capt. John Alcock and navigator Lt. Arthur Whitten Brown made the first nonstop transatlantic flight on June 14/15, 1919, in this modified Vickers Vimy bomber. The flight, for which both were knighted, took the men from St. John's, Newfoundland, to a bog in Clifden, County Galway, Ireland, in 16 hours, 27 minutes. The achievement also won them £10,000 from the *Daily Mail*.

AIR SURVEILLANCE

Between June 30 and October 1, 1926, Alan Cobham made the first England-to-Australia and return flight, as a survey for Imperial Airways, in this de Havilland D.H.50J biplane powered by a 385-hp radial engine. Previously he had flown the same machine on a 16,000-mile (25,700-km) survey flight to the Cape of Good Hope, Africa.

Huge fuel tank in fuselage beneath wing center section

Wright J-5C Whirlwind radial engine

Metal cowling panels around nose

Two-bladed adjustable-pitch metal propeller

ALL AROUND THE WORLD

Flying a Fokker F.VIIb-3m airliner named *Southern Cross*, Australian Charles Kingsford Smith made the first true transpacific flight, from California to Brisbane, Australia, in 1928, and the first air crossing of the Tasman Sea later the same year. He then flew the aircraft from Sydney to London in 12 days and 23 hours in 1929, made the second east-west transatlantic flight, from Ireland to Newfoundland, on June 24–25, 1930, and flew across the US to complete a 80,000-mile (129,000-km) around-the-world flight, for which he was knighted.

1919·1938 FORD 5-AT-B TRI-MOTOR

ORIGINATED from a design conceived by American Bill Stout in the 1920s, the Ford Tri-Motor combined the Dutch-designed Fokker Tri-motor's size and shape with the all-metal, corrugated-skin construction developed by Hugo Junkers in Germany. The result was an exceptionally rugged and reliable workhorse, built on an assembly line and offering three-engine safety. The 3-AT prototype of 1925 was followed in 1926 by the first production model, the 4-AT. In 1928 the most famous model appeared, the larger and more powerful 5-AT, which was produced in a number of variants.

SPECIFICATION

Engines Three 220-hp Wright J-5 radials
Wingspan 77 ft 10 in (23.7 m)
Length 49 ft 10 in (15.2 m)
Height 12 ft (3.65 m)
Typical takeoff weight 13,000 lb (5,897 kg)
Cruising speed 122 mph (196 km/h)
Ceiling 18,500 ft (5,639 m)
Passengers 15
Crew 2

REFINED MODEL

This period photograph depicts 5-AT-B Tri-Motor NC-9685, which was built in 1929 and served with Pan American Airways, carrying passengers and mail. The two underwing engines are fitted with cowling rings to enhance cooling and improve their aerodynamics, and the main wheels have fenders.

VERSATILE GOOSE

The Tri-Motor's unofficial nickname, "Tin Goose," belies its capabilities, since it has been rolled, looped, and even flown upsidedown. Between the first 3-AT and the last of the family, flown in mid-1933, 200 Tri-Motors were built, and they flew with more than 100 airlines, fitted with wheels, floats, or skis.

Elevator control cables

Swiveling tail wheel with shock absorber

Corrugated Alclad skinning on duralumin channel-section framework, riveted together

Entrance door to passenger cabin

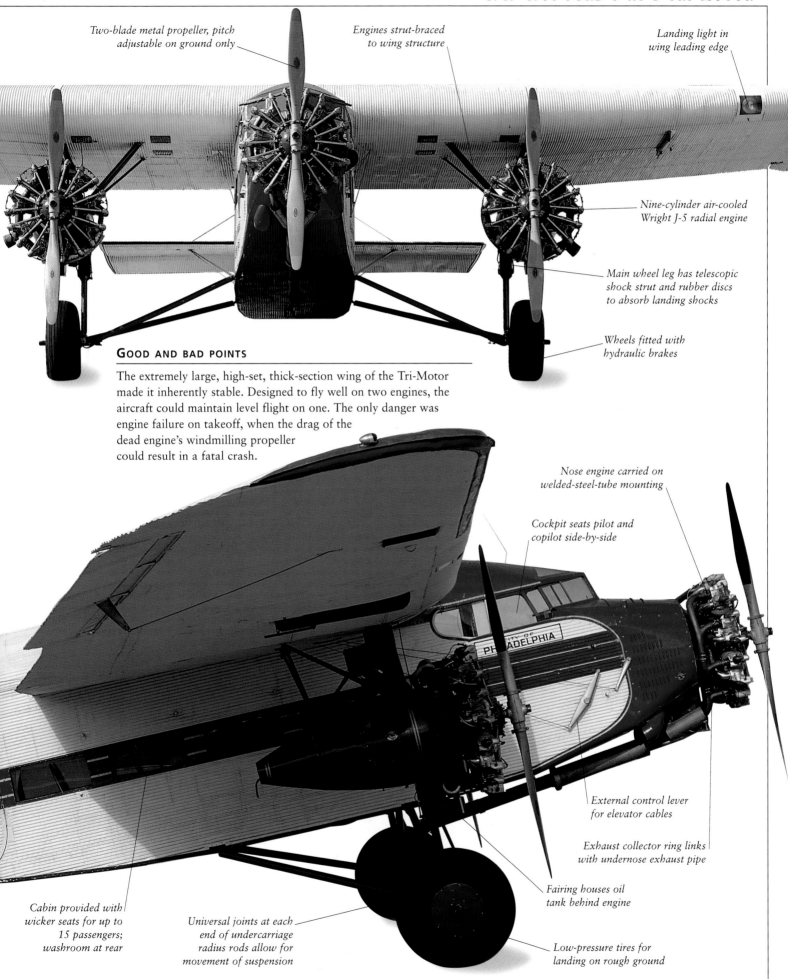

Two-blade metal propeller, pitch
adjustable on ground only

Engines strut-braced
to wing structure

Landing light in
wing leading edge

Nine-cylinder air-cooled
Wright J-5 radial engine

Main wheel leg has telescopic
shock strut and rubber discs
to absorb landing shocks

Wheels fitted with
hydraulic brakes

Good and bad points

The extremely large, high-set, thick-section wing of the Tri-Motor
made it inherently stable. Designed to fly well on two engines, the
aircraft could maintain level flight on one. The only danger was
engine failure on takeoff, when the drag of the
dead engine's windmilling propeller
could result in a fatal crash.

Nose engine carried on
welded-steel-tube mounting

Cockpit seats pilot and
copilot side-by-side

External control lever
for elevator cables

Exhaust collector ring links
with undernose exhaust pipe

Fairing houses oil
tank behind engine

Cabin provided with
wicker seats for up to
15 passengers;
washroom at rear

Universal joints at each
end of undercarriage
radius rods allow for
movement of suspension

Low-pressure tires for
landing on rough ground

61

1919·1938 THE SCHNEIDER TROPHY

INTRODUCED IN 1912 by Jacques Schneider, son of the owner of the Schneider armaments works at Le Creusôt, France, the Schneider Trophy contests were designed to encourage seaplane development. In the interwar years they became keenly fought events for which the world's foremost manufacturers and designers vied to produce airplanes and engines capable of ever greater performance. By the time the trophy was finally won outright by Britain, in 1931, the contest had become a matter of intense national prestige.

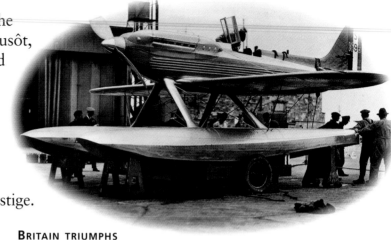

BRITAIN TRIUMPHS

R.J. Mitchell's sleek Supermarine S.6B finally won the trophy outright for Britain by achieving the country's third successive victory at Calshot, Southampton, on September 13, 1931. A fuel "cocktail" was used to wring the utmost from the Rolls-Royce "R" racing engine that powered it. The winning speed was 340.08 mph (547.297 km/h).

TABLOID WINS

Britain's first victory was at Monaco in 1914, when Howard Pixton took this Sopwith Tabloid seaplane around the 28-lap course at an average speed of 86.78 mph (139.66 km/h). He then flew two more laps to set a world seaplane speed record of 86.6 mph (139.39 km/h) over a 186-mile (300-km) course.

Cabane struts carry bracing wires to wings

Open, unfaired cockpit

Spinner attached to propeller improves streamlining

Fabric-covered wooden wing with wire bracing

FIRST HONORS

The honor of winning the very first Schneider Trophy contest, at Monaco in 1913, went to French pilot Maurice Prévost, flying this Deperdussin seaplane powered by a 160-hp 14-cylinder two-row Gnome rotary engine. His true average speed over the course was 61 mph (98 km/h), about a seventh of the winning speed of the final contest in 1931.

BETTERED SUPERMARINE

Britain's entry in the 1923 contest off the English port of Cowes, Isle of Wight, was this Supermarine Sea Lion III. Although the aircraft's 525-hp Napier Lion engine took it around the course at 157.17 mph (252.94 km/h), which was 12 mph (19 km/h) faster than its forebear's winning speed the previous year, it was relegated to third place by the new American Curtiss seaplanes.

Cowlings easily removable for quick servicing

Long float struts lift propeller clear of spray

FLAWED CONTENDERS

Powered by 1,000-hp Fiat AS.3 engines, the three Macchi M.52s entered by Italy in the 1927 event at Venice were all forced to retire due to engine problems. As some small compensation, a new world speed record of 300.94 mph (484.304 km/h) was set by an M.52 in Venice on October 22.

Fairings over engine cylinder heads

Ailerons on upper and lower wings

Single faired I-strut between wings

Two-blade fixed-pitch metal propeller

Wires and struts brace floats

AMERICAN POWER

Backed by funding from the US Navy, in 1925 Curtiss entered the R3C-2, powered by the superb 600-hp Curtiss V-1400 engine. Piloted by the charismatic Lt. James Doolittle, it sailed to first place at 232.57 mph (374.28 km/h). Next day, Doolittle also set a world speed record for floatplanes of 245.7 mph (395.4 km/h).

ITALIAN FINESSE

In 1926 at Hampton Roads, Virginia, the Italians stole the show in their elegant Macchi M.39s with 800-hp Fiat AS.2 engines. They took the first and third places, the winning airplane averaging a speed of 246.496 mph (396.698 km/h).

Three layers of tulipwood veneer make up monocoque fuselage

1919·1938 FLYING BOATS & SEAPLANES

THE GREAT FLYING boats of the 1920s and 1930s had a stately elegance unmatched by any other airplane type. They were a manifestation of their time, the products of an age when only the wealthy could afford to fly, and expected to do so in a style comparable with that of a cruise liner, though much faster. Even so, a long intercontinental flight was a leisurely affair, flown in stages and often requiring changes of aircraft. The advantage of the flying boat was that it could land on any clear expanse of water and did not require constructions of expensive runways in obscure locations.

ENGINES BY THE DOZEN

Designed for transatlantic operation, the 157-ft (48-m) span Dornier Do X first flew in July 1929 but never entered airline service. The final version was powered by twelve 600-hp Curtiss Conqueror water-cooled engines, as seen here. The Do X undertook a transatlantic proving flight during 1930–31.

TWIN-HULLED AMPHIBIAN

The unconventional twin-hulled Savoia Marchetti S.55 flying boat originated in 1924 as a torpedo bomber for Italy's Regia Marina, but commercial versions were also produced. Seen here is one of the 25 S.55Xs, powered by two 750-hp Isotta-Fraschini engines, that made an 11,495-mile (18,499-km) mass-formation flight from Rome to Chicago and back in 1933, led by Air Marshal Italo Balbo.

Engines mounted back-to-back on pylons over center of wing

Cockpit positioned between pylons on wing center-section

Strut-mounted stabilizing floats at wingtips

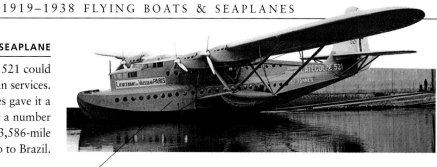

RECORD-HOLDING SEAPLANE

First flown in January 1935, the Latécoère 521 could carry 70 passengers on trans-Mediterranean services. Its six 860-hp Hispano-Suiza 12Ybrs engines gave it a top speed of 162 mph (261 km/h), and it set a number of seaplane records, including a nonstop 3,586-mile (5,771-km) flight from Morocco to Brazil.

Engines in tandem above fuselage, well clear of spray

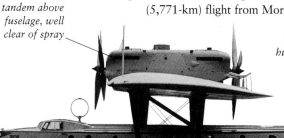

Two decks in all-metal hull; commander's cabin in front of upper deck

AIRBORNE WHALE

A highly successful design, the all-metal Dornier Do J II Wal ("Whale") first flew in 1922 and stayed in production until 1936, some 300 being built. There were several variants, both military and civil; seen here is a Wal 33, the last refinement, powered by a pair of 690-hp BMW VI engines.

Sponsons stabilize aircraft on water

AMERICAN MAIL

The Boeing Model 314 first flew in June 1938. It had a wingspan of 152 ft (46.33 m) and its four 1,500/1,600-hp Wright Cyclone radial engines gave it a cruising speed of 188 mph (303 km/h). Using 314s, Pan American Airways inaugurated transatlantic mail and passenger services in 1939. Three of the 12 built were operated by BOAC (British Overseas Airways Corporation).

Steps in hull enable aircraft to overcome suction on takeoff

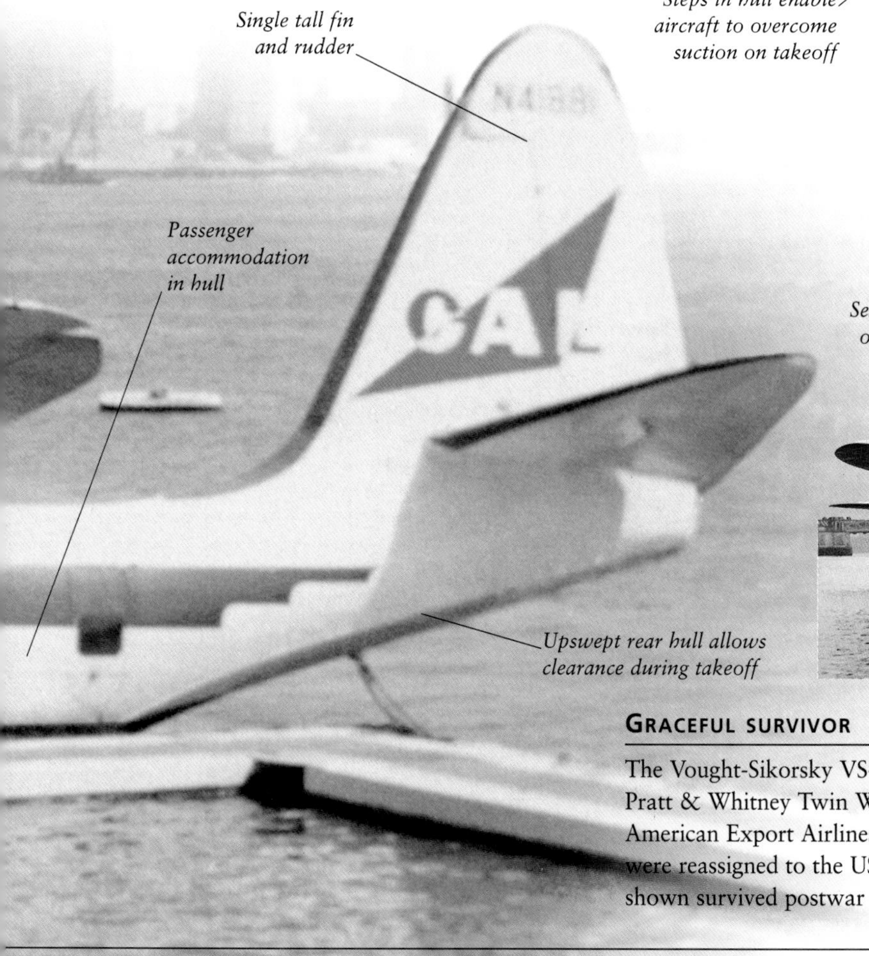

Single tall fin and rudder

Passenger accommodation in hull

COMPOSITE SOLUTION

Initially, the fuel load required to span the Atlantic ruled out a useful payload. The Short-Mayo Composite consisted of a lightly laden flying boat that carried a heavily laden seaplane aloft, the seaplane then being released to continue the flight. The smaller craft, named *Mercury*, made a number of long-distance mail flights before the outbreak of World War II.

Seaplane carried on strut system

Upswept rear hull allows clearance during takeoff

GRACEFUL SURVIVOR

The Vought-Sikorsky VS-44 (*left*) was powered by four 1,200-hp Pratt & Whitney Twin Wasp radial engines. Three were ordered by American Export Airlines in 1940 for transatlantic services, but were reassigned to the US Navy during World War II. The example shown survived postwar civil operations and is preserved today.

Mother plane Maia carries Mercury to cruising height

1919·1938 THE JUNKERS LINE

IN 1910, GERMAN PROFESSOR Hugo Junkers patented an aircraft with a large metal wing. He later developed a metal cantilever wing with a corrugated duralumin skin, which was applied to several World War I combat aircraft designed by his company. After the war Junkers produced a range of all-metal civil aircraft, from small two-seaters to large airliners such as the G 38. Junkers' company was taken over by the state in 1933 and he died two years later. In World War II the Luftwaffe flew the Ju 87 Stuka and the Ju 88 bomber among others. In 1945 the company fell into Soviet hands.

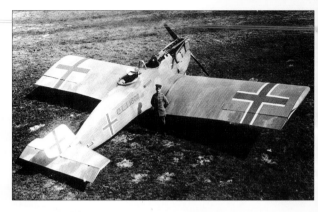

TWO-SEAT PATROLLER

Given the military designation CL I, the J.10 was intended for offensive patrols and close air support of ground troops. It first flew in May 1918. Its 160-hp Mercedes D III engine gave it a top speed of 118 mph (190 km/h), and it was armed with one or two fixed Maxim 08/15 machine guns and a movable Parabellum gun for the observer.

Front cockpit faired over

JAPAN-BOUND JUNIOR

The Junkers A.50 Junior all-metal light two-seater appeared in 1929. The one shown above, powered by an 85-hp Armstrong-Siddley Genet engine and with its front cockpit faired over, was flown from Berlin to Tokyo in 1930 by Japanese pilot Seiji Yoshihara, who averaged 600 miles (970 km) per day.

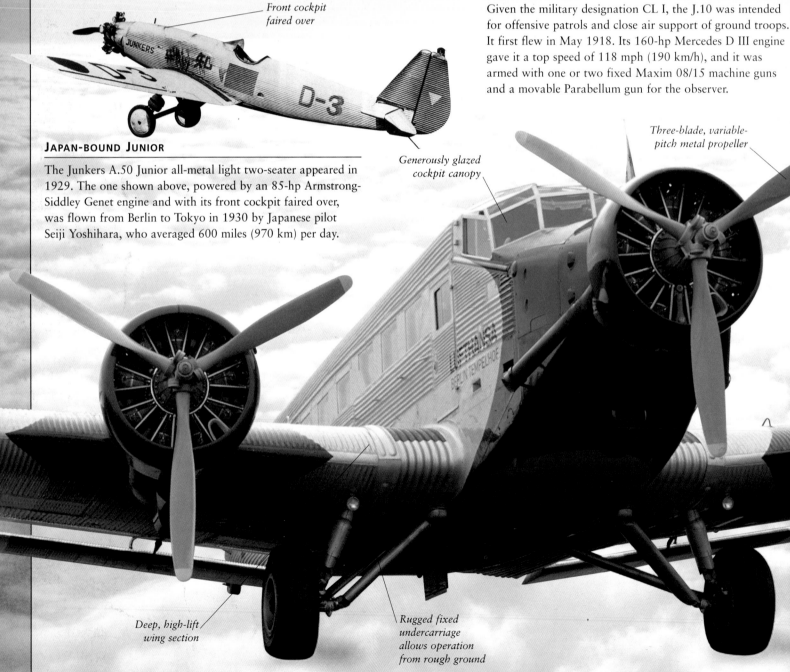

Three-blade, variable-pitch metal propeller

Generously glazed cockpit canopy

Deep, high-lift wing section

Rugged fixed undercarriage allows operation from rough ground

ARMORED GUARDIAN

Designed for "contact patrols" with the infantry, this large biplane had armor plate to protect its two-man crew and engine, making it heavy and slow-climbing. A water-cooled 230-hp Benz Bz IV engine gave it a speed of 97 mph (155 km/h). A total of 227 were built and delivered to the German air force, where the aircraft was designated J I.

INNOVATORY WING

Designed immediately after the 1918 Armistice, the F 13 was a four-seat commercial transport with its crew occupying an open cockpit. First flown on July 18, 1919, it was very advanced, its all-metal wing being based on a girder of nine tubular duralumin spars braced together. When production ceased in 1932, 322 had been built.

SMOOTH OPERATOR

Lacking the distinctive Junkers corrugated finish, the Ju 160 was a six-passenger, single-engined airliner with a 660-hp BMW 132E radial engine, used on Lufthansa's domestic express services from 1935. Its maximum speed was 211 mph (340 km/h).

Crew cabin faired into top of fuselage

Fairing on non-retractable tail wheel

Inward-retracting main undercarriage

COMPANY HIGHLIGHTS

1895 Junkers company founded.

1915 The first Junkers airplane, the iron-clad J.1 all-metal monoplane, makes first flight.

1919 Junkers Flugzeugwerke formed.

1919 Maiden flight of F 13 single-engined transport.

1924 First flight of G 23, the first three-engined all-metal monoplane in airline service.

1932 Ju 52/3m makes maiden flight.

1933 Company taken over by state.

1945 Soviet invaders seize Junkers.

POPULAR AND ADAPTABLE

Over 4,800 Junkers Ju 52/3m aircraft were produced, outnumbering any other European transport model. Affectionately known as "Tante Ju" ("Auntie Ju"), it served as an airliner, freighter, troop carrier, bomber, glider tug, ambulance, and mine-countermeasures aircraft.

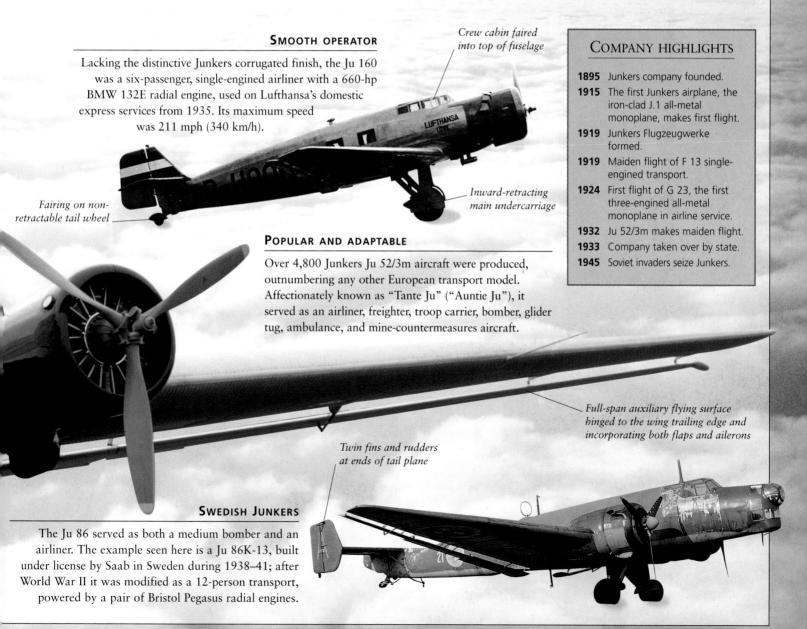

Full-span auxiliary flying surface hinged to the wing trailing edge and incorporating both flaps and ailerons

Twin fins and rudders at ends of tail plane

SWEDISH JUNKERS

The Ju 86 served as both a medium bomber and an airliner. The example seen here is a Ju 86K-13, built under license by Saab in Sweden during 1938–41; after World War II it was modified as a 12-person transport, powered by a pair of Bristol Pegasus radial engines.

1919-1938 LARGE INTERWAR AIRLINERS

COMMERCIAL AIR TRAVEL was an accepted form of transport by the 1930s, and the principal aircraft manufacturers were producing new airliners to serve the multiplicity of routes – internal, transcontinental, and intercontinental – that were spreading across the globe. These large, multiengined aircraft, far removed from the frail biplanes of only 20 years earlier, were taking the colors of the major airlines to all of the world's major cities, transporting their human cargoes in heated cabins with stewards in attendance.

SLEEPER BIPLANE

First flown in 1933, the Curtiss Condor II biplane appeared in the USA just as Boeing and Douglas were introducing their sleek metal monoplanes. However, it did have a retractable undercarriage and full accommodation for 12 passengers. Eastern Air Transport and American Airways used the biplane to pioneer night sleeper services.

COMFORTABLE CRUISER

Accommodating 22 passengers in its four cabins, the Fokker F.XXII had smart lines marred only by its fixed undercarriage. Four 500-hp Pratt & Whitney Wasp T1D1 radial engines gave it a cruising speed of 133.5 mph (215 km/h). Dutch airline KLM took delivery of the first of three F.XXIIs in 1935.

High-wing layout raises propellers well clear of ground, but requires tall undercarriage

Direction-finding loop antenna

Unpressurized, light-alloy, stressed-skin monocoque fuselage

EXCLUSIVE SERVICES

Used only by Britain's Imperial Airways, the Handley Page H.P.42 had four Bristol Jupiter radial engines. Its Warren-girder wing bracing made bracing wires unnecessary. First flown in 1931, it cruised at a stately 100 mph (161 km/h). A 24-passenger Eastern model flew routes in Africa and Asia, while a 38-passenger Western version operated in Europe.

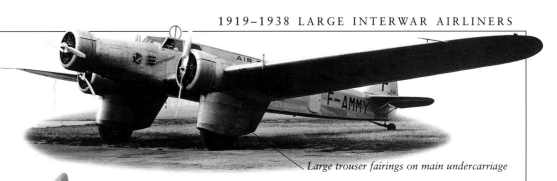

FRENCH TRIMOTOR

Powered by three 575-hp Hispano-Suiza 9V air-cooled radial engines, the French Dewoitine D.332 had a fixed undercarriage despite being of advanced all-metal construction. First flown in 1933, it carried eight passengers and offered sleeper facilities.

Large trouser fairings on main undercarriage

Well-streamlined engine cowlings

ELEGANCE IN WOOD

The sleek de Havilland D.H.91 Albatross was powered by four 525-hp de Havilland Gipsy Twelve water-cooled engines. Its all-wood structure went against the trend for metal. The fuselage was made of cedar ply with a thick balsa core.

FLIGHTS OF THE CONDOR

First flown in July 1937, the Focke-Wulf Fw 200 Condor had four BMW 132 radial engines and carried a total of 25–26 passengers in its two cabins. The Condor was capable of making nonstop flights from Berlin to New York.

Large flaps on wing trailing edge reduce landing speed

Doors enclose all but a portion of the 6-ft 3-in (1.9-m) diameter wheels when undercarriage is retracted

Fabric-covered fin and rudder

FLAGSHIP FOR BRITAIN

The largest landplane built for Imperial Airways before World War II, the Armstrong Whitworth A.W.27 Ensign took to the air in January 1938. Initially the Ensigns had four 850-hp Armstrong Siddeley Tiger IXC radial engines, but the aircraft proved underpowered and they were replaced by 950-hp Wright Cyclones. Early in World War II a few Ensigns flew food, ammunition, and other equipment to the British forces in France.

1919·1938 WARPLANE EVOLUTION

NATIONS BEGAN TO RE-EQUIP their air forces in the late 1920s and 1930s, after allowing them to run down in the aftermath of World War I. Aircraft manufacturers produced a great assortment of fighters and bombers, some of them retaining traditional features, but many introducing new structural techniques and weaponry. Gradually, biplanes began to give way to monoplanes, although these often retained the drafty open cockpits and some of the external wing bracing of their biplane predecessors.

Metal fuselage shaped with wooden formers and covered with fabric

NAVAL WARRIOR

The Boeing F4B-3 carrier-borne fighter entered US Navy service in 1931. Powered by a 550-hp Pratt & Whitney R-1340 air-cooled radial engine, it had a maximum speed of 188 mph (302 km/h). F4B-3s were used on carriers up to 1938.

Enclosed pilot's cockpit

IMPECCABLE STYLING

One of the family of elegant Hawker military biplanes, the Hart two-seat light day bomber was powered by a 525-hp 12-cylinder water-cooled Rolls-Royce Kestrel. Entering RAF (Royal Air Force) service in 1930, it was built in large numbers and flown by both home and overseas units.

NEW-FOUND LUXURY

The first RAF bomber to have a power-operated enclosed gun turret, the Boulton Paul Overstrand (*right*) entered service in 1936. Powered by two 580-hp Bristol Pegasus air-cooled radial engines, it had the luxury of an enclosed cockpit for the pilot and heating for the crew, but its fixed undercarriage and biplane structure cut top speed to 153 mph (246 km/h).

Power-operated nose turret for single .303-in Lewis machine gun

Mid-upper gunner has one .303-in Lewis gun

Nonretractable main undercarriage

TWO-WAY POWER

The French Armée de l'Air's first four-engined bomber, the Farman F.221 entered service in 1936. It was powered by four 700-hp Gnome Rhône radial engines in push-pull pairs on either side of its nose.

BRITISH BULLDOG

Bristol Bulldog single-seat fighters equipped front-line RAF fighter squadrons from 1929 to 1937. Although relatively slow, they comprised some 70 percent of Britain's fighter defenses. Armed with twin forward-firing .303-in Vickers machine guns, the Bulldog had a 490-hp Bristol Jupiter air-cooled radial engine which gave it a top speed of 174 mph (280 km/h).

Ailerons on upper wing only

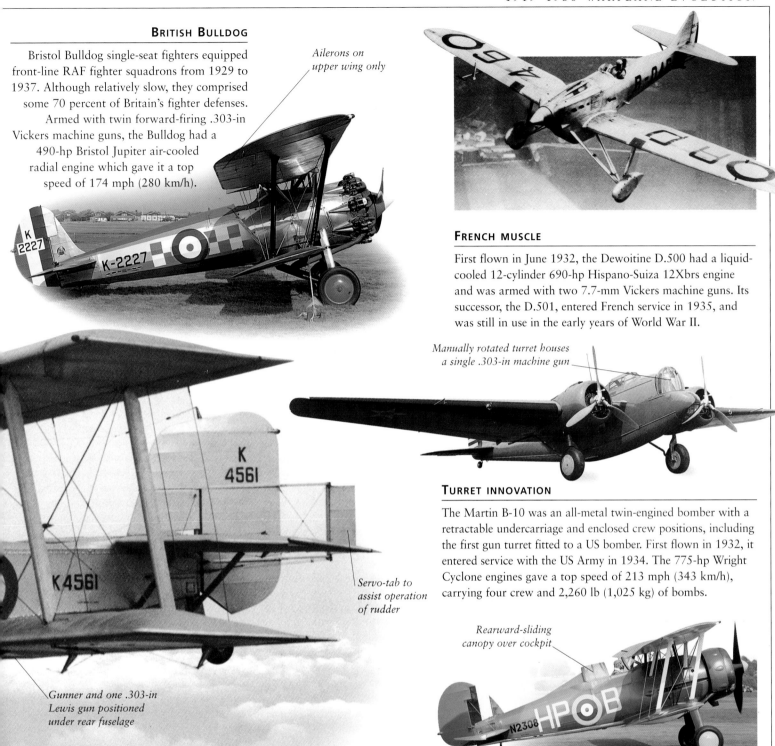

K-2227

K 4561

K 4561

Servo-tab to assist operation of rudder

Gunner and one .303-in Lewis gun positioned under rear fuselage

FRENCH MUSCLE

First flown in June 1932, the Dewoitine D.500 had a liquid-cooled 12-cylinder 690-hp Hispano-Suiza 12Xbrs engine and was armed with two 7.7-mm Vickers machine guns. Its successor, the D.501, entered French service in 1935, and was still in use in the early years of World War II.

Manually rotated turret houses a single .303-in machine gun

TURRET INNOVATION

The Martin B-10 was an all-metal twin-engined bomber with a retractable undercarriage and enclosed crew positions, including the first gun turret fitted to a US bomber. First flown in 1932, it entered service with the US Army in 1934. The 775-hp Wright Cyclone engines gave a top speed of 213 mph (343 km/h), carrying four crew and 2,260 lb (1,025 kg) of bombs.

Rearward-sliding canopy over cockpit

HP⊙B

N2308

ITALIAN THOROUGHBRED

First delivered to Italy's Regia Aeronautica in 1934, the Fiat CR.32 was one of the outstanding single-seat fighters of the era. Its 590-hp Fiat A 30 RA 12-cylinder water-cooled engine gave it a speed of 220 mph (354 km/h). In 1936, CR.32s served in the Spanish Civil War.

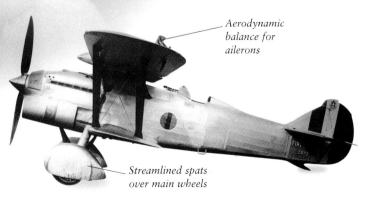

Aerodynamic balance for ailerons

Streamlined spats over main wheels

HERO OF MALTA

The last biplane fighter to serve with the RAF, the Gloster Gladiator first entered service in 1937. Capable of 253 mph (407 km/h) on the power of its 840-hp Bristol Mercury radial engine, it was armed with four forward-firing machine guns. The Gladiator is best known for the part it played in the valiant defense of Malta during 1940–41.

1919·1938 METAL MONOPLANES

MOST OF THE COMMERCIAL aircraft of the 1920s were wooden biplanes and monoplanes, often with drag-inducing struts and bracing wires. In the 1930s, especially in the United States, a series of smooth-skinned, all-metal monoplanes of advanced design and exceptional performance emerged. Enclosed and streamlined, these outstanding designs soon began to replace their lumbering forebears on the world's air routes.

LIGHTNING SERVICES

The prototype of the Heinkel He 70G high-speed four-passenger airplane first flew on December 1, 1932, and the second aircraft set eight speed records. Lufthansa used a number of He 70s from 1934 on its appropriately named Blitz ("Lightning") internal German services.

RECORD BREAKER

The Northrop Gamma appeared in 1932. The very first one, seen here, was built for pilot Frank Hawks, who used it to set several records, including a non-stop flight from Los Angeles to New York in 13 hours, 27 minutes in June 1933, an average speed of 181 mph (291 km/h).

"Trousered" nonretractable undercarriage

"Park bench" ailerons above full-span flaps

Closely-cowled engine for optimum streamlining

Duralumin monocoque fuselage contrasts with wooden elliptical wing

VERSATILE TRANSPORT

Destined to become the most famous piston-engined airliner of all time, the Douglas DC-3 was the ultimate development of the DC-1 and DC-2. Originally known as the DST (Douglas Sleeper Transport), the first DC-3 made its maiden flight on December 17, 1935. The aircraft proved tough and versatile, and became one of the Allies' principal military transport aircraft in World War II. When production ended in 1947, Douglas had built 10,654 DC-3s and derivatives. The type was also built in the USSR and Japan.

Adjustable cooling gills, hydraulically operated

Hamilton Standard fully feathering propeller

Main gear semienclosed when retracted

Oil cooler

Wing/fuselage fairing

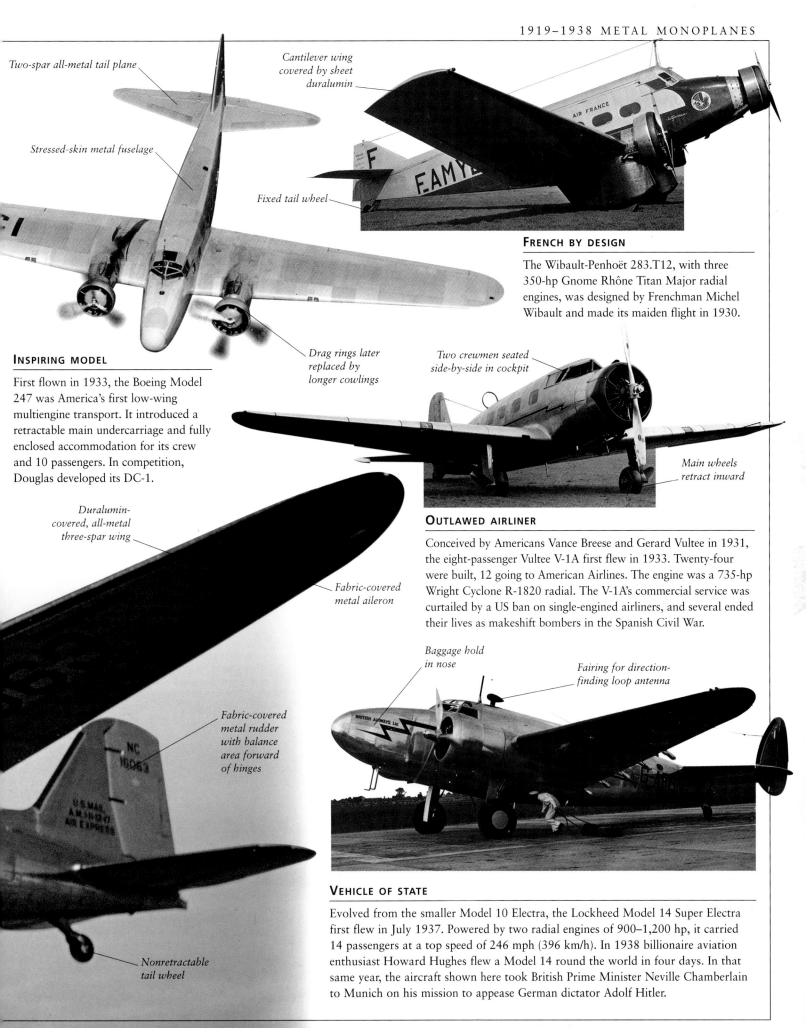

Two-spar all-metal tail plane

Stressed-skin metal fuselage

Cantilever wing covered by sheet duralumin

Fixed tail wheel

Drag rings later replaced by longer cowlings

FRENCH BY DESIGN

The Wibault-Penhoët 283.T12, with three 350-hp Gnome Rhône Titan Major radial engines, was designed by Frenchman Michel Wibault and made its maiden flight in 1930.

INSPIRING MODEL

First flown in 1933, the Boeing Model 247 was America's first low-wing multiengine transport. It introduced a retractable main undercarriage and fully enclosed accommodation for its crew and 10 passengers. In competition, Douglas developed its DC-1.

Two crewmen seated side-by-side in cockpit

Main wheels retract inward

OUTLAWED AIRLINER

Conceived by Americans Vance Breese and Gerard Vultee in 1931, the eight-passenger Vultee V-1A first flew in 1933. Twenty-four were built, 12 going to American Airlines. The engine was a 735-hp Wright Cyclone R-1820 radial. The V-1A's commercial service was curtailed by a US ban on single-engined airliners, and several ended their lives as makeshift bombers in the Spanish Civil War.

Duralumin-covered, all-metal three-spar wing

Fabric-covered metal aileron

Fabric-covered metal rudder with balance area forward of hinges

Baggage hold in nose

Fairing for direction-finding loop antenna

Nonretractable tail wheel

VEHICLE OF STATE

Evolved from the smaller Model 10 Electra, the Lockheed Model 14 Super Electra first flew in July 1937. Powered by two radial engines of 900–1,200 hp, it carried 14 passengers at a top speed of 246 mph (396 km/h). In 1938 billionaire aviation enthusiast Howard Hughes flew a Model 14 round the world in four days. In that same year, the aircraft shown here took British Prime Minister Neville Chamberlain to Munich on his mission to appease German dictator Adolf Hitler.

1919·1938 LOCKHEED ELECTRA

THE FORTUNES OF American aircraft manufacturer Lockheed reached near-collapse in the Depression years of the early 1930s. The company pinned its hopes of recovery on a new twin-engined monoplane with a retractable undercarriage. Designed for fast, economical airline operation with two crew and 10 passengers, this handsome and versatile airplane was dubbed the Lockheed Model 10 Electra. It first flew on February 23, 1934. Both Northwest Airlines and Pan American had ordered it before its maiden flight, and the former company put it into service the following August. In all, 149 were built, serving around the world.

MAIL RUNNER

British Airways imported five Model 10A Electras in 1937/38. They served on the London-Hamburg-Copenhagen-Malmö-Stockholm Viking Mail Service, and also between London and Paris.

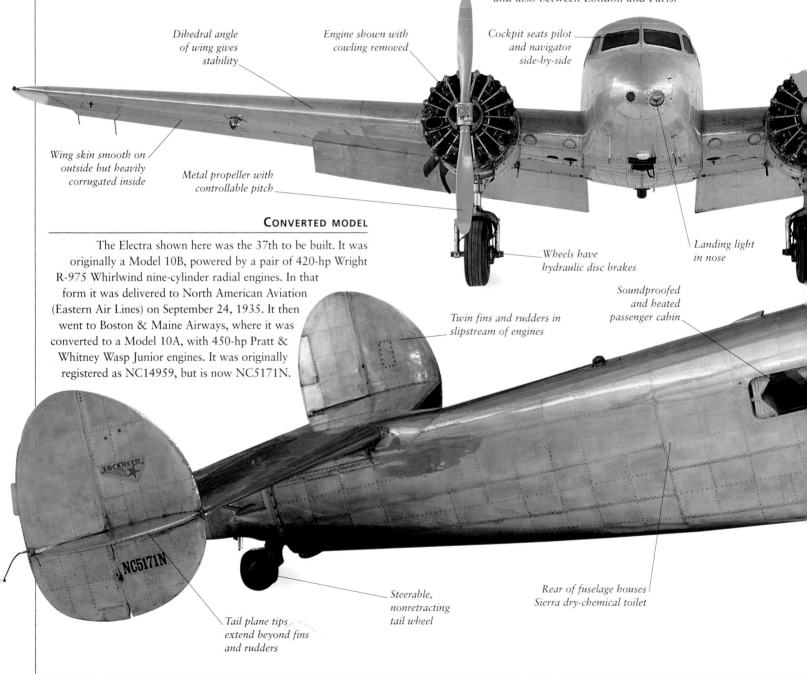

Dihedral angle of wing gives stability

Engine shown with cowling removed

Cockpit seats pilot and navigator side-by-side

Wing skin smooth on outside but heavily corrugated inside

Metal propeller with controllable pitch

Landing light in nose

Wheels have hydraulic disc brakes

CONVERTED MODEL

The Electra shown here was the 37th to be built. It was originally a Model 10B, powered by a pair of 420-hp Wright R-975 Whirlwind nine-cylinder radial engines. In that form it was delivered to North American Aviation (Eastern Air Lines) on September 24, 1935. It then went to Boston & Maine Airways, where it was converted to a Model 10A, with 450-hp Pratt & Whitney Wasp Junior engines. It was originally registered as NC14959, but is now NC5171N.

Twin fins and rudders in slipstream of engines

Soundproofed and heated passenger cabin

Steerable, nonretracting tail wheel

Rear of fuselage houses Sierra dry-chemical toilet

Tail plane tips extend beyond fins and rudders

SPECIFICATION

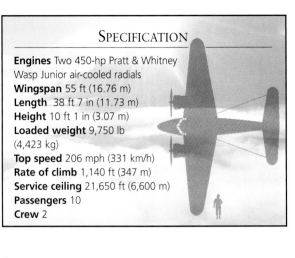

Engines Two 450-hp Pratt & Whitney Wasp Junior air-cooled radials
Wingspan 55 ft (16.76 m)
Length 38 ft 7 in (11.73 m)
Height 10 ft 1 in (3.07 m)
Loaded weight 9,750 lb (4,423 kg)
Top speed 206 mph (331 km/h)
Rate of climb 1,140 ft (347 m)
Service ceiling 21,650 ft (6,600 m)
Passengers 10
Crew 2

ELECTRA POWERPLANT

A nine-cylinder engine, the Pratt & Whitney Wasp Junior had a diameter of 45¾ in (1.16 m) and weighed 596 lb (271 kg). With a takeoff rating of 450 hp at 2,300 rpm, and driving Hamilton-Standard controllable-pitch, two-bladed metal propellers, it gave the Electra a top speed at sea level of 190 mph (305.77 km/h).

9-ft (2.74-m) diameter propeller

Spinner fitted over hub

5.8-gallon (26.5-liter) oil tank

Steel-tube engine bearer

Firewall bulkhead between engine and nacelle

Mounting for spinner

Carburetor unit

Oil sump

Cylinders with integral cooling fins

ALLOY ADVANTAGE

Built entirely of a light alloy, the Electra had a monocoque fuselage and cantilever wings, making it light yet strong, and free from the drag-inducing struts and bracing wires of many of the earlier-generation airliners. As aircraft like this entered service, speed became more important than previously in the airlines' fight for customers.

Light alloy outer wing panels bolted on

Heated and soundproofed cockpit equipped for night flying

Compartment for baggage in nose

16-ft (4.9-m) cabin accommodates 10 passengers

Large electrically operated flaps reduce landing speed

Streamlined nacelle fairings behind engines

Engine cowling with cylinder baffles

Electrically operated undercarriage retracts into nacelles

Wicks discharge static electricity

1919·1938 THE RECORD BREAKERS

THE MAKING AND BREAKING of world records not only helps to sell airplanes, but also promotes national self-esteem. In their efforts to put their companies and nations to the fore in the interwar years, designers worldwide battled to create machines that would fly faster, higher, and farther than before, and in so doing they pushed the technology ever onward. Presented here are some of the record setters of those golden years.

Canopy demisted by hot air from muffs around engine exhaust pipes

HIGH FLYER

Wearing a primitive pressure suit, Flight Lieutenant M.J. Adam set a world altitude record of 53,937 ft (16,440 m) in this Bristol Type 138A monoplane on June 30, 1937. Its 500-hp engine had a double supercharger system to help it maintain power at high altitude.

Landing light in nose

Air pressure on plate changes pitch of French Ratier propellers

Three large fuel tanks in fuselage, ahead of cockpit

Cockpit seats pilot and navigator in tandem

SPEEDING AROUND THE WORLD

Designed and built specifically for the 1934 MacRobertson England-to-Australia race, the de Havilland D.H.88 Comet was powered by two 230-hp engines. Three Comets flew in the race, and the one shown above, G-ACSS *Grosvenor House*, painted bright red and flown by C.W.A. Scott and Tom Campbell Black, won the speed prize, flying from Mildenhall to Melbourne in 70 hours 54 minutes 18 seconds.

Radiator surfaces on floats, wings, and fuselage

SUPER SEAPLANE

The Macchi MC.72 was designed for the 1931 Schneider Trophy contest, but engine problems and a crash forced Italy to withdraw. Work on the racer continued, however, and on October 23, 1934, its pilot, Warrant Officer Agello, set a world speed record for seaplanes of 440.7 mph (709.2 km/h), which remains unbeaten today.

FROM ENGLAND TO AFRICA

In February 1933, Squadron Leader O.R. Gayford – with Flight Lieutenant G.E. Nicholetts as navigator and equipped with an automatic pilot – set out to beat the world nonstop distance record in a custom-built Fairey Long-range Monoplane. They flew from Cranwell, England, to Walvis Bay, South Africa, covering more than 5,410 miles (8,710 km) in 57 hours 25 minutes, breaking the record with a Great Circle distance of 5,309.2 miles (8,544.4 km).

Wing has wooden spars with steel pyramid internal bracing

Pilot's cockpit forward, other crew member accommodated aft

Geodetic wing and fuselage construction

Wooden wings planked with spruce laminations

Nonretractable tailwheel

GOING THE DISTANCE

In November 1938, two RAF (Royal Air Force) Vickers Wellesley bombers, piloted by Squadron Leader Kellett and Flight Lieutenant Combe, completed a nonstop flight of 7,158 miles (11,524 km). Achieved by flying from Ismailia, Egypt, to Darwin, Australia, this world distance record was not broken until 1946.

Fuel tank in forward fuselage

Cockpit faired into base of fin

A FLYING ENGINE

Given a rotund fuselage to match the diameter of its massive Pratt & Whitney air-cooled radial engine, the bizarre American Gee Bee Super Sportster racer was really an engine with wings and was not easy to fly. Two were built. One, powered by an 800-hp Wasp Senior, claimed the world landplane speed record on September 3, 1932, when Jimmy Doolittle reached 296.3 mph (473.8 km/h) over a 1⅛-mile (3-km) course.

Fixed, spatted undercarriage also carries underwing bracing cables

BACK TO WAR

WITH THE OUTBREAK of World War II, the airplane's development diverged again. Initially a few biplanes survived in front-line units, but they soon disappeared and the developments of late-1930s civil aviation were adapted for military use. Offensive and defensive weapons had changed surprisingly little during the interwar period, but now came heavily armed fighters and the widespread adoption of cannons. High-speed bombers needed efficient power-operated turrets for their defensive weaponry, and their bomb capacities grew. As in the previous war, flying boats proved valuable for patrol and antisubmarine work. Ground attack, control of the air over the battlefield, and the movement of troops by air became important roles. Most significant, however, was the introduction of the first jet-propelled fighters and bombers.

POPULAR APPEAL

Avro Lancaster bombers setting off on a mission encourage the British populace to "invest for victory" in this World War II poster.

BATTLING BARREL

Rotund Republic P-47 Thunderbolt fighters of the United States Army Air Force proved hardy opponents for Axis aerial forces.

1939·1945 THE NEW WARPLANES

THE MID-TO-LATE 1930s witnessed significant advances in warplane design. Biplanes gave way to fast, streamlined monoplanes incorporating the latest structural and technological developments, such as retractable undercarriages, variable-pitch propellers, deicing systems, gun turrets, and reflector gunsights. These changes were inevitable; aircraft performance had increased to the point where open cockpits were becoming impracticable and the slipstream made it impossible for gunners to aim with any accuracy.

LOOKING TO THE FUTURE

First flown in 1932, Boeing's 522-hp P-26 single-seat fighter was a harbinger of things to come. Equipped with two machine guns, this monoplane had a monocoque stressed-skin fuselage and an unbraced tail.

TWO-YEAR LIFESPAN

Hailed as a great advance over its biplane forebears when it entered service in 1937, the Fairey Battle light bomber proved to be seriously underpowered and underarmed, and was obsolescent by 1939. It remained in front-line service until September 1940, and its crews suffered heavily.

Twin fins and rudders in propellers' slipstream

Well-glazed cockpit provides good all-around view

SECOND TIME AROUND

First flown in 1934, the Dornier Do 17 medium bomber suffered protracted development problems, and the 1938 Do 17Z version (*above*) had a new forward fuselage, better defensive armament, and a top speed of 255 mph (410 km/h). A prototype proved uncatchable by fighters at the International Military Aircraft Competition at Zürich in 1937.

No spinner over propeller hub

Adjustable cooling louvers in front of cowling

Open cockpit with windshield replaced canopy of earlier models

SOVIETS IN SPAIN

The first single-seat fighter with retractable undercarriage, the Soviet Union's Polikarpov I-16 (*left*) of 1933 had a metal wing and a wooden monocoque fuselage. Armed with two wing-mounted 7.62-mm machine guns, the I-16 fought in the Spanish Civil War.

Pitot pressure head for recording airspeed

Slim rear
fuselage boom
saves weight

Narrow, deep fuselage with
bomb bay below cockpit and
mid-upper-gunner's position

ITALIAN FIRST

Fiat's G.50 Freccia (meaning "arrow") was Italy's first all-metal, retractable-undercarriage, single-seat fighter. Powered by an 870-hp Fiat A 74 RC 38 radial engine, it had a top speed of 294 mph (473 km/h). It first flew in February 1937 and saw service in the Spanish Civil War.

Closely cowled engine
faired to propeller spinner

Cockpit set well back to
allow pilot to see down
behind wing trailing edge

TAKEN OUT OF SERVICE

The Handley Page H.P.52 Hampden (*above*), a four-crew medium bomber, lacked the power-operated gun turrets of its Whitley and Wellington contemporaries, but had superior speed and maneuverability. Its defensive armament proved totally inadequate in war, and it was grounded pending improvements.

Two-blade
fixed-pitch
wooden
propeller
originally
fitted

ARMED TO THE TEETH

First flown in 1938, the Dewoitine D.520 could attain 332 mph (534 km/h) and featured a monocoque fuselage and monospar wing. Armed with one engine-mounted 20-mm HS 404 cannon and four 7.5-mm M39 machine guns in the wings, it joined France's Armée de l'Air in 1940.

Radiator
beneath
cockpit

FANTASTIC FIGHTER

The Hawker Hurricane entered RAF (Royal Air Force) service in December 1937, two years after its first prototype (*above*) made its maiden flight. In World War II it destroyed more enemy aircraft than any other Allied fighter.

Long glazed canopy
enclosing crew positions

Horn-balanced
rudder

All-metal
stressed-skin
wing

1939·1945 THE SUPERMARINE LINE

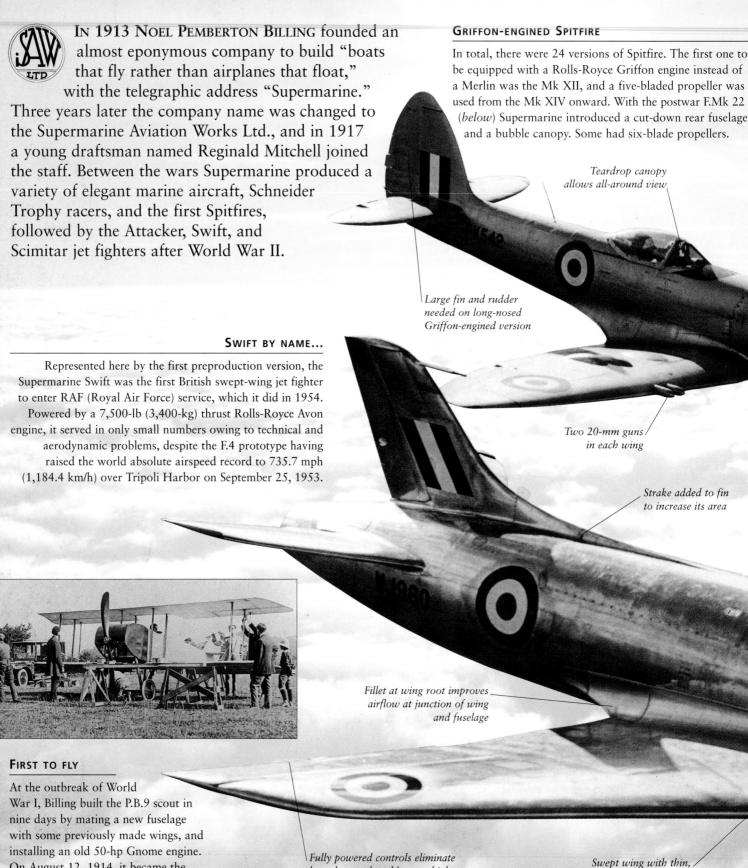

IN 1913 NOEL PEMBERTON BILLING founded an almost eponymous company to build "boats that fly rather than airplanes that float," with the telegraphic address "Supermarine." Three years later the company name was changed to the Supermarine Aviation Works Ltd., and in 1917 a young draftsman named Reginald Mitchell joined the staff. Between the wars Supermarine produced a variety of elegant marine aircraft, Schneider Trophy racers, and the first Spitfires, followed by the Attacker, Swift, and Scimitar jet fighters after World War II.

GRIFFON-ENGINED SPITFIRE

In total, there were 24 versions of Spitfire. The first one to be equipped with a Rolls-Royce Griffon engine instead of a Merlin was the Mk XII, and a five-bladed propeller was used from the Mk XIV onward. With the postwar F.Mk 22 (*below*) Supermarine introduced a cut-down rear fuselage and a bubble canopy. Some had six-blade propellers.

Teardrop canopy allows all-around view

Large fin and rudder needed on long-nosed Griffon-engined version

SWIFT BY NAME...

Represented here by the first preproduction version, the Supermarine Swift was the first British swept-wing jet fighter to enter RAF (Royal Air Force) service, which it did in 1954. Powered by a 7,500-lb (3,400-kg) thrust Rolls-Royce Avon engine, it served in only small numbers owing to technical and aerodynamic problems, despite the F.4 prototype having raised the world absolute airspeed record to 735.7 mph (1,184.4 km/h) over Tripoli Harbor on September 25, 1953.

Two 20-mm guns in each wing

Strake added to fin to increase its area

Fillet at wing root improves airflow at junction of wing and fuselage

FIRST TO FLY

At the outbreak of World War I, Billing built the P.B.9 scout in nine days by mating a new fuselage with some previously made wings, and installing an old 50-hp Gnome engine. On August 12, 1914, it became the first Pemberton-Billing airplane to fly, but it failed to win orders.

Fully powered controls eliminate lateral control problems at high Mach numbers

Swept wing with thin, high-speed airfoil section

AIR-SEA RESCUER

First flown as the Seagull V on June 21, 1933, the Walrus was designed to meet Royal Australian Air Force requirements. The amphibian proved very successful, serving with Britain's Fleet Air Arm as a catapult-launched fleet cooperation aircraft, as well as in an air-sea rescue role with the RAF, saving many downed aircrew during World War II.

RECONNAISSANCE MACHINE

The last in a line of elegant biplane flying boats designed by Mitchell, the Stranraer was designed for general reconnaissance, entering service with the RAF in 1937. It also served for the Royal Canadian Air Force. Spanning 85 ft (26 m) and carrying a crew of six, it was powered by two 980-hp Bristol Pegasus Xs, giving it a 137-mph (220-km/h) cruising speed.

Five-bladed propeller used on late-mark Griffon-powered Spitfires

SCHNEIDER TROPHY WINNER

In September 1927 the RAF entered a team in the Schneider Trophy contest for the first time. Mitchell designed the S.5 racing seaplane, with its 900-hp Napier Lion V12 engine, as their mount. Both first and second places were taken by S.5s, the winner being Flight Lieutenant S.N. Webster, averaging 281.6 mph (453.5 km/h). He also set a new world speed record over 62 miles (100 km) of 283.66 mph (457 km/h).

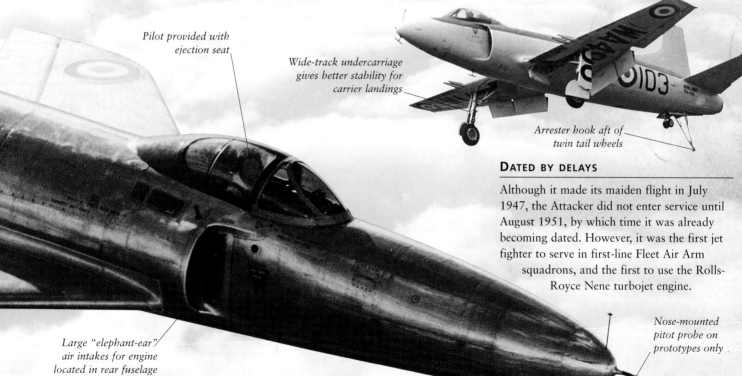

Pilot provided with ejection seat

Wide-track undercarriage gives better stability for carrier landings

Arrester hook aft of twin tail wheels

DATED BY DELAYS

Although it made its maiden flight in July 1947, the Attacker did not enter service until August 1951, by which time it was already becoming dated. However, it was the first jet fighter to serve in first-line Fleet Air Arm squadrons, and the first to use the Rolls-Royce Nene turbojet engine.

Large "elephant-ear" air intakes for engine located in rear fuselage

Nose-mounted pitot probe on prototypes only

1939·1945 SUPERMARINE SPITFIRE MK V

ONE OF THE MOST readily distinguishable aircraft ever built, the Spitfire was the creation of designer Reginald Mitchell. The first incarnation of this famous fighter appeared in 1938, but it was in 1941 that the Mk V (featured here) first entered service for the RAF (Royal Air Force). The Mk V's airframe was essentially an improved version of that used for the Mk I/II, one important modification being the strengthening of the engine mounting to take the Rolls-Royce Merlin 45, as well as later engine types.

CLIPPED WINGS

The Spitfire Mk V, represented above by a member of Poland's 315 Squadron, RAF, had its detachable wingtips removed to improve its maneuverability at low altitude. This enabled the aircraft to compete on better terms with the Luftwaffe's new Focke-Wulf Fw 190 fighter.

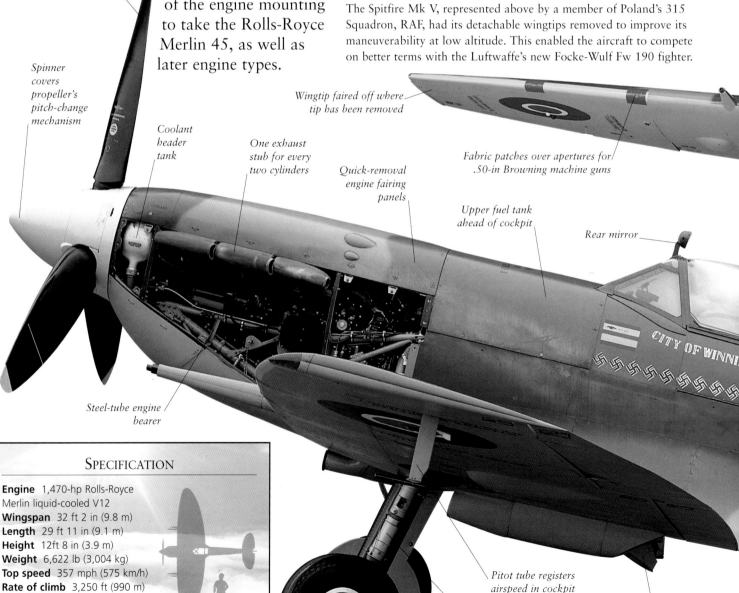

Laminated wood propeller blade

Spinner covers propeller's pitch-change mechanism

Coolant header tank

One exhaust stub for every two cylinders

Quick-removal engine fairing panels

Wingtip faired off where tip has been removed

Fabric patches over apertures for .50-in Browning machine guns

Upper fuel tank ahead of cockpit

Rear mirror

Steel-tube engine bearer

Pitot tube registers airspeed in cockpit

Main undercarriage leg

Radiator flap operated from cockpit controls engine cooling

SPECIFICATION

Engine 1,470-hp Rolls-Royce Merlin liquid-cooled V12
Wingspan 32 ft 2 in (9.8 m)
Length 29 ft 11 in (9.1 m)
Height 12ft 8 in (3.9 m)
Weight 6,622 lb (3,004 kg)
Top speed 357 mph (575 km/h)
Rate of climb 3,250 ft (990 m) per min at 10,000 ft (3,050 m)
Service ceiling 36,500 ft (11,125 m)
Armament 2 cannons, 4 machine guns
Crew 1 pilot

PROPELLER PITCH CHANGING

The de Havilland or Rotol constant-speed three-bladed propeller used on the Spitfire had three basic pitch settings, giving optimum performance for cruising, and high-speed flight. The blades were made of impregnated and compressed laminated wood.

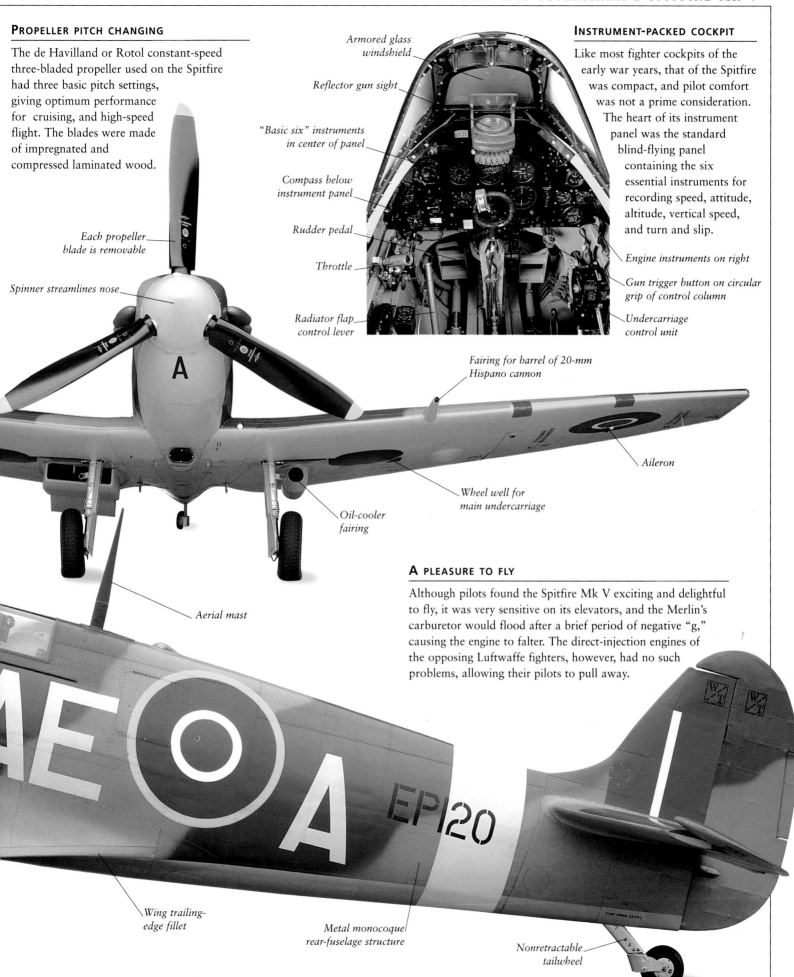

Armored glass windshield

Reflector gun sight

"Basic six" instruments in center of panel

Compass below instrument panel

Rudder pedal

Throttle

Radiator flap control lever

INSTRUMENT-PACKED COCKPIT

Like most fighter cockpits of the early war years, that of the Spitfire was compact, and pilot comfort was not a prime consideration. The heart of its instrument panel was the standard blind-flying panel containing the six essential instruments for recording speed, attitude, altitude, vertical speed, and turn and slip.

Engine instruments on right

Gun trigger button on circular grip of control column

Undercarriage control unit

Each propeller blade is removable

Spinner streamlines nose

Fairing for barrel of 20-mm Hispano cannon

Aileron

Wheel well for main undercarriage

Oil-cooler fairing

Aerial mast

A PLEASURE TO FLY

Although pilots found the Spitfire Mk V exciting and delightful to fly, it was very sensitive on its elevators, and the Merlin's carburetor would flood after a brief period of negative "g," causing the engine to falter. The direct-injection engines of the opposing Luftwaffe fighters, however, had no such problems, allowing their pilots to pull away.

EP120

Wing trailing-edge fillet

Metal monocoque rear-fuselage structure

Nonretractable tailwheel

1939·1945 BATTLE OF BRITAIN AIRCRAFT

BETWEEN JULY AND OCTOBER 1940 the RAF (Royal Air Force) denied Germany command of the air over the British Isles, effectively preventing the invasion of Britain from France. This great feat of air defense would have been impossible without a steady supply of good fighters and their effective deployment, made possible by Britain's "Chain Home" radar warning system. By the end of October, 1,733 Luftwaffe aircraft had been shot down, compared with the RAF's loss of 915. The turning point came on September 15, when the Luftwaffe lost 80 to the RAF's 35; the invasion was canceled three days later.

PUNISHED AGGRESSOR

The Junkers Ju 87 two-seat dive bomber, equipped with sirens to add terror to its steep diving attacks, played a prominent part in the Blitzkrieg war in mainland Europe. However, the "Stuka" proved easy prey for the RAF's Hurricanes and Spitfires, suffering heavy losses.

Antenna wire beneath fuselage

Twin fins with horn-balanced rudders on ends of tail plane

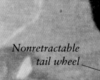

Nonretractable tail wheel

DEFIANT BUT VULNERABLE

The Boulton Paul Defiant relied for both attack and defense on the four .303-in Browning machine guns in the turret behind its cockpit. Although effective against bombers, it was easy prey for fighters once the enemy pilots learned to distinguish it from the Hurricane.

Wing has single main spar and stressed skin

Small, heavily framed cockpit canopy

Horn-balanced rudder

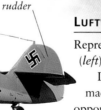

LUFTWAFFE ACE

Represented here by the later Messerschmitt Bf 109G (*left*), the Bf 109, in its Bf 109E form with a 1,150-hp Daimler-Benz DB 601A engine and mixed machine-gun and cannon armament, was a worthy opponent to the Hurricane and Spitfire in combat.

Extensive glazing in nose

Gondola for rearward-firing machine-gun position

BOMBING AT A PRICE

The Heinkel He 111 medium bomber, powered by a pair of 1,100-hp Daimler-Benz DB 601A liquid-cooled engines, could carry a 4,410-lb (2,000-kg) bomb load at a maximum speed of 247 mph (397 km/h). Its three 7.9-mm MG 15 machine guns did not ward off British fighters.

POWERFUL THREAT

Powered by a pair of 1,200-hp Junkers Jumo 211 liquid-cooled engines, the versatile Junkers Ju 88 high-speed level and dive bomber carried 3,968 lbs (1,800 kg) of bombs on underwing pylons, plus a small additional load internally. Its defensive armament comprised three 7.9-mm MG 15 machine guns in front and rear cockpit positions and in a ventral gondola.

Non-retractable tail wheel

All-metal elliptical wing

BEAUTIFUL BUT SCARCE

The Supermarine Spitfire, potent with its eight wing-mounted .303-in Browning machine guns, was available in far smaller numbers than the Hurricane in the Battle. Nine squadrons had the Mk I by the outbreak of war, and deliveries of the Mk II (*above*) began in June 1940.

TWIN-ENGINED ESCORT

Designed to serve as both a long-range fighter and a defensive aircraft, the Messerschmitt Bf 110 (*above*) was a disastrous failure in the former role when confronting modern fighters. Its poor speed and maneuverability and weak defensive armament resulted in high losses during the daylight raids over Britain.

Undercarriage retracts into rear of engine nacelles

Forward fuselage metal-covered, rear fuselage fabric-covered

FORCE OF DESTRUCTION

The mainstay of Fighter Command during the Battle of Britain, the Hawker Hurricane, represented here by a Mk I of 3 Squadron at Biggin Hill in 1939, was the RAF's first aircraft with a top speed greater than 300 mph (483 km/h). Similarly armed to the Spitfire, though inferior in speed and climb, it had a Rolls-Royce Merlin III of 1,030 hp. No fewer than 1,715 were flown by Fighter Command pilots during the Battle, and four-fifths of the enemy aircraft destroyed fell to them.

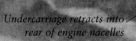

1939-1945 HEAVY BOMBERS

REARMAMENT IN THE late 1930s spawned a number of four-engined long-range heavy bombers that gave the major powers the ability to undertake mass-formation strategic raids by day and night. Their targets were industrial sites, transportation hubs, cities, and military installations in their opponents' countries and occupied territories, the aim being to cripple the opposing war effort by hindering production and mobility, and by demoralizing the populace. Some of the foremost heavy-bomber designs are featured here.

FORTRESS FOREBEAR

The prototype for one of World War II's most famous bombers (the B-17 Flying Fortress), the Boeing Model 299 was powered by four 750-hp Pratt & Whitney Hornet radial engines and carried a crew of eight. It cost Boeing $432,034 to build and it first flew on July 28, 1935, only to crash on October 30. But the expensive gamble paid off when the B-17 went into production.

Exhaust pipes equipped with flame dampers to conceal aircraft from night fighters

Position of bombadier/nose-gunner

NORTHERN MIGHT

First flown in 1939, the Handley Page Halifax was the RAF's (Royal Air Force's) second four-engined bomber. Versions powered by liquid-cooled Rolls-Royce Merlins and air-cooled Bristol Hercules engines (seen here) were produced, a total of 6,176 being built. The maximum bomb load was 12,000 lb (5,443 kg).

Leading edge armored for protection against barrage-balloon cables

Bristol Hercules air-cooled radial engine

All-metal monocoque fuselage, bomb bay in lower section

Four .303-in machine guns in tail turret

Inner-engine nacelles also house retracted undercarriage

Retractable twin tailwheels

LONG-LEGGED "LIB"

The Consolidated B-24 Liberator was built in greater numbers for the USAAF (US Army Air Force), US Navy, and Allied air forces than any other single American aircraft – 18,431 in total. Equipped with a high-lift wing that reduced drag, the Liberator had a crew of eight or 10, and in its B-24J form could carry an 8,800-lb (3,992-kg) bomb load over 2,100 miles (3,379 km).

Two .303-in guns in mid-upper turret

DAM BUSTER

The famous Avro Lancaster originated as a four-engined version of the failed, twin-engined Avro Manchester. The most celebrated of the 156,000 sorties flown by Lancasters were those against the Ruhr dams on May 16/17, 1943, by 617 Squadron: the "Dam Busters." Production totaled 7,377.

SOLE SOVIET HEAVY

The Tupolev TB-7/ANT-42, later redesignated Pe-8 after design-team leader Vladimir Petlyakov, was the Soviet Union's only heavy bomber of World War II. It had four 1,340-hp AM-35A engines and could carry a 4,409-lb (2,000-kg) bomb load over a maximum range of 2,236 miles (3,600 km). Only 93 were built.

GERMAN GRIFFON

The Heinkel He 177 Greif ("Griffon") strategic bomber was four-engined; each nacelle housed two Daimler-Benz liquid-cooled 12-cylinder engines, coupled to a single propeller. Engine problems and fuel shortages limited its operational use. The example seen here is a captured He 177 under test.

20-mm MG 151 cannon gimbal-mounted in tail

De Havilland Hydromatic constant-speed propeller

Oil-cooler inlet

Two .303-in machine guns in nose turret

STALKY STIRLING

The Short Stirling was the first four-engined monoplane bomber to enter RAF service and the first to be used operationally. Its shoulder-wing layout required a complicated stalky undercarriage with an electrical retraction mechanism that proved troublesome in service. Powered by 1,650-hp Bristol Hercules air-cooled radial engines, it could carry a 14,000-lb (6,350-kg) bomb load over a range of 590 miles (950 km). A total of 2,208 were built.

1939·1945 MESSERSCHMITT BF 109E

THE SPITFIRE'S GREAT ADVERSARY during the Battle of Britain of 1940, the Bf 109 was designed by Willy Messerschmitt of the Bayerische Flugzeugwerke. Designed to match the smallest possible airframe with the most powerful engine available, it first flew in mid-September 1935, at which time it was probably the world's most advanced fighter. Blooded in the Spanish Civil War, it remained in service in various forms, latterly with foreign air forces, for nearly 20 years. In total, some 35,000 of all marks were built.

HIGH-POWERED ENGINE

The Bf 109E-3's liquid-cooled Daimler-Benz DB 601Aa was a 12-cylinder inverted-V engine, hence the low position of the exhaust stubs. It drove a metal, electrically operated propeller, with a 20-mm MG FF cannon firing through the hole in the spinner.

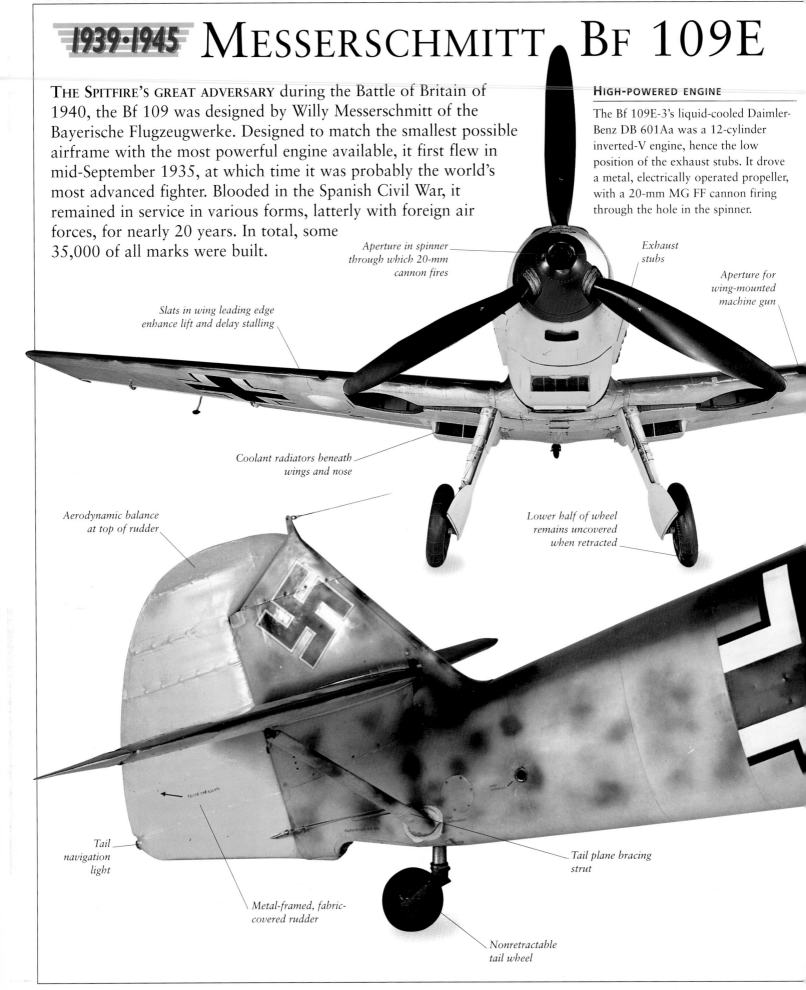

Aperture in spinner through which 20-mm cannon fires

Exhaust stubs

Aperture for wing-mounted machine gun

Slats in wing leading edge enhance lift and delay stalling

Coolant radiators beneath wings and nose

Aerodynamic balance at top of rudder

Lower half of wheel remains uncovered when retracted

Tail navigation light

Tail plane bracing strut

Metal-framed, fabric-covered rudder

Nonretractable tail wheel

1939·1945 BOEING B-17G

Hamilton Standard Hydromatic constant-speed propeller

ONE OF THE GREATEST medium bombers of World War II, Boeing's B-17 Flying Fortress was used for high-altitude daylight raids in massed formations. Among its best-known operations were those from England against targets in Germany and occupied Europe, carried out by the 8th Air Force of the USAAF (US Army Air Force) from 1943. First flown as the B-299 on July 28, 1935, the B-17 appeared in several basic variants with steadily increasing defensive armament. At the time production ceased in 1945, a total of 12,726 B-17s had been built.

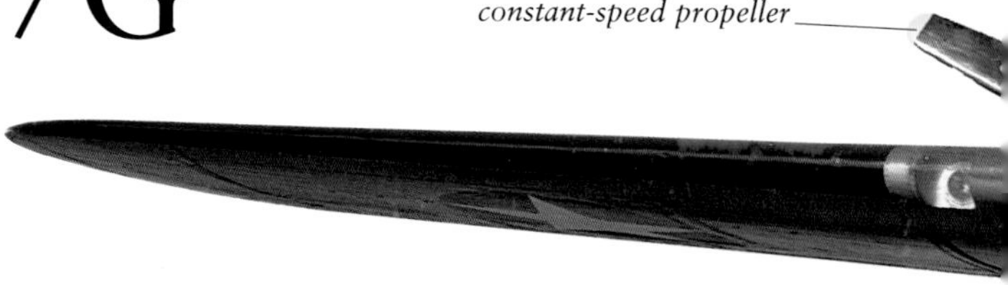

SALLY B., ALIAS MEMPHIS BELLE

The aircraft featured here (and shown in flight above) was one of the last 100 B-17s to be produced. It rolled out of Lockheed's plant in Burbank, California, in June 1945 – too late to see combat. After being used for cartographic work in France it was bought by the British entrepreneur Ted White in 1975. *Sally B.*, as it is now known, starred in the title role of the 1990 movie *Memphis Belle*.

Fabric-covered rudder

124485

Rudder trim tab

Dorsal fin fairing

Tail-gunner's position

26-in (66-cm) diameter tail wheel

Radio beam antenna

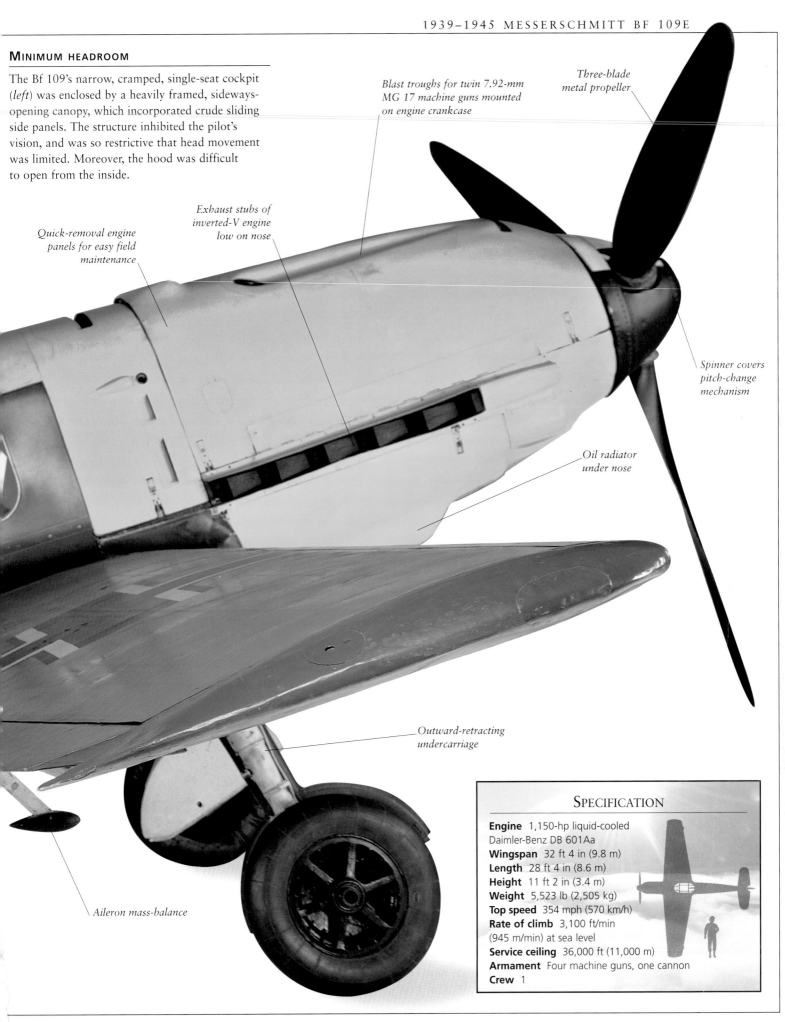

MINIMUM HEADROOM

The Bf 109's narrow, cramped, single-seat cockpit (*left*) was enclosed by a heavily framed, sideways-opening canopy, which incorporated crude sliding side panels. The structure inhibited the pilot's vision, and was so restrictive that head movement was limited. Moreover, the hood was difficult to open from the inside.

Blast troughs for twin 7.92-mm MG 17 machine guns mounted on engine crankcase

Three-blade metal propeller

Exhaust stubs of inverted-V engine low on nose

Quick-removal engine panels for easy field maintenance

Spinner covers pitch-change mechanism

Oil radiator under nose

Outward-retracting undercarriage

Aileron mass-balance

SPECIFICATION

Engine 1,150-hp liquid-cooled Daimler-Benz DB 601Aa
Wingspan 32 ft 4 in (9.8 m)
Length 28 ft 4 in (8.6 m)
Height 11 ft 2 in (3.4 m)
Weight 5,523 lb (2,505 kg)
Top speed 354 mph (570 km/h)
Rate of climb 3,100 ft/min (945 m/min) at sea level
Service ceiling 36,000 ft (11,000 m)
Armament Four machine guns, one cannon
Crew 1

HARD TO HANDLE

The weak and narrow-track main undercarriage of the Bf 109, coupled with a tendency for the aircraft to swing to the left on takeoff and landing, led to some five percent of all Bf 109s being destroyed at these critical stages of flight.

Gun sight with leather crash pad

Cutoff switch

Turn and bank indicator

Engine revolution counter

Gun button in top of control column

Back armor protects pilot

Pitot head under port wing

Transmitter/receiver radio package in rear fuselage

Wing root fillet

Metal monocoque fuselage structure

POOR VISIBILITY

The Bf 109's steep ground angle greatly restricted the pilot's forward vision and made taxiing the fighter difficult. This type, the Bf 109E, flew accurately and steadily in combat, making it a good gun platform, but considerable strength was needed to pull it out of a dive. The Messerschmitt Bf 109E-3 shown above force-landed at RAF (Royal Air Force) Manston, Kent, on November 27, 1940, following combat with RAF Spitfires. It has been restored to show the markings it wore at the time of its "arrival" in Britain.

Plexiglas nose

Triangular flat-glass panel for bomb aiming

Deicing strips in wing leading edge

Sperry ball turret

Remote-controlled chin turret

Main undercarriage legs retract rearward into inner engine nacelles

SHOOTING FROM THE HIP

The waist-gun positions in early B-17s had Plexiglas "blister" fairings, but these gave way to simplified windows from the B-17E onward. Initially directly opposite each other, in the B-17F and later models the posts were staggered to give the gunners more room to move.

Ammunition belt

.50-in Browning machine gun

Single .50-in Browning machine gun in waist position

SUPERCHARGED ENGINES

The B-17G's four turbo-supercharged Wright R-1820 radial engines with their 11½-ft (3.5-m) diameter Hamilton Standard propellers enabled the bomber to cruise at 160 mph (257 km/h) at 25,000 ft (7,620 m) with a 4,000-lb (1,814-kg) bomb load. The main wheels' circumference was 21 ft 1½ in (6.4 m).

Radio operator's compartment

Antenna

Sliding hatch

POWER-OPERATED TURRET

The power-operated Sperry ball turret beneath the central fuselage was introduced on the B-17E. Only airmen of small stature could fit in it, and for safety purposes they had to enter the turret from within the aircraft after takeoff and leave it before touchdown.

Twin .50-in Browning machine guns in hydraulically operated ball turret

Outer wing panel

Navigation light

Control yokes for ailerons and elevators

"BOMBS AWAY!"

The bombardier's position in the nose has a triangular flat-glass panel for aiming, using the centrally positioned bombsight. The bomb rack selector switches are on the left. The bombardier was in absolute command of the aircraft for the run on to the target.

Bombsight

GOOD INSTRUMENT VISIBILITY

The neatly arranged cockpit has the pilot's seat on the left and the copilot's on the right, while the throttle controls are situated on a central pedestal. The most important flying instruments are in the center of the panel, clearly visible to both pilots, while the engine instruments are grouped on the right.

Selector switches

Bombardier's swivel seat

Cockpit roof contains two emergency exits

Navigator's sighting dome

Cheek position for one .50-in machine gun

Streamlined fairing for loop antenna

55-in (1.4-m) diameter wheel

SPECIFICATION

Engines Four 1,200-hp air-cooled radials with General Electric B-22 turbo-superchargers
Wingspan 103 ft 9 in (31.6 m)
Length 74 ft 4 in (22.7 m)
Height 19 ft 1 in (5.8 m)
Weight 55,000 lb (24,948 kg)
Top speed 302 mph (486 km/h)
Service ceiling 35,600 ft (10,850 m)
Armament 13 M-2 Browning .50-in machine guns; normal internal bomb load 4,000 lb (1,814 kg)
Crew 10

1939·1945 LATE-WWII FIGHTERS

DURING WORLD WAR II fighter development had proceeded at great pace, and this, coupled with the entry of the US into the conflict, meant that a wide variety of designs were rolling from production lines worldwide. By the war's end, piston engines were approaching the limits of their mechanical complexity and performance, and high-speed flight was presenting new aerodynamic problems as the speed of sound was approached. Shown here is a selection of some of the most renowned fighters from the combatant nations.

Manually folded wingtips (later discarded)

JAPANESE ZERO

Known by the Allies as the "Zero" from its Japanese Navy designation Type 0 Carrier Fighter, the Mitsubishi A6M Reisen first flew on April 1, 1939, and served throughout the war. When production ended with the A6M7 in 1945, 10,500 Reisen had been built.

FORMIDABLE OPPONENT

Designed by Kurt Tank, the Focke-Wulf Fw 190 made its maiden flight on June 1, 1939. The Fw 190A-3 (*below*) was powered by a 1,700-hp BMW engine. Armament comprised two 7.9-mm MG 17 machine guns in front of the cockpit and four 20-mm MG FF cannons in the wings.

Annular oil cooler around nose

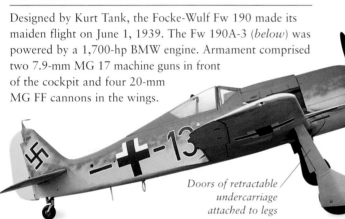

Doors of retractable undercarriage attached to legs

Matt black anti-glare paint on top of forward fuselage

Small spinner on propeller hub

TEMPESTUOUS FIGHTER

The Hawker Tempest V Series 2 (*right*) was the only version of this fighter to see combat in the war. It had a 2,200-hp Napier Sabre II 24-cylinder H-type engine and was armed with four 20-mm cannons. The Tempest II, which followed the V into service, was the last single-seat, single-piston-engined fighter to enter production for the Royal Air Force.

Radiator in undernose housing

Large clear-view teardrop canopy

Exit flap for cooling air

HUGE PRODUCTION

One of the greatest fighters of the war, the North American P-51 Mustang first flew in October 1940. Early models had a cockpit faired into a high rear fuselage, but the P-51D (*left*) introduced a bubble canopy. Capable of speeds up to 437 mph (703 km/h), more P-51Ds were built than the total of all other P-51 variants together.

RUSSIAN ATTACK

By mid-1944 there were more Yakovlev Yak-9s on Russia's major war fronts than all of the other fighters equipping the Soviet Air Force. The Yak-9D (*right*) had a top speed of 374 mph (600 km/h) at 10,170 ft (3,100 m), and was equipped with a 20-mm engine-mounted ShVAK cannon and one 12.7-mm machine gun. When production ended with the postwar Yak-9P in 1948, 16,769 of all models had been built.

Four-blade, variable-pitch propeller

Adjustable engine cooling gills

Radio antenna

Trim tab in rudder trailing edge

A BOLT FROM THE BLUE

The Republic Thunderbolt first entered service in 1942 in its "razorback" P-47B form. From the later P-47Ds onward a low rear fuselage and a bubble canopy were introduced. P-47Ns (*left*) were powered by the 2,800-hp Pratt & Whitney R-2800-77 two-row, 18-cylinder air-cooled radial engine and armed with eight .50-in machine guns.

Bulletproof windshield

Tail wheel retracted

Bomb carrier

Long nose interferes with pilot's view for approach and landing

Undercarriage retracts rearward

WATCHING FROM THE SKIES

Appearing late in the war, the Spitfire PR Mk XIX (*below*) was an unarmed reconnaissance version of Supermarine's famous fighter. Basically a Mk XIV with modified Mk VC wings, it had a universal camera installation, a top speed of 460 mph (740 km/h), and a ceiling of 43,000 ft (13,100 m).

On retraction, wheel turns through 90° to lie flat

NAVY WARBIRD

The distinctive inverted-gull wing of the Chance-Vought F4U Corsair naval fighter allowed a short undercarriage to be used while permitting adequate ground clearance for the large-diameter propeller. First flown in May 1940, it could attain 374 mph (600 km/h) and served with the US Navy, US Marine Corps, and Britain's Fleet Air Arm.

Long nose houses Rolls-Royce Griffon engine

1939·1945 THE FIRST JETS

THE FIRST TURBOJET engines were barely more powerful than the larger piston engines of the time, but as manufacturing and operating experience was improved their power quickly increased. One of the major challenges was to develop metals that could withstand the heat and stresses generated within the engines. Before long, the aerodynamic problems of high-speed flight beyond Mach 1, the so-called "sound barrier," would also present themselves to scientists and designers.

Single-seat cockpit behind nose intake

TURBOJET PIONEER

The first airplane to fly purely on turbojet power was the Heinkel He 178, which had an HeS 3b gasoline-burning engine providing a thrust of 1,100 lb (499 kg). It made its first hop on August 24, 1939, followed by a true flight three days later.

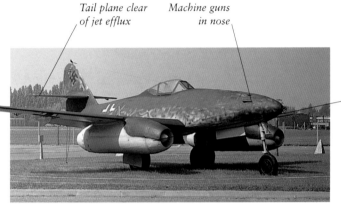

Tail plane clear of jet efflux   *Machine guns in nose*

Junkers Jumo jet engine in underwing nacelle

FIRST COMBAT JET

The sharklike Messerschmitt Me 262 was the first turbojet aircraft to enter combat service, doing so with the Luftwaffe in the autumn of 1944. Powered by a pair of 1,980-lb (898-kg) thrust Junkers Jumo 109 engines, it was deployed as both a day and night fighter, and also as a bomber.

Bubble canopy over single-seat cockpit

Engine air intake well forward of wing leading edge

Air intake on fuselage flank

AMERICA'S FIRST JET

The first US jet aircraft, the Bell P-59 Airacomet, made its maiden flight on October 1, 1942, powered by two 1,300-lb (590-kg) thrust General Electric I-As. Although it was originally intended to be a fighter, its combat performance proved inferior to that of piston-engined contemporaries and it served mainly as a trainer.

JET-POWERED BOMBER

The Arado Ar 234B Blitz ("lightning") was the world's first true jet bomber. It entered Luftwaffe service in July 1944 and also performed reconnaissance duties. Although its two BMW 003 turbojets gave it a maximum speed of 460 mph (740 km/h) at 32,800 ft (10,000 m), they had a life of only 25 hours because certain components were prone to cracking.

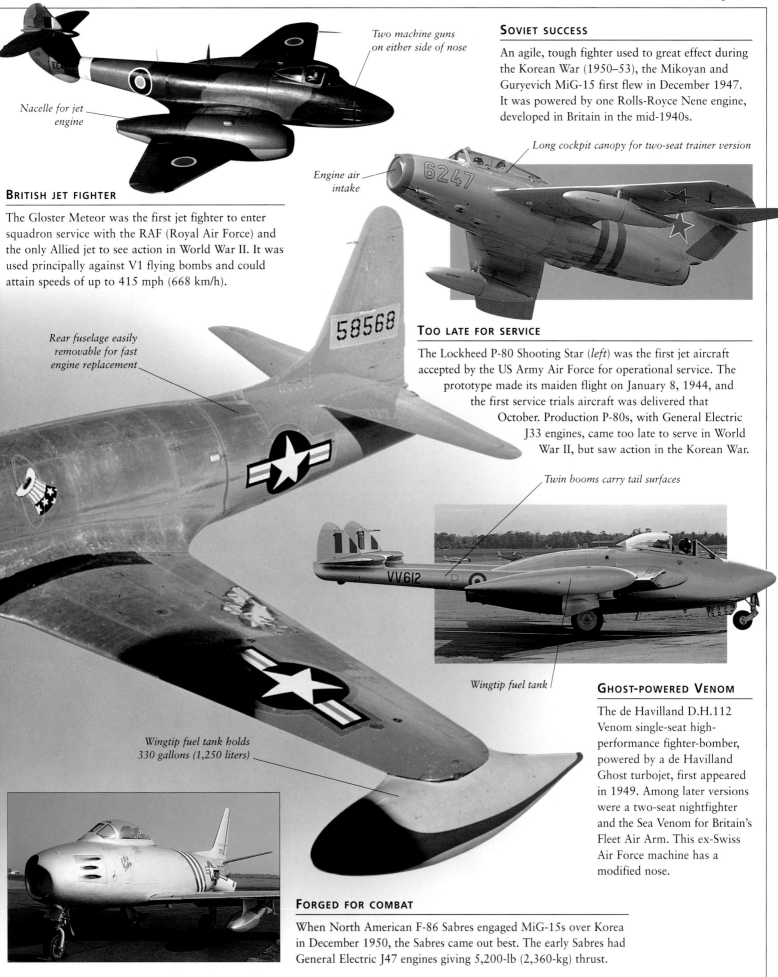

Two machine guns on either side of nose

SOVIET SUCCESS

An agile, tough fighter used to great effect during the Korean War (1950–53), the Mikoyan and Guryevich MiG-15 first flew in December 1947. It was powered by one Rolls-Royce Nene engine, developed in Britain in the mid-1940s.

Nacelle for jet engine

Engine air intake

Long cockpit canopy for two-seat trainer version

BRITISH JET FIGHTER

The Gloster Meteor was the first jet fighter to enter squadron service with the RAF (Royal Air Force) and the only Allied jet to see action in World War II. It was used principally against V1 flying bombs and could attain speeds of up to 415 mph (668 km/h).

TOO LATE FOR SERVICE

The Lockheed P-80 Shooting Star (*left*) was the first jet aircraft accepted by the US Army Air Force for operational service. The prototype made its maiden flight on January 8, 1944, and the first service trials aircraft was delivered that October. Production P-80s, with General Electric J33 engines, came too late to serve in World War II, but saw action in the Korean War.

Rear fuselage easily removable for fast engine replacement

Twin booms carry tail surfaces

Wingtip fuel tank

Wingtip fuel tank holds 330 gallons (1,250 liters)

GHOST-POWERED VENOM

The de Havilland D.H.112 Venom single-seat high-performance fighter-bomber, powered by a de Havilland Ghost turbojet, first appeared in 1949. Among later versions were a two-seat nightfighter and the Sea Venom for Britain's Fleet Air Arm. This ex-Swiss Air Force machine has a modified nose.

FORGED FOR COMBAT

When North American F-86 Sabres engaged MiG-15s over Korea in December 1950, the Sabres came out best. The early Sabres had General Electric J47 engines giving 5,200-lb (2,360-kg) thrust.

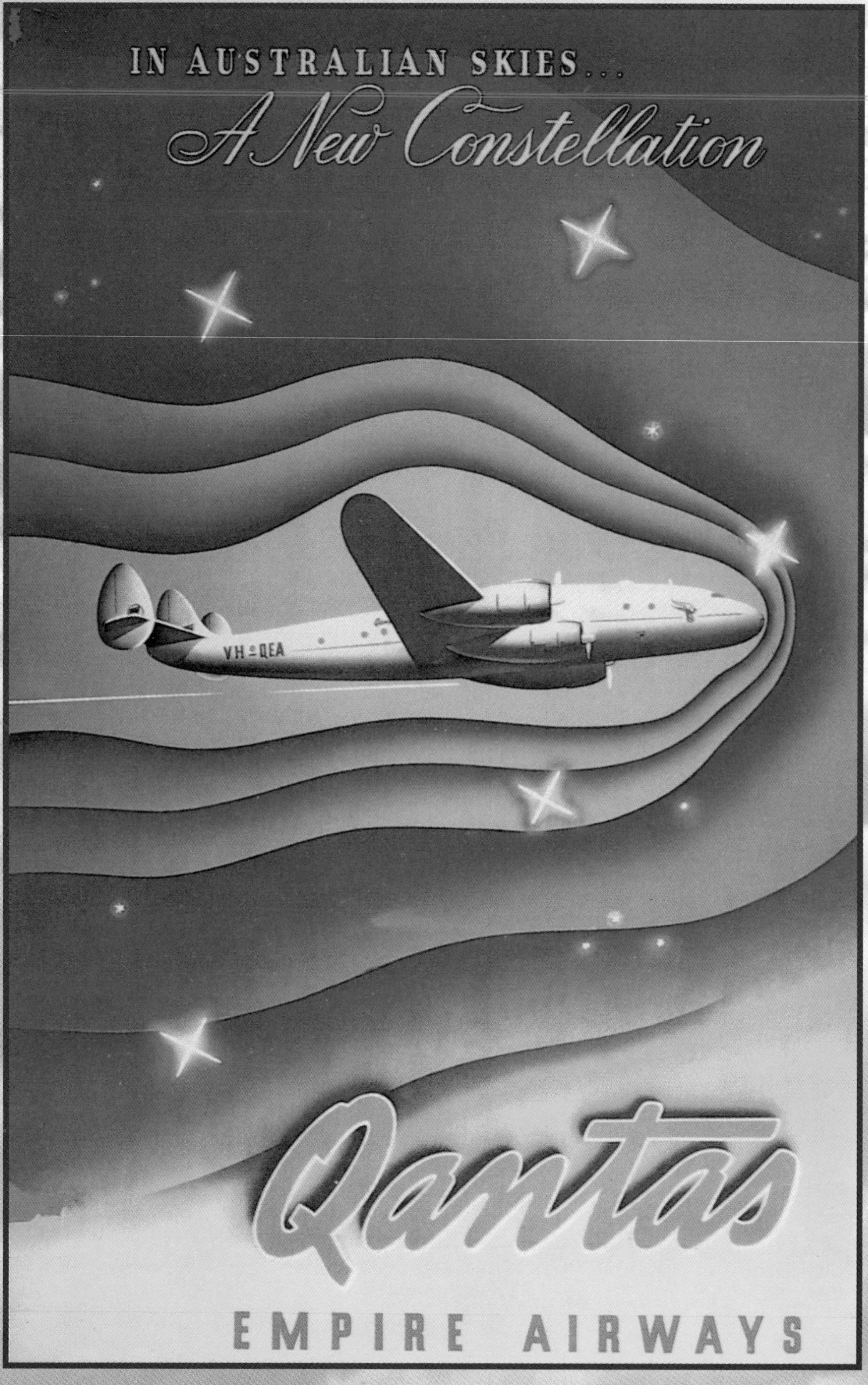

IN AUSTRALIAN SKIES...

A New Constellation

Qantas

EMPIRE AIRWAYS

1946-1969

THE JET AGE DAWNS

THE WIDESPREAD CONSTRUCTION of airfields during World War II had rendered the flying boat obsolete as a passenger transport, and its place was taken by four-engined landplanes with pressurized passenger cabins. Soon, however, even these began to give way to the first of the turboprop and pure-jet airliners that would equip the world's major commercial airlines. The jet engine was also used in fighters and bombers, but military transports were piston-engined for some time. German wartime research into high-speed aerodynamics heralded the introduction of swept wings and podded engines, and the era of supersonics was born. In the same period, the helicopter became a practical aircraft; other significant creations included the supersonic transport, high-capacity wide-bodied airliners, and the vertical-takeoff airplane.

STAR TURN

Airline posters have always been evocative of the eras in which they were designed. This advertisement for the Australian airline Qantas dates from the 1950s, and shows a Lockheed Constellation.

NAVY JET

The de Havilland Vampire and Venom family of twin-boom jet fighters and trainers was prevalent in the 1950s. Shown below is a Sea Vampire in British Fleet Air Arm colors.

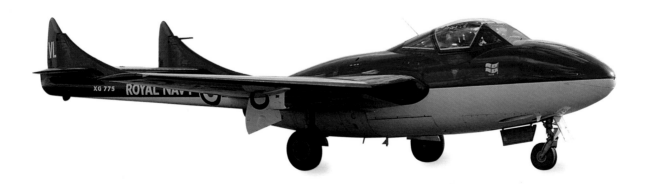

1946·1969 PISTON-ENGINED AIRLINERS

WITH THE END OF World War II, commercial airliners once again came to the fore. While Britain's manufacturers concentrated on converting wartime bombers to meet the demand, the US already had aircraft that were designed as commercial transports but had been hurriedly adapted for military use during the war. It was not long, however, before new, custom-designed airliners such as those featured here were joining the airline fleets.

LANCASTER CONVERSION

Essentially an Avro Lancaster bomber with its mid-upper turret removed and its nose and tail turrets replaced by streamlined fairings, the Avro 691 Lancastrian was a lot faster than its 1930s forebears, but lacked the comfort. It served with Qantas, Skyways, and British South American Airways Corporation among others.

Tail is provided with triple fins and rudders

FROM THE ASHES OF THE WELLINGTON

The first postwar British transport airplane to undertake airline work, Vickers' V.C.1 Viking combined many Wellington bomber components, such as the engine nacelle and undercarriage units and, at first, the fabric-covered geodetic outer-wing panels, with a new stressed-skin metal fuselage seating 21 passengers. It first flew in June 1945.

All-metal, stressed-skin fuselage

Fin folds down sideways for easier hangar accommodation

DOUBLE BUBBLE

A commercial development of Boeing's C-97 military transport, the 377 Stratocruiser was powered by four massive, complicated 3,500-hp radial engines, and first flew in 1947. Its "double-bubble" fuselage accommodated passengers on two levels and included a spiral staircase to a lounge on the lower deck.

Pressurized "double-bubble"-section fuselage

Circular windows resist pressurization stresses

Upswept fuselage improves ground clearance at takeoff

123-ft (37.5-m) wingspan

Unpressurized two-deck fuselage

Pratt & Whitney Double Wasp four-row radial engine

BOUND FOR NORTH AFRICA

With its double-deck accommodation, the Breguet 763 Deux-Ponts airliner first flew as the 761 in 1949. It was powered by four 1,580-hp SNECMA 14R engines, but these were replaced by Pratt & Whitneys in the production models. Air France had 12 of the improved 763s, which it named Provence and used mainly on North Africa routes.

Small central fin

Undercarriage retracts into rear of engine nacelles

MOST ELEGANT AIRLINER

The Airspeed Ambassador, with its high wing and triple fins, was the epitome of piston airliner elegance. Conceived as a DC-3/Dakota replacement, it entered service in 1952 and had a cruising speed of up to 260 mph (418 km/h).

COMPETITION FOR DOUGLAS

American manufacturer Consolidated-Vultee Aircraft (Convair) produced a series of piston twins intended to replace the ubiquitous Douglas DC-3. The Model 240, first flown in March 1947, was followed by the Model 340 (*right*), which made its maiden flight in October 1951 and entered service a year later.

Cabin for 40/44 passengers

Tailplane spans 50 ft (15 m)

Well-streamlined, pressurized fuselage

Astrodome for stellar navigation using sextant

CLASSIC CONSTELLATION

One of the greatest postwar piston-engined airliners, the Lockheed Constellation (*above*) first flew as the civil-registered C-69 military transport in 1943. It began commercial life as the 51-passenger 049 in 1945, and the ultimate development was the 99-seat Model 1649 Starliner of 1956. This South African Airways Model 749 dates from 1950.

Deicing strips on wing leading edges

2,500-hp Wright Cyclone R-3350 radial engine

Pratt & Whitney Double Wasp radial engines

FLYING THE SEVEN SEAS

Developed from the C-54 Skymaster military transport via the DC-4 and DC-6 families, the Douglas DC-7C Seven Seas with its transatlantic capability was the ultimate expression of piston-engined passenger aircraft. First flown in 1955, the DC-7C could normally carry between 60 and 105 passengers in a fully pressurized cabin. It was later eclipsed by the first jet transports, including the DC-8, but continued flying as a cargo plane throughout the 1960s.

1946·1969 JETS & TURBOPROPS

THE ADVENT OF JET AIRLINERS, employing either pure jet engines or propeller turbines, quickly relegated the postwar piston-engined machines to second rank. Those airliners with propeller turbines – known as turboprops – were noted for their comfort, smooth running, and lack of vibration. However, in the public's eyes their "old-fashioned" propellers seemed to relate more to the piston-engined era than the jet era. Although more economical on shorter routes, turboprops eventually gave way to the pure jets.

TROUBLE-FREE TRANSPORTATION

The world's first turboprop transport airplane, the Vickers Viscount, first flew on July 16, 1948, proving almost trouble-free from the outset. Powered by four Rolls-Royce Dart propeller turbines, the Viscount was produced until 1964 and was used by more than 60 different airlines.

Flightdeck well forward in nose

Stretched fuselage accommodated additional passengers

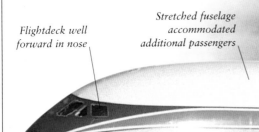

Engines buried in wing roots

THE REVOLUTION STARTS HERE...

The de Havilland Comet was the world's first jet airliner. The prototype made its maiden flight in July 1949, and in 1952 BOAC (British Overseas Airways Corporation) began the first jet passenger service. But in-flight structural failures cost the Comet its early preeminence, and despite the introduction of the improved 4C (*above*), sales never recovered.

SOVIET GIANT

Until the appearance of Boeing's 747, the Tupolev Tu-114 was the world's largest airliner, making its first flight in 1957 and entering airline service in 1961. Its four 14,795-hp turboprops gave it a maximum cruising speed of 478 mph (770 km/h) at 29,500 ft (9,000 m).

Eight-bladed counterrotating propeller

BORN-AGAIN BOMBER

Shown above in prototype form, Tupolev's Tu-104 used the wings, undercarriage, tail unit, engine installation, and nose of a Tu-16 bomber, while the fuselage was new. It began operations for the Soviet airline Aeroflot in September 1956, when, due to the problems with the early Comets, it was the only jet transport in service.

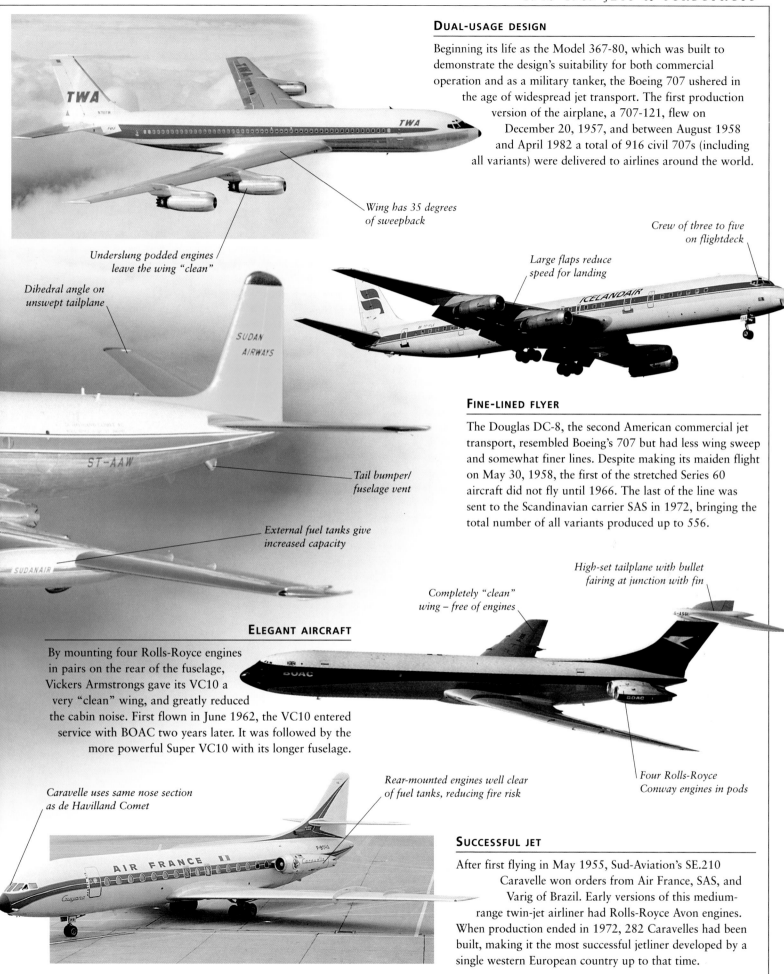

DUAL-USAGE DESIGN

Beginning its life as the Model 367-80, which was built to demonstrate the design's suitability for both commercial operation and as a military tanker, the Boeing 707 ushered in the age of widespread jet transport. The first production version of the airplane, a 707-121, flew on December 20, 1957, and between August 1958 and April 1982 a total of 916 civil 707s (including all variants) were delivered to airlines around the world.

Wing has 35 degrees of sweepback

Underslung podded engines leave the wing "clean"

Crew of three to five on flightdeck

Large flaps reduce speed for landing

Dihedral angle on unswept tailplane

Tail bumper/ fuselage vent

External fuel tanks give increased capacity

FINE-LINED FLYER

The Douglas DC-8, the second American commercial jet transport, resembled Boeing's 707 but had less wing sweep and somewhat finer lines. Despite making its maiden flight on May 30, 1958, the first of the stretched Series 60 aircraft did not fly until 1966. The last of the line was sent to the Scandinavian carrier SAS in 1972, bringing the total number of all variants produced up to 556.

High-set tailplane with bullet fairing at junction with fin

Completely "clean" wing – free of engines

ELEGANT AIRCRAFT

By mounting four Rolls-Royce engines in pairs on the rear of the fuselage, Vickers Armstrongs gave its VC10 a very "clean" wing, and greatly reduced the cabin noise. First flown in June 1962, the VC10 entered service with BOAC two years later. It was followed by the more powerful Super VC10 with its longer fuselage.

Four Rolls-Royce Conway engines in pods

Rear-mounted engines well clear of fuel tanks, reducing fire risk

Caravelle uses same nose section as de Havilland Comet

SUCCESSFUL JET

After first flying in May 1955, Sud-Aviation's SE.210 Caravelle won orders from Air France, SAS, and Varig of Brazil. Early versions of this medium-range twin-jet airliner had Rolls-Royce Avon engines. When production ended in 1972, 282 Caravelles had been built, making it the most successful jetliner developed by a single western European country up to that time.

1946·1969 JET FIGHTERS & BOMBERS

DURING THE 1950s and 1960s a whole gamut of classic military jet aircraft filled the skies, and the world became familiar with such famous names as Hunter, Phantom, Canberra, Vulcan, and Super Sabre, to mention but a few. With the Cold War still very much at the fore, manufacturers both in the West and in the Eastern Bloc vied to keep pace with developments in aircraft, weapons, and technology in order to maintain a "balance of power." Under this degree of pressure, aircraft were constantly being developed and improved.

SOVIET SUCCESS

One of the USSR's most successful warplanes was the Mikoyan and Guryevich MiG-21 fighter. Over 9,000 of various models were built in the USSR between 1958 and 1980; it was also built under license in China, Czechoslovakia, and India.

FIRST SUPERSONIC FIGHTER

The first operational fighter in the world capable of level supersonic performance, the North American F-100 Super Sabre made its maiden flight on May 25, 1953, and entered US Air Force service in November of that year. The Pratt & Whitney J-57 turbojet engine gave the F-100D a top speed of 892 mph (1,436 km/h) at 35,000 ft (10,670 m).

Communications antenna

Wings swept back 40°

DEADLY NOSE

First flown on July 21, 1951, the Hawker Hunter was powered by a Rolls-Royce Avon turbojet and armed with four 30-mm Aden cannons in an ingenious undernose pack. The Hunter served with many of the world's air forces, and 1,972 were built before production ended in 1959.

U.S. AIR FORCE FW-281 42281

Oval air intake in nose

Antenna at base of fin leading edge

FRENCH BOMBER

France's nuclear bomber, the Dassault Mirage IVA, was first flown in October 1961. To allow it to use short runways when dispersed in an emergency, it was equipped with a rocket-assisted takeoff system. Two SNECMA Atar 9K turbojets, each giving 15,432-lb (7,000-kg) thrust with maximum afterburner, gave the bomber a maximum speed at sea level of 1,454 mph (2,340 km/h), or Mach 2.2.

Auxiliary fuel tanks

ARRIVAL OF THE V-BOMBERS

The first large bomber to have a delta wing, the Avro Vulcan, along with the Vickers Valiant and Handley Page Victor, made up the RAF's (Royal Air Force's) group of "V-bombers." The prototype Vulcan first flew on September 3, 1953, and the type entered service in 1956. The example shown here is a B.Mk 2, which was powered by four Bristol Siddeley Olympus turbojets of 17,000-lb (7,711-kg) or 20,000-lb (9,072-kg) thrust each.

Delta wing was given compound leading-edge sweep in later versions

Radome also houses electronic countermeasures equipment

Double-delta wing

Engine air intakes at front of wing

SUPERSONIC SWEDE

With its unusual double-delta wing, Sweden's supersonic J 35 Draken fighter (*right*) from Saab entered service in 1960, and was also used by Finland, Austria, and Denmark. The definitive model, the J 35F, had a 12,710-lb (5,765-kg) thrust RM 6C engine and could carry four Falcon air-to-air missiles.

FIGHTER OF REPUTE

First flown in October 1947, North American's F-86 Sabre was the first swept-wing jet fighter to go into production and serve with the USAF. It made a name for itself in the Korean War, and a range of variants served with many air forces. The F-86K (like this Royal Netherlands Air Force example) was evolved from the F-86D for NATO forces, and had both cannons and missiles.

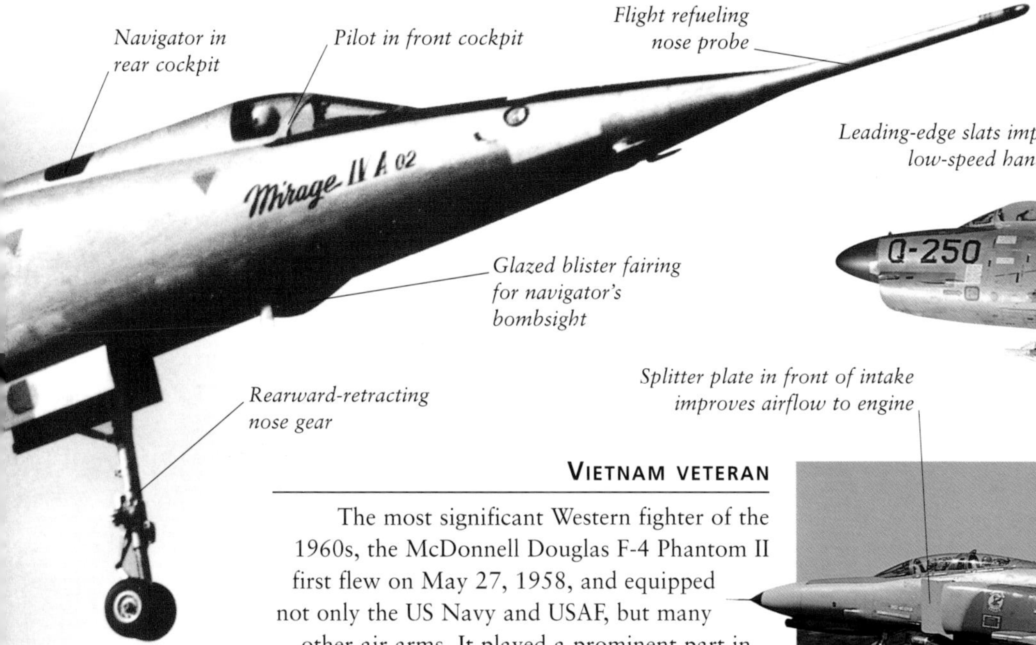

Navigator in rear cockpit

Pilot in front cockpit

Flight refueling nose probe

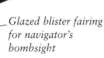

Leading-edge slats improve low-speed handling

Glazed blister fairing for navigator's bombsight

Splitter plate in front of intake improves airflow to engine

Rearward-retracting nose gear

VIETNAM VETERAN

The most significant Western fighter of the 1960s, the McDonnell Douglas F-4 Phantom II first flew on May 27, 1958, and equipped not only the US Navy and USAF, but many other air arms. It played a prominent part in the Vietnam War, proving equally effective whether sea- or land-based. Shown here is an F-4E of the USAF's Tactical Air Command.

Engine nacelle

Simple wing has single main spar

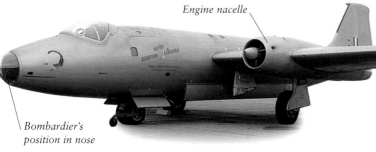

HIGH FLYER

Britain's first jet bomber, the Canberra from English Electric, served with the RAF from 1951. Powered by Rolls-Royce Avons, it also proved effective for high-altitude reconnaissance. This Canberra B.2/6 was used as a test bed for the Napier Double Scorpion rocket motor.

Bombardier's position in nose

1946·1969 LOCKHEED SR-71A

ONE OF THE MOST AMAZING aircraft of the twentieth century, the SR-71 "Blackbird" originated in 1957 in a request by the US Central Intelligence Agency (CIA) that studies be made of the altitude, speed, and radar cross-section of an aircraft to replace the Lockheed U-2 spyplane. Two years later, Lockheed's famous "Skunk Works," where many advanced secret projects were hatched, submitted its A-12 design. The fastest air-breathing crewed aircraft, it was designed to fly at Mach 3, three times faster than modern fighters, and at twice their altitude. The SR-71 first flew on April 24, 1962.

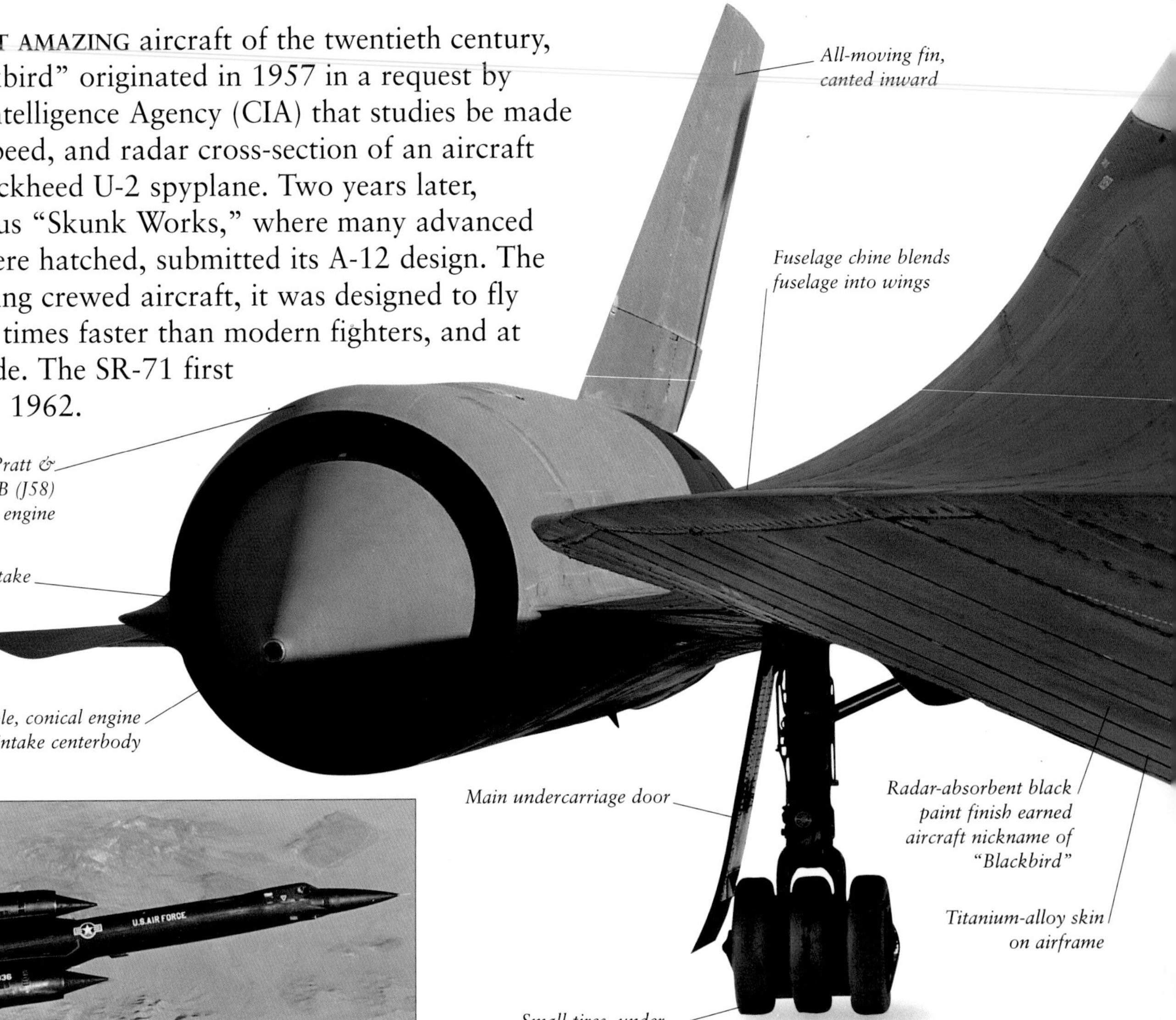

All-moving fin, canted inward

Fuselage chine blends fuselage into wings

Nacelle housing Pratt & Whitney JT11D-20B (J58) turbo-ramjet engine

Engine air intake

Movable, conical engine intake centerbody

Main undercarriage door

Radar-absorbent black paint finish earned aircraft nickname of "Blackbird"

Titanium-alloy skin on airframe

Small tires, under very high pressure

EARLY BLACKBIRD

Seen above is a Lockheed A-12, prototype of the SR-71. In May 1965 its successor, the YF-12A, set records for sustained height and speed, including 2,070.101 mph (3,331 km/h) over a 9/15-mile (15/25-km) course, and an absolute sustained altitude of 80,258 ft (24,463 m). The last flight of an A-12/YF-12 took place in November 1979.

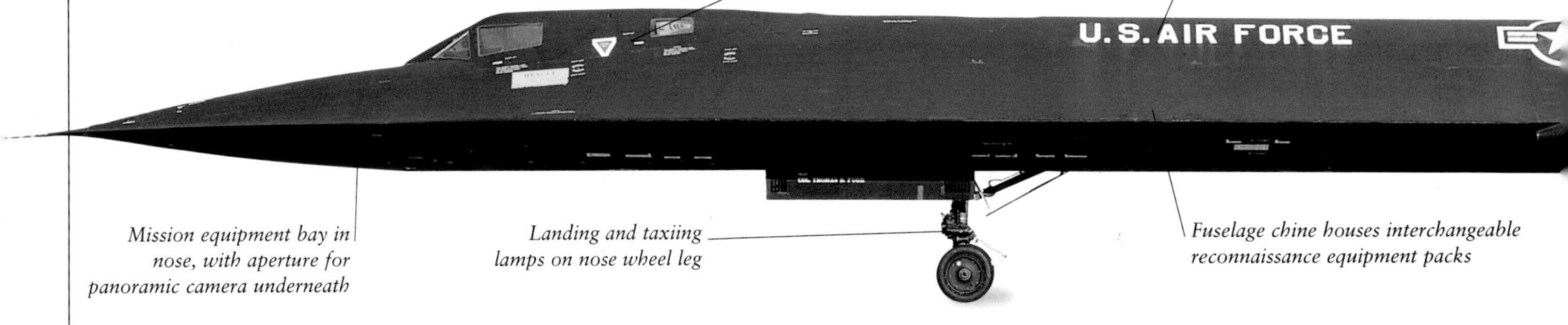

Rear cockpit for reconnaissance systems officer

Integral fuel tanks in fuselage, from aft of rear cockpit almost to tail; total capacity 10,158 gallons (46,180 liters)

U.S. AIR FORCE

Mission equipment bay in nose, with aperture for panoramic camera underneath

Landing and taxiing lamps on nose wheel leg

Fuselage chine houses interchangeable reconnaissance equipment packs

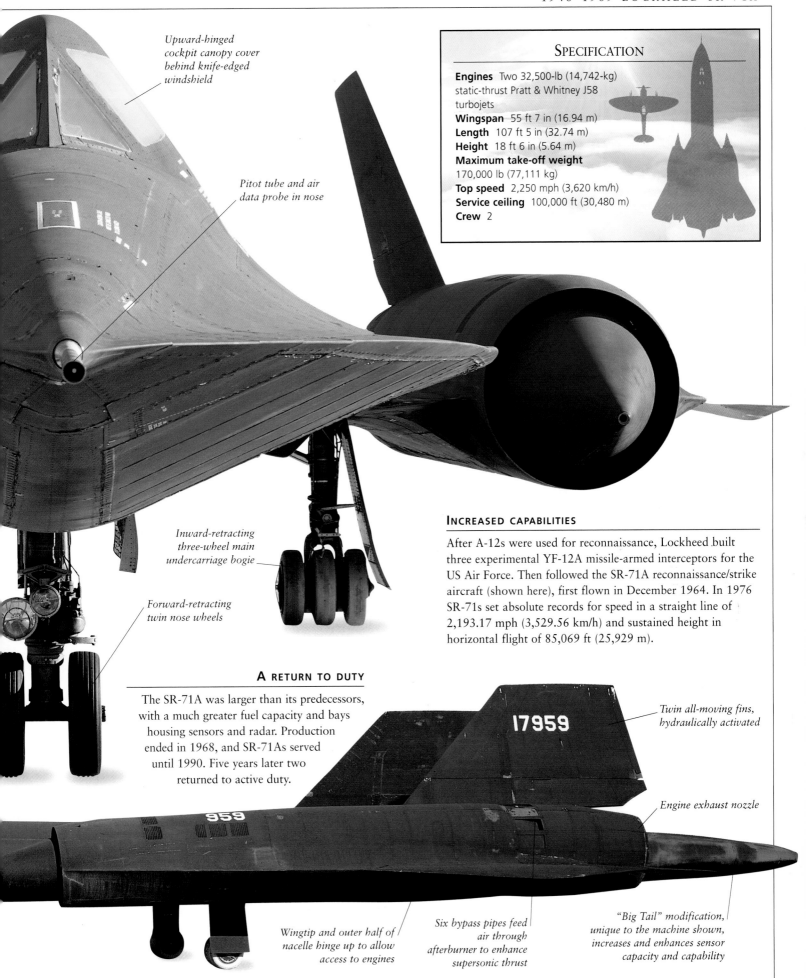

Upward-hinged cockpit canopy cover behind knife-edged windshield

Pitot tube and air data probe in nose

SPECIFICATION

Engines Two 32,500-lb (14,742-kg) static-thrust Pratt & Whitney J58 turbojets
Wingspan 55 ft 7 in (16.94 m)
Length 107 ft 5 in (32.74 m)
Height 18 ft 6 in (5.64 m)
Maximum take-off weight 170,000 lb (77,111 kg)
Top speed 2,250 mph (3,620 km/h)
Service ceiling 100,000 ft (30,480 m)
Crew 2

Inward-retracting three-wheel main undercarriage bogie

Forward-retracting twin nose wheels

INCREASED CAPABILITIES

After A-12s were used for reconnaissance, Lockheed built three experimental YF-12A missile-armed interceptors for the US Air Force. Then followed the SR-71A reconnaissance/strike aircraft (shown here), first flown in December 1964. In 1976 SR-71s set absolute records for speed in a straight line of 2,193.17 mph (3,529.56 km/h) and sustained height in horizontal flight of 85,069 ft (25,929 m).

A RETURN TO DUTY

The SR-71A was larger than its predecessors, with a much greater fuel capacity and bays housing sensors and radar. Production ended in 1968, and SR-71As served until 1990. Five years later two returned to active duty.

17959

Twin all-moving fins, hydraulically activated

959

Engine exhaust nozzle

Wingtip and outer half of nacelle hinge up to allow access to engines

Six bypass pipes feed air through afterburner to enhance supersonic thrust

"Big Tail" modification, unique to the machine shown, increases and enhances sensor capacity and capability

1946·1969 THE BOEING LINE

BOEING

ON JULY 15, 1916, William Boeing set up Pacific Aero Products, and the following year he changed its name to the Boeing Airplane Company. Now with more than 80 years of continuous operation behind it, Boeing is the longest-running aircraft manufacturer in the US, and its products have included an exceptional number of outstanding designs for use in all manner of roles.

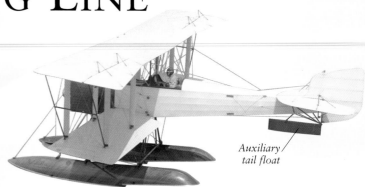

Auxiliary tail float

THE FIRST BOEING

William E. Boeing and naval officer Conrad Westervelt collaborated in the design of the company's first product, a twin-float seaplane built in a boathouse on Lake Union, Seattle, Washington. The two B&Ws built were bought by the New Zealand government and made that country's first experimental airmail flights.

Segmented high-lift slats along wing leading edge

LIGHTWEIGHT LINER

Boeing's latest product, the long-range 777 airliner first flew in June 1994. It is built with lightweight materials such as aluminum alloys, carbon fibers, and glass fiber, and is equipped with a digital fly-by-wire flight control system.

Tail of fuselage houses auxiliary power unit

Six-wheel groups, rear pair of wheels steerable

Double-slotted flaps inboard of engines

Pratt & Whitney Hornet radial engine

COMMERCIAL COMFORT

Designed to meet a United Air Lines requirement, the Model 247 commercial transport (*below*), first flown in 1933, had two Pratt & Whitney Wasp air-cooled radial engines and carried 10 passengers in considerable comfort for the time. Stewardess service and a tiny galley and washroom were included.

CARRYING THE MAIL

First flown in 1930, the all-metal Monomail (*above*) made very early use of a semi-retractable undercarriage. The only two built were used successfully by Boeing Air Transport, the second, the Model 221, having a cabin for six passengers. Both were later converted to eight-seaters.

All-metal monocoque fuselage

Company highlights

- **1916** Two B&W seaplanes built. Pacific Aero Products Co registered.
- **1917** Company re-registered as Boeing Airplane Co.
- **1933** Boeing Aircraft Co formed as subsidiary.
- **1947** The two companies merge.
- **1960** Boeing buys Vertol helicopter company.
- **1961** Name changes to The Boeing Company due to diversification of output.
- **1986** Boeing buys North American Aviation.
- **1997** Boeing buys McDonnell Douglas.

An armed force

The Boeing B-29 made its first flight in 1942. With its three pressurized crew compartments and a 10- or 13-gun defensive armament in four remotely controlled power-operated turrets and a directly controlled tail turret, it was a great advance on its immediate ancestor, the B-17. The B-29 could carry a 20,000-lb (9,000-kg) bomb load.

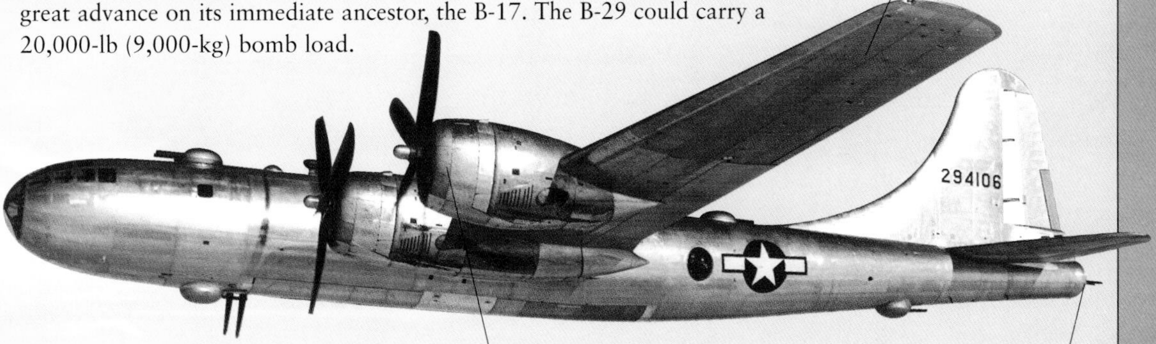

Narrow, long-span wings for high lift at altitude
294106
Each 2,200-hp Wright Double Cyclone engine has two superchargers
Rear gun position provides good defense against attack from behind

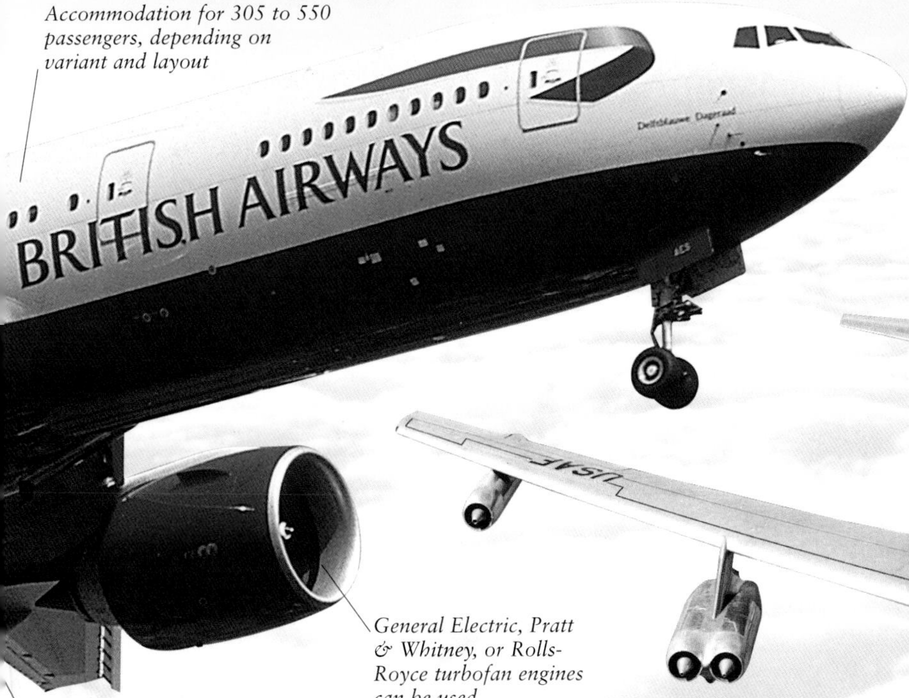

Accommodation for 305 to 550 passengers, depending on variant and layout
BRITISH AIRWAYS
General Electric, Pratt & Whitney, or Rolls-Royce turbofan engines can be used
Single-slotted flaps along trailing edge, outboard of engines

Sleek bomber

Designed to carry thermonuclear bombs, the B-47 was revolutionary when it first appeared in 1947, in part due to its 35-degree swept wing and six underslung jet engines. The slow-accelerating turbojets were augmented by 18 rocket-assisted takeoff units, while its only defense was a pair of 20-mm cannons in a tail turret.

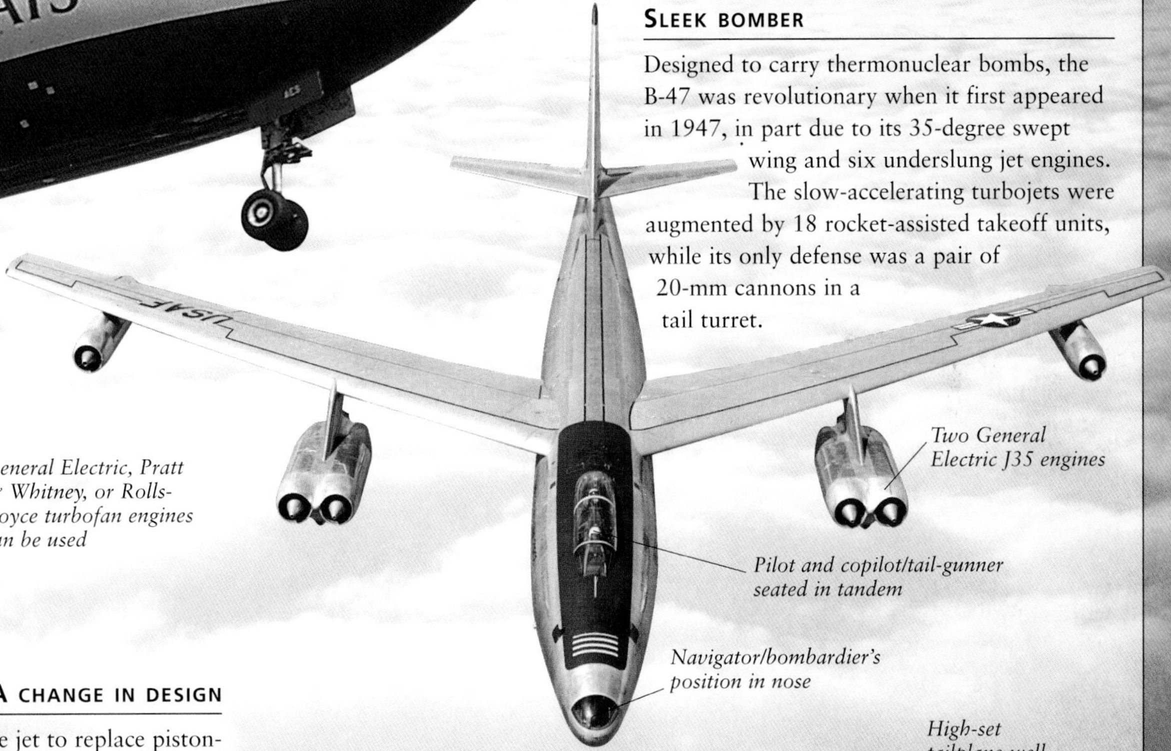

USAF
Two General Electric J35 engines
Pilot and copilot/tail-gunner seated in tandem
Navigator/bombardier's position in nose

A change in design

Designed as a short-to-medium-range jet to replace piston- and turboprop-powered types, the 727 departed from Boeing's usual styling by having its three engines clustered around the rear fuselage. Its auxiliary power unit for stationary use and integral boarding stairs made it virtually independent of ground power vehicles.

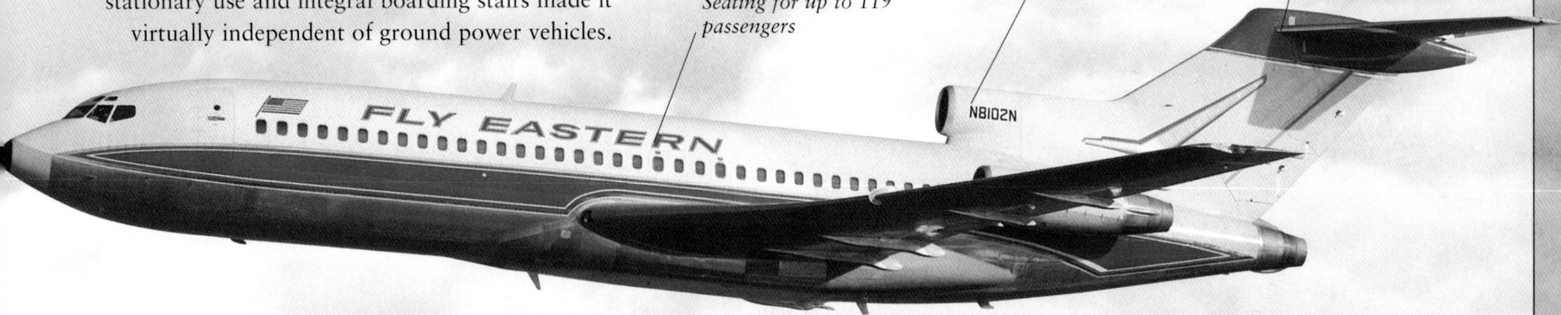

High-set tailplane well clear of jet efflux
Air intake with "S"-duct leading to central engine
Seating for up to 119 passengers
FLY EASTERN
N8102N

1946·1969 BOEING B-52G

WHEN BOEING CONCEIVED the B-52 Stratofortress conventional and nuclear strategic bomber late in 1948, it was expected that it would serve until the late 1950s. Yet it is still going strong and, in its latest B-52H version, will equip frontline US Air Force units well into the twenty-first century. The first of the breed, the tandem-cockpit YB-52, took to the air on April 15, 1952, followed two years later by the B-52A with its now-familiar airline-style flightdeck. The first Stratofortress to enter service with US Strategic Air Command was the B-52B in 1955. Since then the successful design has undergone constant updating of equipment and extensive structural modification.

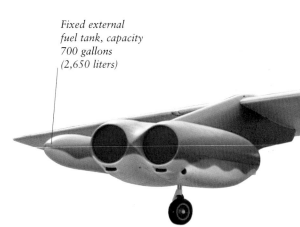

Fixed external fuel tank, capacity 700 gallons (2,650 liters)

TALL TAIL

Well displayed on this B-52E is the earlier, taller vertical tail. This variant of the Stratofortress, of which 100 were built, had a completely new navigation and bombing system that required substantial redesign of the crew compartment.

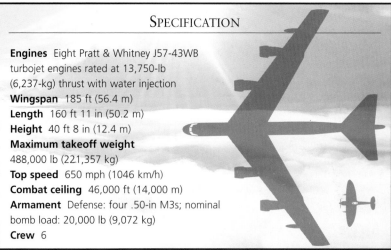

SPECIFICATION

Engines Eight Pratt & Whitney J57-43WB turbojet engines rated at 13,750-lb (6,237-kg) thrust with water injection
Wingspan 185 ft (56.4 m)
Length 160 ft 11 in (50.2 m)
Height 40 ft 8 in (12.4 m)
Maximum takeoff weight 488,000 lb (221,357 kg)
Top speed 650 mph (1046 km/h)
Combat ceiling 46,000 ft (14,000 m)
Armament Defense: four .50-in M3s; nominal bomb load: 20,000 lb (9,072 kg)
Crew 6

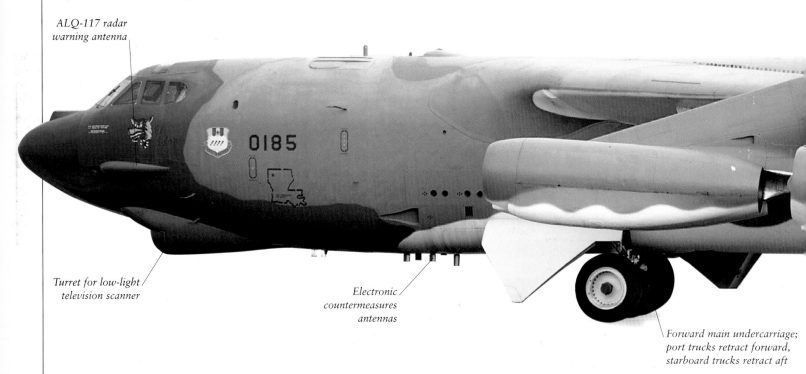

ALQ-117 radar warning antenna

Turret for low-light television scanner

Electronic countermeasures antennas

Forward main undercarriage; port trucks retract forward, starboard trucks retract aft

Flightdeck in front of Stretched
Upper Deck, well forward on nose

A JUMBO BY ANY OTHER NAME...

Currently the world's largest, heaviest, and most
powerful airliner, the 747-400 is the only model of the
family still in production. The span of its structurally
redesigned wings, with winglets added, is 16 ft (4.9 m)
greater than that of the -300, and the fairings between
the wing and fuselage, and the engine pylons and nacelles,
have also been redesigned. Extensive use of composite
materials has reduced empty weight considerably.

Engine nacelles
carried on
underwing pylons

Main passenger accommodation in large
single deck, seating up to ten abreast with
two aisles in economy class

Large-diameter intakes
for high-bypass
turbofan engines

Foremost main
trucks wider apart
than rearmost units

Twin hydraulically
steered nose wheels

Rear truck

Segmented Kreuger flaps
incorporated in wing leading edges

Main undercarriage comprises
four four-wheel trucks

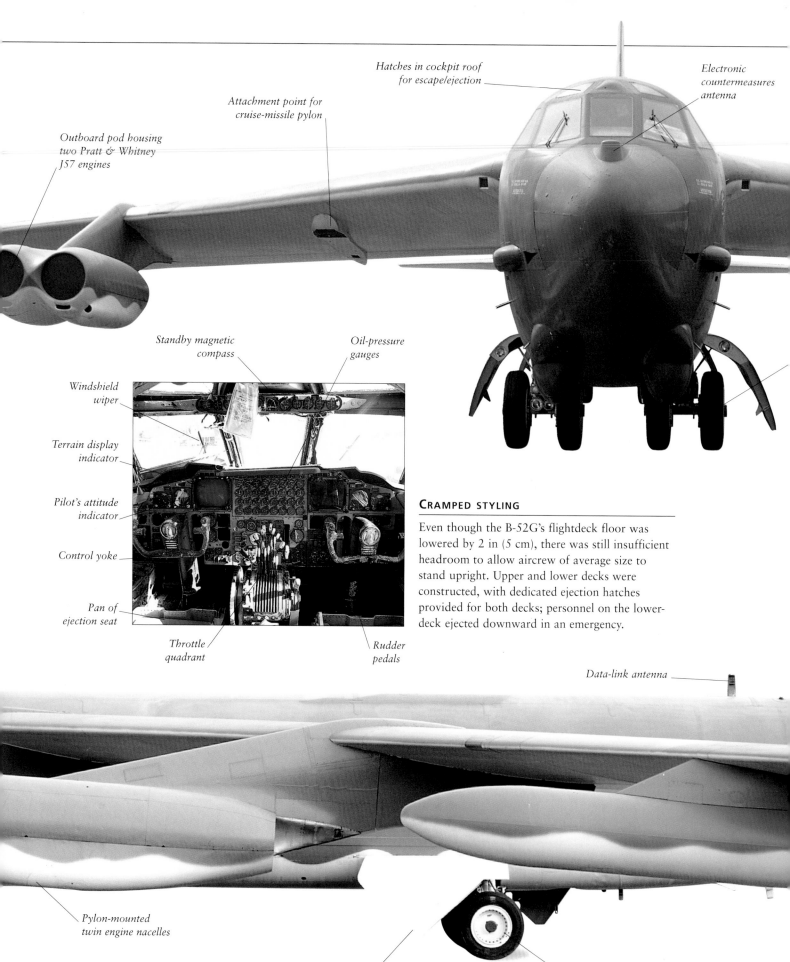

Hatches in cockpit roof
for escape/ejection

Electronic
countermeasures
antenna

Attachment point for
cruise-missile pylon

Outboard pod housing
two Pratt & Whitney
J57 engines

Standby magnetic
compass

Oil-pressure
gauges

Windshield
wiper

Terrain display
indicator

Pilot's attitude
indicator

Control yoke

Pan of
ejection seat

Throttle
quadrant

Rudder
pedals

CRAMPED STYLING

Even though the B-52G's flightdeck floor was
lowered by 2 in (5 cm), there was still insufficient
headroom to allow aircrew of average size to
stand upright. Upper and lower decks were
constructed, with dedicated ejection hatches
provided for both decks; personnel on the lower-
deck ejected downward in an emergency.

Data-link antenna

Pylon-mounted
twin engine nacelles

Door for rear main
undercarriage

Rear main undercarriage;
two twin-wheel trucks

WINGS OF FUEL

The B-52's wing is based on a two-spar torsion box, and is extraordinarily flexible in flight, though the weight of the paired engine pods dampens this out. The B-52G, which appeared in 1958, was the greatest single advance of the type. Its wing incorporated the largest integral fuel tankage up to that time, giving the bomber a total internal fuel capacity, including the fuselage tanks, of 46,575 gallons (176,305 liters). On this variant the ailerons were omitted, lateral control being provided by spoilers.

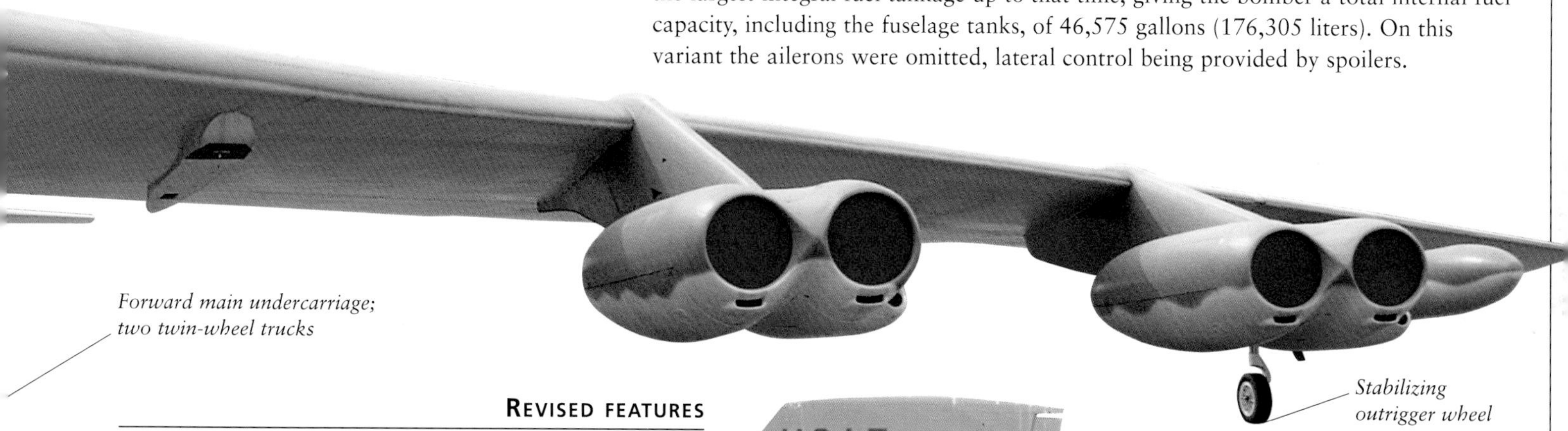

Forward main undercarriage; two twin-wheel trucks

Stabilizing outrigger wheel

REVISED FEATURES

The B-52G's vertical tail was nearly 8 ft (2.43 m) shorter than those of earlier B-52s, and its rudder and elevators were hydraulically powered. By moving the gunner into the main crew compartment, the designers were able to eliminate his pressure cabin in the tail, with all its essential services. The huge bomb bay could accommodate a nominal 20,000-lb (9,072-kg) bomb load, and there was provision to carry two Hound Dog air-breathing cruise missiles on underwing pylons.

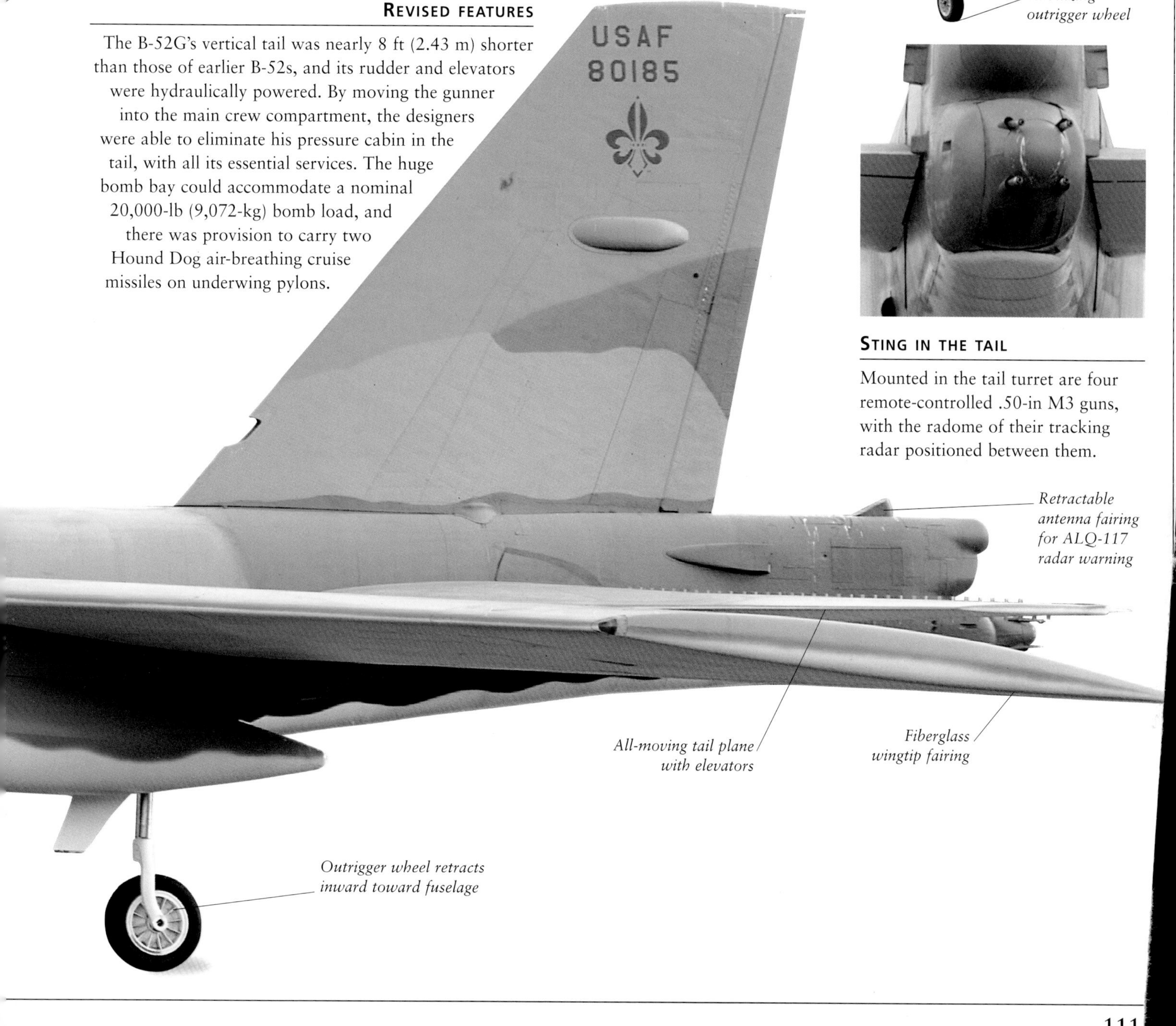

USAF
80185

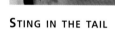

STING IN THE TAIL

Mounted in the tail turret are four remote-controlled .50-in M3 guns, with the radome of their tracking radar positioned between them.

Retractable antenna fairing for ALQ-117 radar warning

All-moving tail plane with elevators

Fiberglass wingtip fairing

Outrigger wheel retracts inward toward fuselage

1946·1969 BOEING 747-400

THE PROTOTYPE of the famous 747 airliner made its maiden flight on February 9, 1969. The program was launched by Boeing at enormous financial risk, but the company's gamble paid off handsomely over the ensuing years. The 747 ushered in the age of the widebody, bringing air travel within the reach of many more people. Although the 747-400 looks to all intents and purposes like just another variant of the 747 family, and has the same fuselage dimensions as the -300, it is a major redesign incorporating numerous aerodynamic enhancements and upgraded engines, and is cleared to higher operating weights.

PLENTY OF ROOM ON BOARD

On December 30, 1969, the 747, represented above by the prototype, powered by four 43,000-lb (19,732-kg) thrust Pratt & Whitney JT9D turbofan engines, was certificated to carry up to 490 passengers. The launch customer, Pan American, flew the type's first scheduled service, using the first production variant, the 747-100, from New York to London on February 22, 1970.

Rudder divided into upper and lower segments

When wing is full of fuel, outer portions bend down and winglets are angled further outward, increasing span by 19 in (48 cm)

Fin built up on two-spar box structure

Rearmost passenger entry/exit door

VH-OJC

SPECIFICATION

Engines Four Rolls-Royce RB.211-524 turbofans, of 58,000-lb (26,300-kg) thrust each
Wingspan 211 ft 5 in (64.4 m)
Length 231 ft 10 in (70.6 m)
Height 63 ft 8 in (19.4 m)
Maximum takeoff weight 800,000 lb (362,880 kg)
Typical cruise speed Mach 0.85
Initial cruise altitude* 34,700 ft (10,577 m)
Range* 6,828 miles (10,982 km)
Passengers 420 (in typical three-class arrangement)
Crew 4 pilots and up to 14 cabin crew
* at maximum takeoff weight

ADAPTED FOR LONG HAULS

The 747-400 has, in common with the -300, the Stretched Upper Deck fuselage. While this additional passenger accommodation inevitably increases weight, it also improves the fuselage aerodynamics. The -400 was developed to enable the 747 to fly popular long-haul routes, such as those from the US to Asia, nonstop, without requiring a reduction in payload.

Overhead systems switch panel

Instrument panel has five cathode-ray-tube EFIS displays

MAKING LIFE EASIER

The two-crew flightdeck has an Electronic Flight Instrumentation System (EFIS), which presents primary flight and navigation information on color cathode-ray tubes. This reduces the pilots' workload by about a third. Because of the aircraft's increased range, a small rest area is provided behind the cockpit.

Captain's seat on left, First Officer's on right

Twin landing lights in wing root leading edge

Fairing covers flap track mechanism

6-ft (1.8-m) high winglets, canted out at 290-degree angle

Special color scheme applied to promote the March 2000 Qantas Grand Prix in Melbourne

Additional passenger accommodation in Stretched Upper Deck: 52 business-class or 69 economy-class seats

Flight deck includes two folding seats for observers at rear

Nose wheel leg retracts forward

Full-length nacelle cowling for Rolls-Royce RB.211 engine

1946·1969 VTOL AIRCRAFT

THE ADVANTAGES OF ENDOWING an airplane with the ability to take off and land vertically, with no forward speed, have always been apparent; but it took many years of experimenting before a practical means of accomplishing this was developed. The true jet-lift pioneer was Rolls-Royce's Thrust Measuring Rig (the "Flying Bedstead"), which first hovered uncertainly in 1953, but was never intended as a practical aircraft. Shown here is a small selection of the VTOL (Vertical Take-Off and Landing) devices built, some of which proved more successful than others.

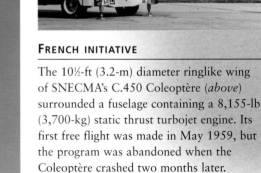

Nose boom

Retractable stabilizing wheels in wingtips

Large spinner for counterrotating propellers

Cockpit has tilting ejection seat for pilot

FIRST SOVIET V/STOL

First flown in 1965, the Yakovlev Yak-36 was the USSR's first jet V/STOL (Vertical or Short Take-Off and Landing) aircraft. Ten were built, all with two Tumanskii R-11V turbojets engines. Stability was maintained by reaction control nozzles in the wingtips, tail, and at the extremity of a long nose boom.

FRENCH INITIATIVE

The 10½-ft (3.2-m) diameter ringlike wing of SNECMA's C.450 Coleoptère (*above*) surrounded a fuselage containing a 8,155-lb (3,700-kg) static thrust turbojet engine. Its first free flight was made in May 1959, but the program was abandoned when the Coleoptère crashed two months later.

POGO POWER

Appropriately named "Pogo," Convair's XFY-1 of 1954 was designed to be lifted vertically by the counterrotating propellers of its 5,850-shp Allison turboprop engine. Successful transitions from vertical to horizontal flight and vice versa were made, but the backward descent to land, after a pull-up into the vertical, was tricky.

Aircraft attached to elevated flatbed of special trailer

VERTICAL HOOK-UP

In November 1956 the USA's Ryan X-13 Vertijet became the first pure-jet aircraft to make a transition from horizontal to vertical flight and back. Five months later it made the first full transition from vertical to horizontal flight, and vice versa for a vertical descent to a hook-on landing on its dedicated trailer.

HARRIER TAKES THE LEAD

Designed around the brilliant Rolls-Royce Pegasus vectored-thrust engine, the British Aeorspace (BAe) Harrier (the "Jump Jet") was the world's first V/STOL combat airplane to enter regular squadron service. It was developed through the Hawker Siddeley Kestrel from the original Hawker P.1127, which first flew conventionally in July 1961, making complete transitions from horizontal to vertical (and back) that September. Further developments led to the Sea Harrier and the BAe/McDonnell Douglas AV-8 Harrier II.

Leading-edge root extensions (LERX) increase maneuver lift and improve handling

FOUR-ENGINE LIFT

As with many early VTOL concepts, the four tilting Rolls-Royce RB.108 lift engines in Britain's Short S.C.1 were dead weight during normal flight under the power of a single horizontal RB.108. First flown conventionally on April 2, 1957, it achieved its first complete transition from level flight to vertical descent, and then vertical climb back to level flight, three years later.

Bay containing four Rolls-Royce RB.108 lift engines

Retracted flight-refueling probe

AIM-9L Sidewinder air-to-air missile

GERMAN–ITALIAN COLLABORATION

Seen here in a ground test-rig, the VAK 191B VTOL aircraft of the late 1960s/early 1970s was developed by VFW-Fokker of Germany in cooperation with Fiat of Italy. Its main lift/cruise engine, a 10,160-lb (4,609-kg) thrust Rolls-Royce/MTU RB.193-12 with four thrust-vectoring nozzles, was augmented in vertical flight by two RB.162-81 lift engines fore and aft. The project foundered.

1946·1969 BAe HARRIER GR.5

WITH ITS NEW AND LARGER WING, an airframe structure incorporating 26 percent carbon-fiber composite, and several other major innovations to the basic Harrier design (*see p. 115*), the GR.5 was the result of a joint study by British Aerospace (BAe) and McDonnell Douglas. The aim was to meet Air Staff Requirement 409: higher performance and a greater fuel/weapon load to enable the Harrier V/STOL (Vertical or Short Take-Off and Landing) ground-attack and battlefield-support fighter to remain in frontline service with the RAF (Royal Air Force) in Germany well into the 1990s.

LONG IMPROVEMENT PERIOD

Seen above are Harrier GR.5s serving with 4 Squadron, RAF, in Germany in the mid-1990s. The type's counterpart in the US Marine Corps was the AV-8B, which first flew in November 1978. However, the RAF did not finalize its plans for the improved Harrier until 1978, and it was not until April 1985 that the first prototype GR.5 made its maiden flight.

SPECIFICATION

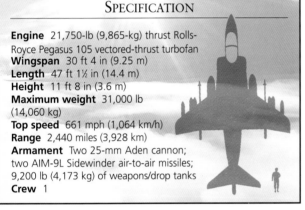

Engine 21,750-lb (9,865-kg) thrust Rolls-Royce Pegasus 105 vectored-thrust turbofan
Wingspan 30 ft 4 in (9.25 m)
Length 47 ft 1½ in (14.4 m)
Height 11 ft 8 in (3.6 m)
Maximum weight 31,000 lb (14,060 kg)
Top speed 661 mph (1,064 km/h)
Range 2,440 miles (3,928 km)
Armament Two 25-mm Aden cannon; two AIM-9L Sidewinder air-to-air missiles; 9,200 lb (4,173 kg) of weapons/drop tanks
Crew 1

Detonation cord in canopy roof shatters canopy before emergency ejection by pilot

Forward swiveling nozzles of Rolls-Royce Pegasus vectored-thrust engine

Smith's Industries SU-128/A head-up display

Free-floating supplementary air doors permit additional air to be drawn in during hovering flight

PUTTING IT ALL TOGETHER

Production of the GR.5 was shared between BAe and McDonnell Douglas. The former made the aft fuselage and tail, and the latter the front fuselage and single-piece wing. Final assembly and flight testing took place at BAe's plant and airfield at Dunsfold. The first RAF unit to have the GR.5 was 3 Squadron in March 1989. Many were later upgraded to GR.7 standard.

Steerable, levered-suspension nose wheel retracts forward

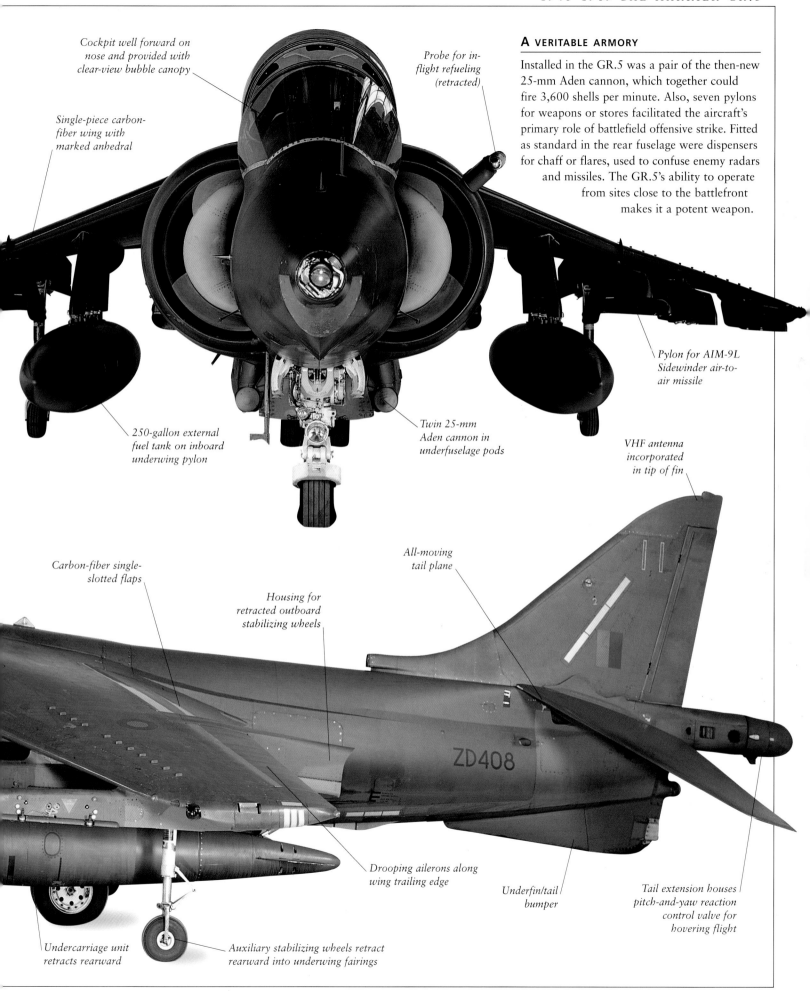

Cockpit well forward on nose and provided with clear-view bubble canopy

Probe for in-flight refueling (retracted)

Single-piece carbon-fiber wing with marked anhedral

A VERITABLE ARMORY

Installed in the GR.5 was a pair of the then-new 25-mm Aden cannon, which together could fire 3,600 shells per minute. Also, seven pylons for weapons or stores facilitated the aircraft's primary role of battlefield offensive strike. Fitted as standard in the rear fuselage were dispensers for chaff or flares, used to confuse enemy radars and missiles. The GR.5's ability to operate from sites close to the battlefront makes it a potent weapon.

Pylon for AIM-9L Sidewinder air-to-air missile

250-gallon external fuel tank on inboard underwing pylon

Twin 25-mm Aden cannon in underfuselage pods

VHF antenna incorporated in tip of fin

Carbon-fiber single-slotted flaps

Housing for retracted outboard stabilizing wheels

All-moving tail plane

Drooping ailerons along wing trailing edge

Underfin/tail bumper

Tail extension houses pitch-and-yaw reaction control valve for hovering flight

ZD408

Undercarriage unit retracts rearward

Auxiliary stabilizing wheels retract rearward into underwing fairings

1946·1969 CONCORDE

THE CONCORDE IS A STRIKING example of international cooperation in advanced technology. Conceived in the mid-1950s, the world's only successful supersonic commercial transport became a collaborative venture when the British and French governments agreed to it in November 1962. Seven years later, in March 1969, the two prototypes from British Aerospace and Aérospatiale made their maiden flights, and fare-paying services were initiated by British Airways and Air France in 1979. Sixteen production Concordes were built on assembly lines in Bristol, England, and Toulouse, France, and 13 remain in operation today.

Fairing for rudder power control unit

Aluminum skinning can tolerate kinetic heating to 270°F (120°C) at Mach 2.0

Fuselage kept to minimum cross-section possible with four-abreast seating

Long fore–aft root of wing allows thin wing to be used while retaining structural stiffness

Underwing nacelle houses paired Olympus engines

Nose in drooped position

Main undercarriage retracts sideways and inward

Nose undercarriage leg retracts forward

Four-wheel main undercarriage truck

Steerable twin nose-wheel truck

SPECIFICATION

Engines Four 38,050-lb (17,259-kg) thrust reheat Rolls-Royce/SNECMA Olympus 593 Mk.602 turbojets
Wingspan 83 ft 10 in (25.56 m)
Length 202 ft 4 in (61.7 m)
Height 37 ft 1 in (11.3 m)
Weight 174,750 lb (79,265 kg)
Maximum cruising speed Mach 2.05 (1,354 mph / 2,179 km/h)
Rate of climb 5,000 ft/min (25.4 m/sec)
Service ceiling 60,000 ft (18,300 m)
Passengers 128 (144 in high-density layout)
Flight crew 3

Faired antenna

Visor retracts into nosecone

Aerodymanic strake

BRITISH AIRWAYS

Wing skinned with machined aluminum panels

ON THE SAME RUNWAYS

Accommodating 128 passengers, the Concorde cruises efficiently at over 1,300 mph (2,100 km/h), more than twice the speed of sound, yet operates from airport runways designed for subsonic airliners. Regardless of the speed of the aircraft, the variable-geometry engine air intakes keep the speed of the airflow to the engines below 300 mph (483 km/h).

ON THE FLIGHTDECK

In the Concorde the pilot and copilot sit side-by-side; a third crew member behind them on the starboard side attends to the systems-management panel. There is provision for a further seat behind the pilots. The instrumentation appears somewhat antiquated now.

NOSING AROUND

Because of the Concorde's high "angle of attack" during landing and takeoff, its nose is hinged to droop, greatly enhancing the crew's view. Once the aircraft is airborne a retractable visor streamlines the nose and protects the main windshield against the kinetic heating experienced in supersonic flight.

Airspeed indicator (Machmeter below, obscured)

Control column and yoke operates elevons, which act as both elevators and ailerons

Rudder pedals

Four throttles on central pedestal

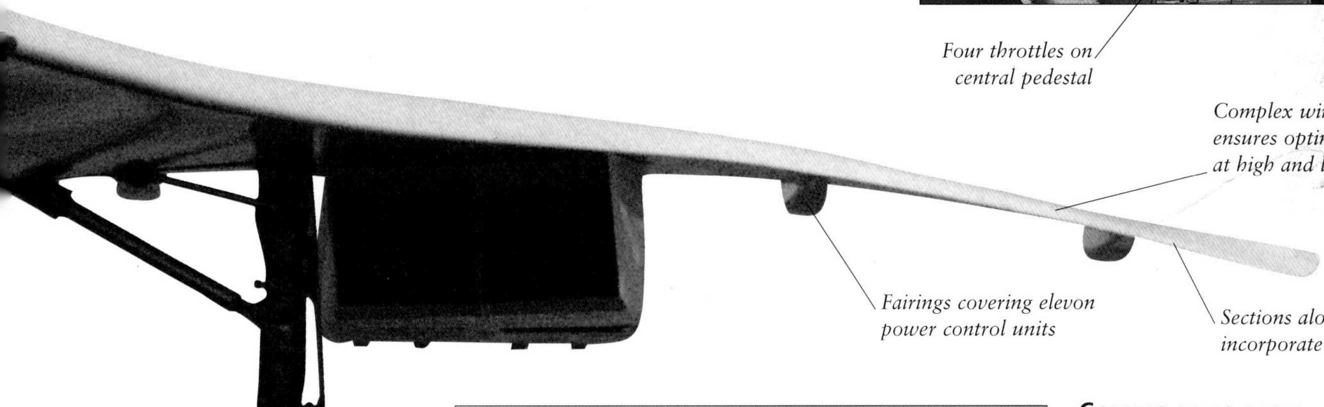

Complex wing curvature ensures optimum efficiency at high and low speeds

Fairings covering elevon power control units

Sections along wing leading edge incorporate expansion joints

COMING IN TO LAND

The Concorde's steep tail-down approach to touchdown means that the crew on the flightdeck are 37 ft (11.2 m) above the ground when the wheels make contact with the runway. Here, the nose is in its 12½-degree fully down position.

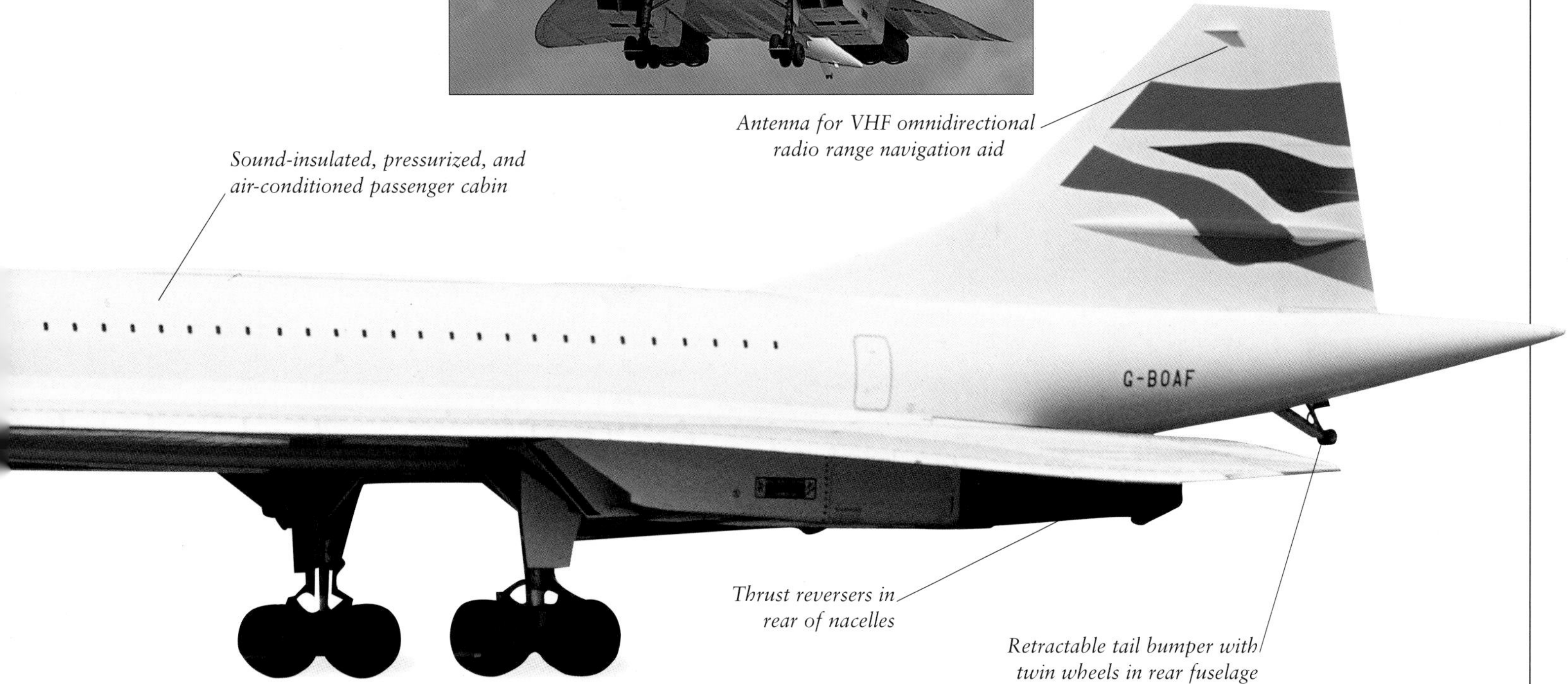

Antenna for VHF omnidirectional radio range navigation aid

Sound-insulated, pressurized, and air-conditioned passenger cabin

G-BOAF

Thrust reversers in rear of nacelles

Retractable tail bumper with twin wheels in rear fuselage

THE NEW TECHNOLOGY

ALTHOUGH THE INCREASING complexity of civil and military aircraft resulted in longer development periods and higher costs, progress in the last decades of the century accelerated on all fronts. The proliferation of wide-bodied airliners brought long-range air travel within the reach of millions, while technical developments led to great changes in aircraft operation. New materials cut down on weight, while refined aerodynamics continued to improve performance. Stealth technology changed the image of bombers and fighters, and weaponry continued to evolve. Meanwhile, home-built ultralight airplanes proliferated as never before, and sustained human-powered flight became a reality. At the beginning of the new century the 500-passenger airliner is upon us, and the tilt-rotor convertiplane is becoming a practical vehicle.

AIRCRAFT FOR SALE

Some of the larger air shows are primarily trade affairs, where the world's aerospace companies can exhibit their products to potential customers. However, several days with enhanced flying displays are set aside for the public.

UNITED EUROPE

An outstanding result of international cooperation, the swing-wing Tornado, represented here by a GR.1 all-weather tactical strike aircraft, is a product of Panavia, a European consortium of British, German, and Italian companies.

HELICOPTERS

1970-2000

BECAUSE OF THE COMPLEX mechanical and aerodynamic problems associated with rotating-wing aircraft, the development of the helicopter was protracted, and many saw little use for it. However, once it had been perfected, it soon proved its worth in a variety of roles, including medical evacuation, crop-spraying, troop transport, heavy lifting and construction work, policing, and anti-submarine operations. More recently it has also become a potent antitank weapon.

Forward transmission gearbox in front pylon

Engines on either side of rear pylon

TANDEM TRANSPORT

First flown in 1961, the tandem-rotor Boeing Vertol CH-47 Chinook medium transport helicopter is powered by a pair of Lycoming T-55 turboshaft engines driving two 60-ft (18.3-m) diameter three-blade rotors. RAF (Royal Air Force) Chinooks like this one (*above*) can carry a 22,000-lb (10,000-kg) payload or 30 seated troops.

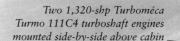

Two 1,320-shp Turboméca Turmo 111C4 turboshaft engines mounted side-by-side above cabin

SUCCESS... BUT TOO LATE

In the 1920s Spanish marquis Pateras Pescara built and tested several cumbersome helicopters with some success. This 1925 effort, with coaxial biplane rotors powered by a Salmson radial engine, achieved a degree of stability, but Pescara's work was overshadowed by the advent of the Cierva Autogiro (*see pp. 12–13*).

Cockpit for two-person crew

AMPHIBIOUS HELICOPTER

The Sikorsky S-61N, launched in 1962 (updating the S-61 of two years earlier), is an all-weather helicopter airliner. It can accommodate between 26 and 28 passengers in its cabin, and its sealed hull enables it to undertake amphibious operations. It is powered by two 1,500-shp General Electric CT58 Turboshaft engines.

Wheels retract into stabilizing floats

Tail boom supports five-blade tail rotor

CHAMPION WEIGHT LIFTER

Far and away the largest and most powerful helicopter ever built was the Soviet Union's Mil V-12 of 1967. This heavy-lift general-purpose helicopter was equipped with two 6,500-shp Soloviev D-25VF turboshaft engines at each wingtip, driving two five-bladed rotors of 115-ft (35-m) diameter. With a top speed of 160 mph (260 km/h), the V-12 set several world records for weight-lifting in 1969, lifting well over 88,000 lb (40,000 kg) on one flight.

Rotorhead

Tail rotor counteracts torque of main rotor

Fairing for engines and gearbox

Transmission shaft for tail rotor runs along top of tail boom

Sliding door for cabin access

AMBULANCE CHOPPER

Used for tactical assault and troop transport, the Westland/Aérospatiale Puma HC Mk 1 (*left*) was developed from the French SA 300, which made its maiden flight in 1965. Entering service with the RAF in mid-1971, the Puma can carry up to 16 troops, or four stretchers and four seated casualties.

Rocket pods and missiles on underwing pylons

STALLION POWER

The first prototype of Sikorsky's CH-53 family, a twin-engined design, made its maiden flight in 1964, and this heavy-duty, multipurpose version, the CH-53E Super Stallion (*right*), was produced to meet US Navy and US Marine Corps requirements. Powered by three 4,380-shp General Electric T64 turboshaft engines, it can carry up to 55 troops or seven cargo pallets. The US Navy model, the MH-53E Sea Dragon, serves in a mine-countermeasures role.

ATTACK APACHE

Developed by Hughes Helicopters, which became McDonnell Douglas Helicopter Co. in 1984, the AH-64 first flew in 1975. The AH-64A Apache (*above*) entered operational service with the US Army two years later. Its prime role is anti-armor attack by day or night, in any weather, and it is equipped with a 30-mm M230 chain gun under its nose and rocket pods on its stub wings.

1970-2000 BELL AH-1S COBRA

THE MAJOR ANTIARMOR helicopter of the US Army in the 1980s, the Bell AH-1S began life as the Model 209, first flown on September 7, 1965. The design at first incorporated 85 percent of the components used in the UH-1 HueyCobra utility and troop transport helicopter, including its rotor, transmission, and power plant. The AH-1 proved its worth in the hands of the Assault Helicopter Companies in Vietnam, and many of them subsequently served in Europe.

SPECIFICATION

Engine 1,800-shp Avco Lycoming T53-L-703 turboshaft engine
Rotor diameter 44 ft (13.4 m)
Max. length 53 ft 1 in (16.18 m)
Height 13 ft 5 in (4.09 m)
Weight 10,000 lb (4,536 kg)
Top speed 141 mph (227 km/h)
Initial rate of climb 1,620 ft (494 m) per min
Service ceiling 12,200 ft (3,718 m)
Armament One 20-mm cannon; four weapons points on stub wings usually carry eight BGM-71 TOW missiles and two pods with 7–19 folding-fin aircraft rockets in each
Crew 2

THREE BARRELS OF FIRE

The AH-1S has redesigned, composite rotor blades and an uprated, 1,800-hp Avco Lycoming T53 turboshaft engine. The example above is fitted with a nose turret containing a three-barrel General Electric M197 20-mm cannon, which has a rate of fire of up to 3,000 rounds per minute.

Composite main blades developed by Kaman can tolerate damage by weapons of up to 23-mm caliber

Rotor blades have tapered tips

Tail rotor driven by shafts and bevel drives from main gearbox

Orifice for output of turboshaft engine

Pylon carrying tail rotor has cambered trailing edge to help counteract torque of main rotor

Driveshaft to tail rotor runs along spine of tail boom

Tail skid protects tail rotor and tailboom from damage

Elevator with inverted airfoil section assists movement in the pitching plane

Tail boom built to withstand damage from weapons of up to 23-mm caliber

UNITED STATES ARMY

SLIM DESTROYER

Because its crew are seated in tandem, the Cobra has a narrow front profile that makes it a difficult target for ground fire as it performs its dangerous low-level sorties against enemy armored vehicles. The stub wings carry antitank missiles and rockets.

Blade pitch control rod

Rotor-head fairing

Armored windshield of hardened glass

Pilot's seat higher than gunner's, allowing him to see forward

Stub wings relieve load on main rotor and provide points for weaponry

Four TOW missile launch tubes outboard, rocket pods inboard

Landing skids instead of wheels, which are less robust

Viewfinder for sighting system

Sight control handle and trigger

NOSE GUNNER

The forward cockpit position is occupied by the gunner/copilot, who is provided with several electronic aiming devices in addition to his own vision. He operates the nose turret, which can also be fired by the pilot.

Rotorhead turns at 294–324 revolutions per minute

TARGETING THE HEAT

Mounted in the extreme nose is an M65 sight – a magnifying thermal imaging system – in a Hughes-designed turret. This enables targets for the TOW missiles to be located and attacked at night. Heavy Norton Co. "Noroc" armor on the seats and cockpit side panels protects the crew from small-arms fire.

Cockpit entered by upward-hinged side doors, pilot's to starboard, gunner's to port

M28 turret houses twin 7.62-mm Miniguns with 4,000 rounds apiece

1970-2000 WIDE-BODIED AIRLINERS

COMMERCIAL MASS transportation by air became a reality with the advent of the wide-bodied airliners. The ability to carry several hundred passengers in each airplane meant that fares could be reduced to a price affordable by many more people, making air travel competitive with other forms of transportation. Since the rollout of the prototype Boeing 747 in 1969 several major aircraft manufacturers have fielded "widebody" airliners, as they have come to be known.

Underwing engine pod

Intake with "S" duct to engine in rear fuselage

TROUBLED BEGINNINGS

Lockheed of the US reentered the commercial-aircraft market with the L-1011 TriStar, but initial problems with the three Rolls-Royce RB.211 jet engines put it at a disadvantage. First flown on November 16, 1970, the TriStar was offered in a range of variants, according to airlines' operational requirements. The basic medium-range version carries 400 passengers in its high-density configuration.

LET DOWN BY ITS ENGINES

The Ilyushin Il-86-300, the USSR's first entry in the widebody game, was handicapped by the relatively short lives of Soviet engines, in this case four Samara NK-86 turbofans. Even so, 99 Il-86s were delivered before production ceased in 1994, the principal operators being Aeroflot (*left*) and Vnukovo Airlines. In an all-economy nine-abreast seating layout, 350 passengers can be accommodated, and the aircraft typically cruises at 560 mph (900 km/h).

Podded turbofan engine

Lower deck includes holds for containers

BUILT IN LARGE NUMBERS

Similar in configuration to its competitor the TriStar, the McDonnell Douglas DC-10 was powered by three General Electric CF-6 or Pratt & Whitney JT-9D turbofans. First flown in 1970, it was offered in three principal versions, the DC-10-10 for US domestic services, and the 10-20 and 10-30 for intercontinental routes. Production ended in 1989.

Rudder

Fin

Straight-through tail nacelle permits easy installation of different engines

Leading-edge slats

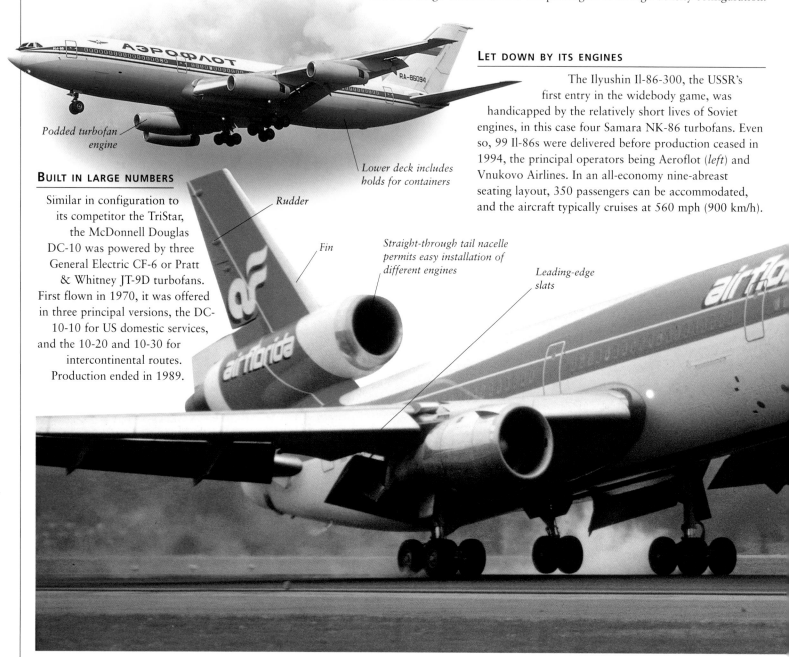

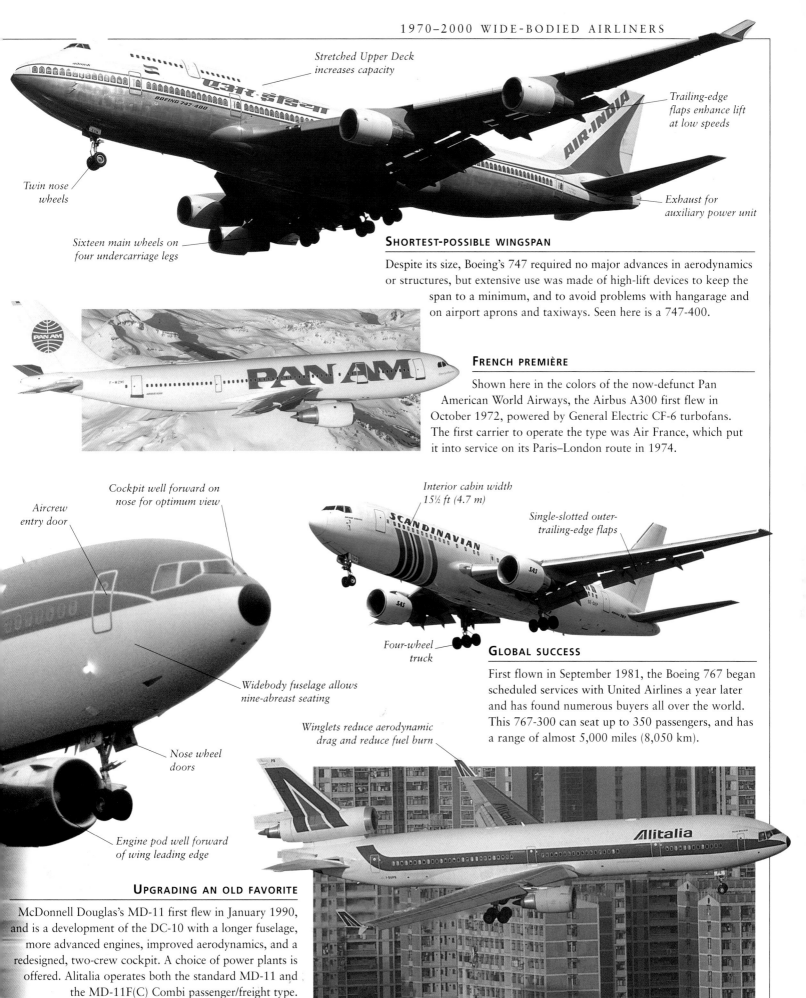

Stretched Upper Deck increases capacity

Trailing-edge flaps enhance lift at low speeds

Twin nose wheels

Exhaust for auxiliary power unit

Sixteen main wheels on four undercarriage legs

SHORTEST-POSSIBLE WINGSPAN

Despite its size, Boeing's 747 required no major advances in aerodynamics or structures, but extensive use was made of high-lift devices to keep the span to a minimum, and to avoid problems with hangarage and on airport aprons and taxiways. Seen here is a 747-400.

FRENCH PREMIÈRE

Shown here in the colors of the now-defunct Pan American World Airways, the Airbus A300 first flew in October 1972, powered by General Electric CF-6 turbofans. The first carrier to operate the type was Air France, which put it into service on its Paris–London route in 1974.

Cockpit well forward on nose for optimum view

Aircrew entry door

Interior cabin width 15½ ft (4.7 m)

Single-slotted outer-trailing-edge flaps

Widebody fuselage allows nine-abreast seating

Four-wheel truck

GLOBAL SUCCESS

First flown in September 1981, the Boeing 767 began scheduled services with United Airlines a year later and has found numerous buyers all over the world. This 767-300 can seat up to 350 passengers, and has a range of almost 5,000 miles (8,050 km).

Nose wheel doors

Winglets reduce aerodynamic drag and reduce fuel burn

Engine pod well forward of wing leading edge

UPGRADING AN OLD FAVORITE

McDonnell Douglas's MD-11 first flew in January 1990, and is a development of the DC-10 with a longer fuselage, more advanced engines, improved aerodynamics, and a redesigned, two-crew cockpit. A choice of power plants is offered. Alitalia operates both the standard MD-11 and the MD-11F(C) Combi passenger/freight type.

1970·2000 THE AIRBUS LINE

IN DECEMBER 1970, the first real challenge to Boeing's supremacy in the jet airliner market arrived with the formal creation of Airbus Industrie. This collaboration of the European manufacturers Hawker Siddeley, Aérospatiale, Deutsche Airbus, Fokker VFW, and CASA was backed by the French, German, Netherlands, and Spanish governments. Since the launch of the A300, the world's first civil twin-engined wide-bodied airliner, the Airbus consortium has grown from strength to strength.

Three fuselage frames removed forward of wing, and four aft, compared with A320

A SMALL ALTERNATIVE

First flown in 1995, the A319 is a short- to medium-range lower-capacity version of the A320, with a fuselage some 12 ft (3.5 m) shorter, accommodating 134 passengers in single-class layout. It entered service with Swissair in May 1996, and deliveries of a corporate jet (CJ) version began in 1999.

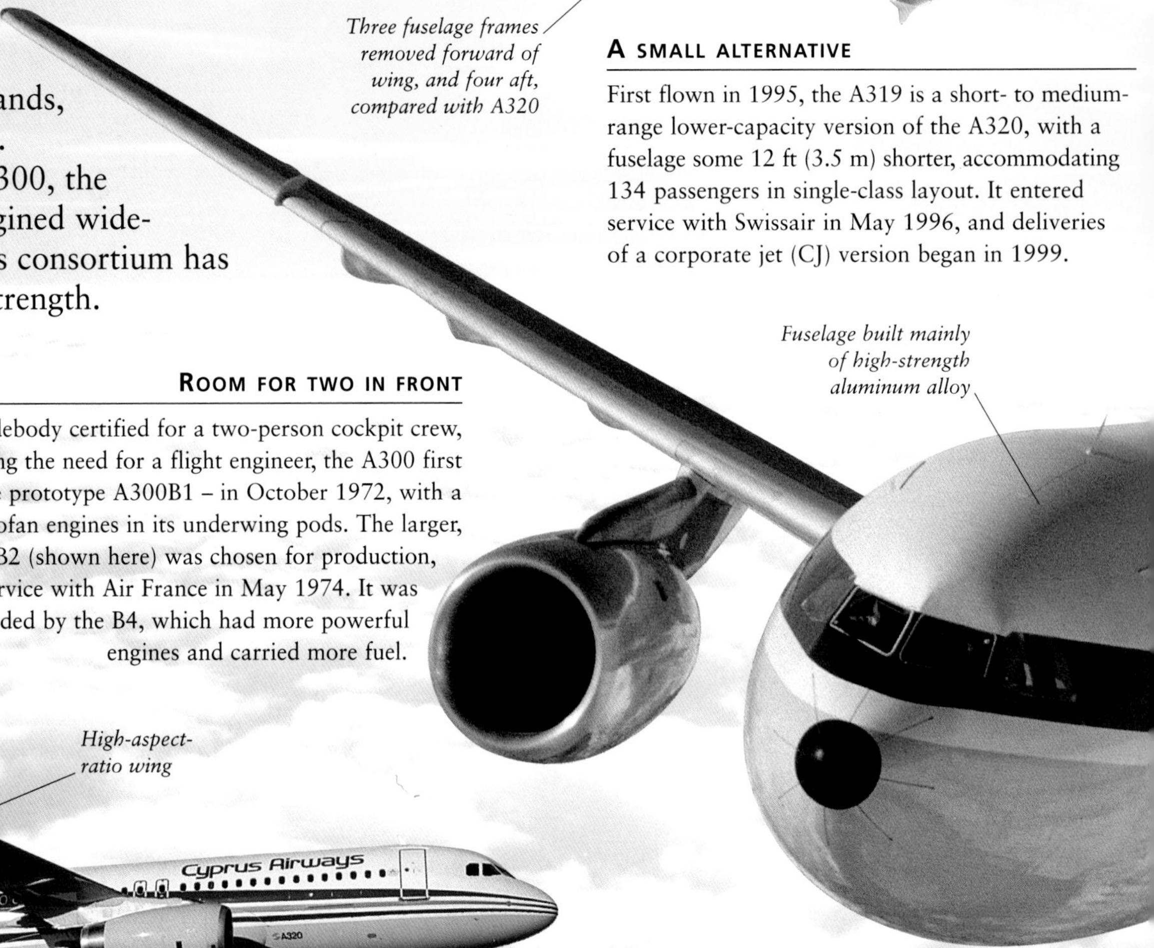

Fuselage built mainly of high-strength aluminum alloy

ROOM FOR TWO IN FRONT

The first widebody certified for a two-person cockpit crew, thus avoiding the need for a flight engineer, the A300 first flew – as the prototype A300B1 – in October 1972, with a pair of turbofan engines in its underwing pods. The larger, heavier B2 (shown here) was chosen for production, entering service with Air France in May 1974. It was later superseded by the B4, which had more powerful engines and carried more fuel.

Winglets

High-aspect-ratio wing

Fin was first composite-built primary structure on a certified commercial airliner

NARROW-BODIED AIRBUS

Introduced while the A300 and A310 were still in production, the A320 was a short/medium-range narrowbody. It first flew in February 1987, and the initial customer, Air France, received its first A320 in March 1988. It was subsequently complemented by the smaller A319 and the larger A321. Final assembly of A320s takes place in Toulouse, France.

WINGING THE CHANGES

Although the A310 employed the same layout as its forebears, it had a redesigned wing and could carry more than 200 passengers. The A310-300 (*below*) succeeded the initial 200 series, making its maiden flight on July 8, 1985. Its winglets distinguish it from all other A310s.

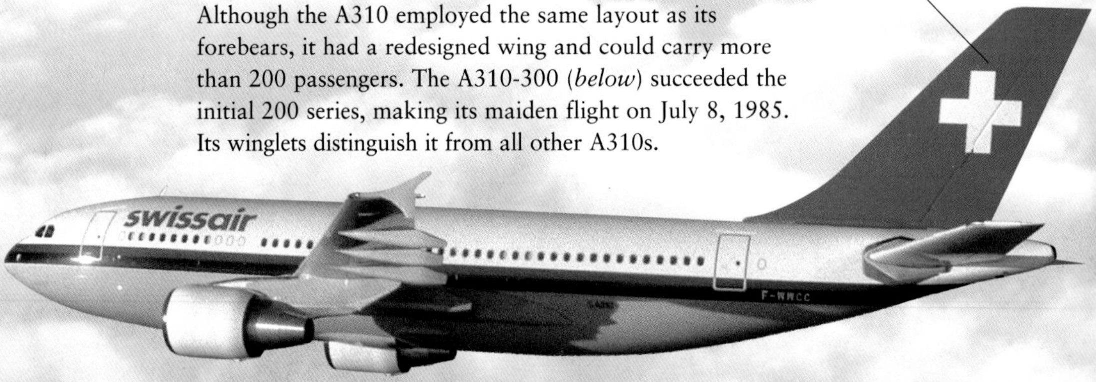

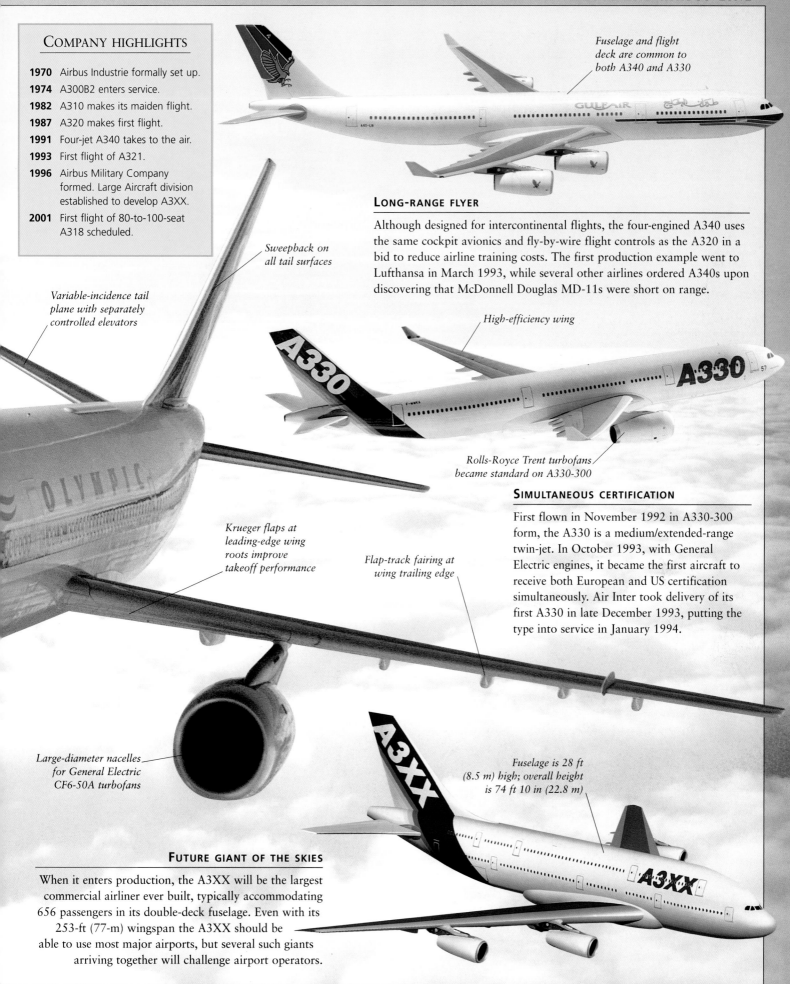

Fuselage and flight deck are common to both A340 and A330

Sweepback on all tail surfaces

Variable-incidence tail plane with separately controlled elevators

LONG-RANGE FLYER

Although designed for intercontinental flights, the four-engined A340 uses the same cockpit avionics and fly-by-wire flight controls as the A320 in a bid to reduce airline training costs. The first production example went to Lufthansa in March 1993, while several other airlines ordered A340s upon discovering that McDonnell Douglas MD-11s were short on range.

High-efficiency wing

Rolls-Royce Trent turbofans became standard on A330-300

SIMULTANEOUS CERTIFICATION

First flown in November 1992 in A330-300 form, the A330 is a medium/extended-range twin-jet. In October 1993, with General Electric engines, it became the first aircraft to receive both European and US certification simultaneously. Air Inter took delivery of its first A330 in late December 1993, putting the type into service in January 1994.

Krueger flaps at leading-edge wing roots improve takeoff performance

Flap-track fairing at wing trailing edge

Large-diameter nacelles for General Electric CF6-50A turbofans

Fuselage is 28 ft (8.5 m) high; overall height is 74 ft 10 in (22.8 m)

FUTURE GIANT OF THE SKIES

When it enters production, the A3XX will be the largest commercial airliner ever built, typically accommodating 656 passengers in its double-deck fuselage. Even with its 253-ft (77-m) wingspan the A3XX should be able to use most major airports, but several such giants arriving together will challenge airport operators.

1970-2000 GENERAL AVIATION

AIRPLANES FOR PERSONAL and business use have existed ever since the earliest days of flight; but it was not until the 1920s that anyone other than the very wealthy could afford to own an airplane. In the 1930s gliders and light biplanes such as the de Havilland Moth brought flying within the reach of many more people; and since World War II the number of privately owned aircraft, from business jets to ultralights, has grown considerably. Indeed, operating your own private aircraft, especially a jet, is now seen as the ultimate status symbol.

FRENCH FLEA

In 1933 Frenchman Henri Mignet introduced his H.M.14 Pou Du Ciel, or Sky Louse, a tiny tandem-wing airplane that could be built by amateurs. Many people around the world built "Flying Fleas," but an inherent fault caused several deaths and they were banned. Modified variants still fly safely today.

IS IT A CAR OR IS IT A PLANE?

There have been several attempts to produce "flying cars" – aircraft that can be driven on roads after touchdown. None have really caught on, but one of the most successful was the 1950s Aerocar designed by Molt Taylor of the US. Its 143-hp engine drove the pusher propeller via one transmission shaft and the front wheels of the car/fuselage via another. Upon landing, the flying surfaces were folded up and towed behind.

Protective skid beneath tail

EVER THE OPTIMIST

Gliding is a sport that demands great skill. Over the years the glider has progressed steadily as designers have searched for greater efficiency through the use of new materials and improved aerodynamics. The British Edgley EA9 Optimist (*above*) makes extensive use of Fibrelam composite throughout, and has a sink rate of less than 2 ft (60 cm) per second. It is supplied in kit form for assembly by groups or individuals.

Slats in upper wing leading edge delay stall and reduce landing speed

Wire-braced wooden framework covered with doped linen

AN OLD FAVORITE

Descended from the Moth and Gipsy Moth of the late 1920s, the de Havilland D.H.82A Tiger Moth first flew in 1931 and was the standard basic trainer for the RAF (Royal Air Force) and British Empire and Commonwealth training programs in World War II. Thousands were built, and after the war many were acquired by private owners and clubs. Now a prized and classic veteran, the "Tiger," as it has become known, is still much loved by pilots worldwide.

FREEDOM OF FLIGHT

Many large companies and wealthy individuals have their own aircraft, making them independent of airline timetables and large commercial airports. Typical of the business jets that now ply the world's air routes is the Falcon family produced by Dassault Aviation of France. The three-engine Falcon 900 (*left*) can carry up to 19 passengers at speeds of up to 590 mph (950 km/h).

Sailwing originally developed as possible means of facilitating return of manned spacecraft after reentry

High-aspect-ratio wing (long span, narrow chord) gives optimum lift

Inset ailerons for lateral control

Pilot controls glider by moving his body position in relation to wing surface

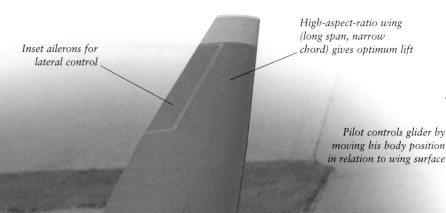

Clear Plexiglas canopy offers good visibility

A CENTURY OF CHANGE?

Hang gliding, pioneered by Percy Pilcher and Otto Lilienthal in the 1890s, is now a popular sport. Modern hang gliders with sail-like wings can put up impressive performances in skilled hands. Even so, the basic principles are not far removed from those developed more than a century ago.

Skid under nose for protection during landing

Pivoted wing moves in similar fashion to system used on hang gliders to control aircraft

FLYING FOR FUN

One step up from the hang glider is the ultralight, which can either take the form of a powered hang glider, like this Solar Wings Pegasus XL-Q, powered by a Rotax 462 engine, or resemble a minimal airplane, with a conventional control system. Available in a wide variety of designs, ultralights can operate from small fields and are simple to maintain.

1970-2000 FIGHTERS & BOMBERS

THE PROHIBITIVE COST of modern combat aircraft means that the air forces of smaller or poorer nations must be equipped with aircraft capable of performing several different roles. Thus, while some aircraft are still designed with very specific tasks in mind, others are versatile and can carry a wide variety of weaponry. The capability to operate in all weather is essential, and stealth technology is in demand to make fighters and bombers almost invisible to enemy radar systems. Modern weapons systems enable several targets to be identified and engaged simultaneously.

HEAVYWEIGHT HELPER

Designed as a close-support attack aircraft, the heavily armored Fairchild A-10 Thunderbolt carries various bombs and missiles on its wing pylons, and also has a 30-mm General Electric GAU-8A multibarrel cannon in its nose. Its top speed is 439 mph (706 km/h).

FAST AND FURIOUS

A versatile multimission land- and carrier-borne fighter, and day/night strike and reconnaissance aircraft, the McDonnell Douglas F/A-18 Hornet has won customers worldwide. Two 16,000-lb (7,257-kg) thrust General Electric F404-GE-400 turbofans give it a top speed of 1,190 mph (1,915 km/h), or Mach 1.8.

Twin fins canted outward, with inset rudders

Engines mounted side-by-side in rear fuselage

Afterburner uses injection and combustion of additional fuel to augment thrust

LONG-TERM INVESTMENT

The Tupolev Tu-22M bomber and missile carrier entered service with the Soviet Air Force in 1975 and is expected to remain a vital part of Russia's long-range strike capability beyond 2010. Two Samara NK-25 turbofans give the aircraft a maximum speed of 1,243 mph (2,000 km/h) at high altitude. Its maximum weapons load is 52,910 lb (24,000 kg).

Widely spaced engine nacelles with intakes beneath wing-root extensions

NIMBLE PLAYER

A potent long-range air-superiority fighter, the Sukhoi Su-27 was built in large numbers for the Soviet Air Force, and many remain in service with Russia and other powers, including China, Syria, and Vietnam. Noted for its exceptional maneuverability, the Su-27 has a maximum speed of 1,336 mph (2,150 km/h).

AMERICAN EAGLE

A single- or two-seat air-superiority fighter, the McDonnell Douglas F-15 Eagle is powered by two 23,930-lb (10,855-kg) thrust Pratt & Whitney F-100 turbofans and has a top speed of Mach 2.5. It carries a formidable load of weapons, including four AIM-7 Sparrow or AIM-120 AMRAAM air-to-air missiles.

Hughes APG-63 radar scanner in nose

Intake ducts have ramp doors inside to control flow of air to engines

Long wing leading-edge root extensions (LERX) improve airflow over wing at high angles of attack in extreme maneuvers

Large bubble canopy allows pilot good all-around vision

AGILE BIRD

The Lockheed Martin F-16 Fighting Falcon multirole air-combat fighter also has a ground-attack capability. It is very maneuverable, and its large, clear canopy allows the pilot a superb all-around view. A Pratt & Whitney F100 engine takes the F-16 to 1,350 mph (2,172 km/h), or Mach 2.05.

AIM-9L Sidewinder air-to-air missile on wingtip pylon

All-moving tail plane

UNSEEN SPIRIT

The Northrop Grumman B-2A Spirit subsonic stealth bomber first flew in 1989, and the first production aircraft appeared in 1993. Its shape, structure, and finish are all designed to endow it with low visibility on radar. A 40,000-lb (18,145-kg) bomb load can be carried internally, and top speed is Mach 0.8.

Jet orifices above wing, shielded from searching radar

APG-65 multimode radar in nose

Large fin with rudder

All-moving foreplane doubles as air brake on ground

ZH588

COOPERATIVE EFFORT

The Eurofighter Typhoon air-superiority fighter is a joint venture by Daimler-Benz of Germany, Alenia of Italy, CASA of Spain, and British Aerospace of the UK. It is very agile in subsonic close air combat, and also has surface-attack and reconnaissance capability. It can attain Mach 2 with its two 13,500-lb (6,124-kg) thrust Eurojet EJ200 turbofans.

1970-2000 MiG-21F-13

THE SOVIET UNION'S first production aircraft capable of Mach 2 in level flight, the MiG-21, codenamed "Fishbed" by NATO, was numerically the most important short-range fighter in Soviet service in the 1960s and early 1970s. The Mikoyan and Guryevich design bureau's first delta-winged prototype, the Ye-4, made its maiden flight on June 16, 1955, and was followed by the Ye-5 and the Ye-6 pre-series prototypes. Small-scale production of the MiG-21F began in 1959, but gave way to the MiG-21F-13 in 1960, the designation denoting compatibility with the K-13 infrared-homing air-to-air missile, carried on underwing pylons.

Fence on upper wing surface directs airflow

Wing has an anhedral angle (slopes down toward tip)

Blank keeps air intake free of debris when aircraft is on ground

UNDER-EQUIPPED PERFORMER

Although it is reliable in service, can perform six sorties a day for several days, and is cheap to operate apart from its high fuel-burn, the MiG-21 is deficient in endurance, navigation, weapon load, and all-weather avionics. All variants have only simple search/track radar for air-to-air interception, of limited value for air-to-ground sorties.

Fuselage doors for main undercarriage

Steerable nose wheel with levered suspension

Rudder

Fairing for tail plane actuator

Engine bay venting air intake

Tail pipe of engine afterburner

Ventral fin/tail bumper

Wing navigation light

Air brake powered by hydraulic ram

PEDIGREE DOGFIGHTER

The MiG-21F-13, essentially a cheap and simple aircraft, was initially lightly armed, having a single 30-mm NR-30 cannon and two K-13 missiles. There was also a vertical reconnaissance camera under the cockpit floor. It is an exceptional and agile dogfighter and handles well, though it is prone to mild snaking that can cause stalls and surges in the compressor of its Tumanskii turbojet.

Main undercarriage retracts inward into wing and fuselage

Underwing pylon for missile

UBIQUITOUS BREED

The MiG-21 has undergone continual and extensive development, both in Russia and abroad. Total production of all variants, including those of foreign manufacture built under license, has topped 13,500 aircraft. Used by no fewer than 56 air forces, it has taken part in at least 30 shooting wars, and many still serve with front-line combat units.

SPECIFICATION

Engine 13,670-lb (6,200-kg) reheated Tumanskii RD-11-300 turbojet
Wingspan 23 ft 5½ in (7.15 m)
Total length 51 ft 8½ in (15.76 m)
Height 13 ft 5 in (4.1 m)
Maximum loaded weight 18,104 lb (8,212 kg)
Top speed 1,386 mph (2,220 km/h) above 36,000 ft (11,000 m) [Mach 2.1]
Rate of climb 590 ft (180 m) per sec
Service ceiling 59,055 ft (18,000 m)
Armament Two 23-mm cannons; up to four K-13 air-to-air missiles; four 550-lb (250-kg) bombs or four 220-mm or 325-mm air-to-surface missiles
Crew 1

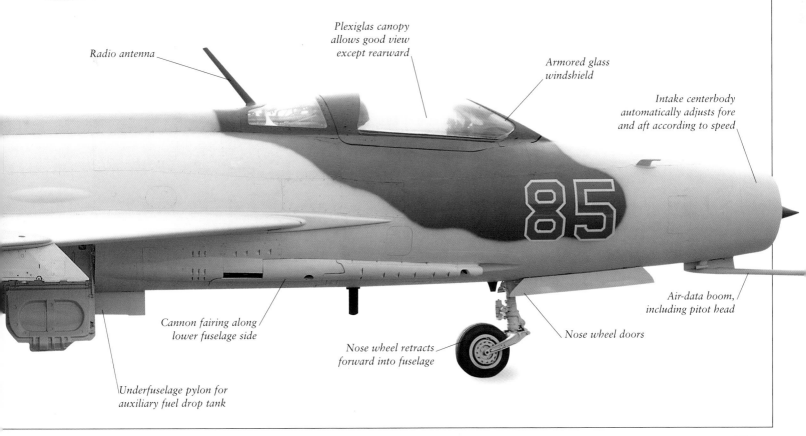

Radio antenna

Plexiglas canopy allows good view except rearward

Armored glass windshield

Intake centerbody automatically adjusts fore and aft according to speed

Cannon fairing along lower fuselage side

Nose wheel retracts forward into fuselage

Nose wheel doors

Air-data boom, including pitot head

Underfuselage pylon for auxiliary fuel drop tank

1970-2000 MILITARY SUPPORT AIRCRAFT

IN ADDITION TO serving in their basic roles as personnel, vehicle, and supply carriers, the larger transporter types of military aircraft are often adapted to act as air-to-air refueling tankers or as airborne platforms for early-warning radar systems or battle-management suites. Other models are purpose-designed for roles within maritime reconnaissance or antisubmarine warfare. One prime requirement for a troop carrier is that it has the ability to operate from short, rough-field airstrips anywhere in the world; the capacity to make a steep takeoff can be indispensable in these circumstances.

FOUR-JET HUNTER

The Hawker Siddeley Nimrod MR.2 was the world's first land-based, four-jet maritime reconnaissance aircraft to enter service, in 1970. Based on the airframe of the de Havilland Comet, it has four Rolls-Royce Spey 250 turbofans, giving a cruising speed of 490 mph (788 km/h) and an endurance of 12 hours.

Circular-section fuselage, internally clear to allow maximum use of space

SENTRY IN THE SKY

The Boeing E-3A Sentry, seen here in its AEW Mk 1 form, is an early-warning and control aircraft. A 30-ft (9.14-m) diameter "rotodome" radar antenna is mounted above the rear of a Boeing 707 airframe. Used by the USAF (US Air Force) since 1977 and NATO since 1983, the Sentry can remain on station 1,000 miles (1,600 km) from base for six hours.

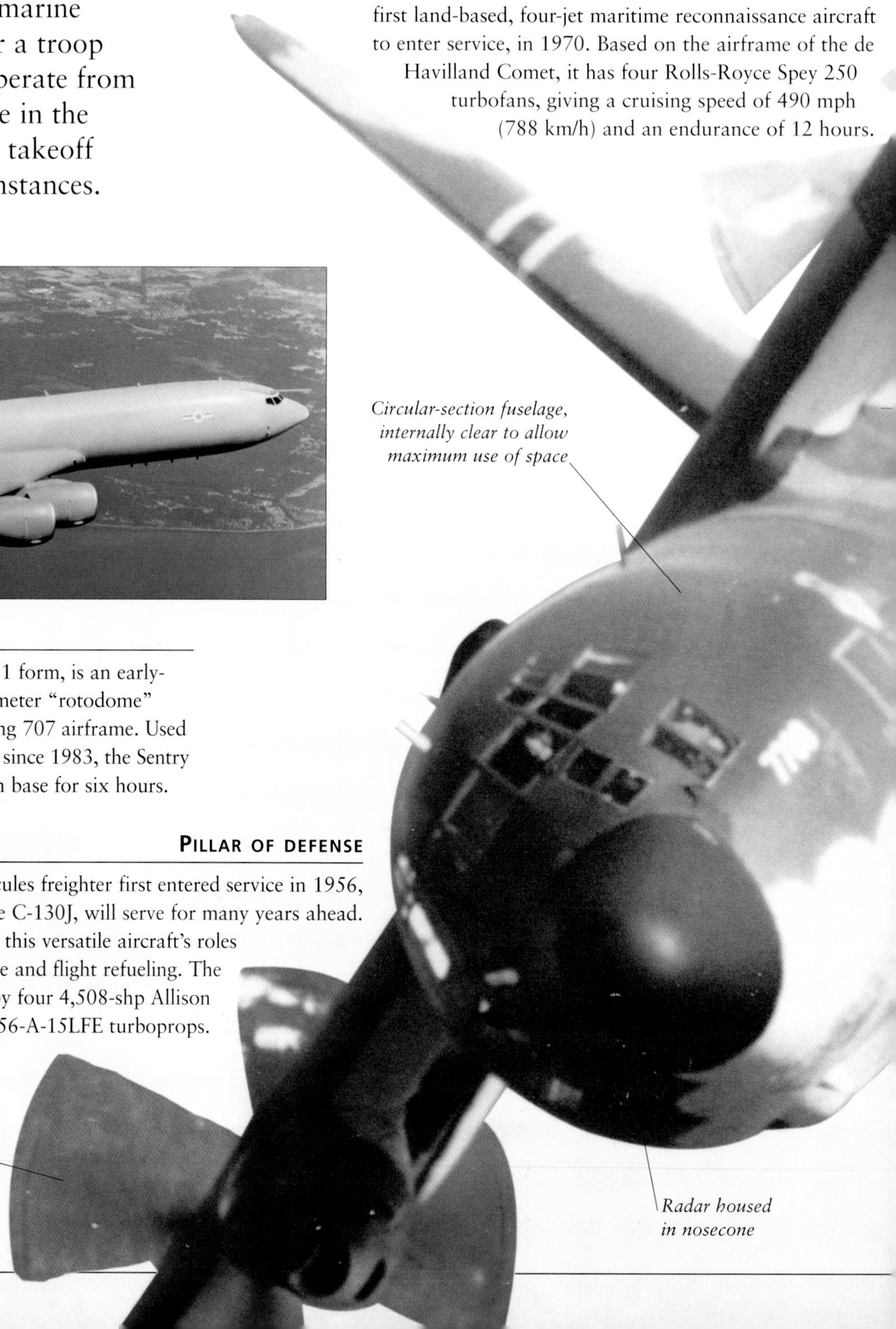

PILLAR OF DEFENSE

The Lockheed C-130 Hercules freighter first entered service in 1956, and in its latest form, the C-130J, will serve for many years ahead. As well as transport, this versatile aircraft's roles include electronic warfare and flight refueling. The C-130H is powered by four 4,508-shp Allison T56-A-15LFE turboprops.

Four-blade reversible-pitch propellers

Radar housed in nosecone

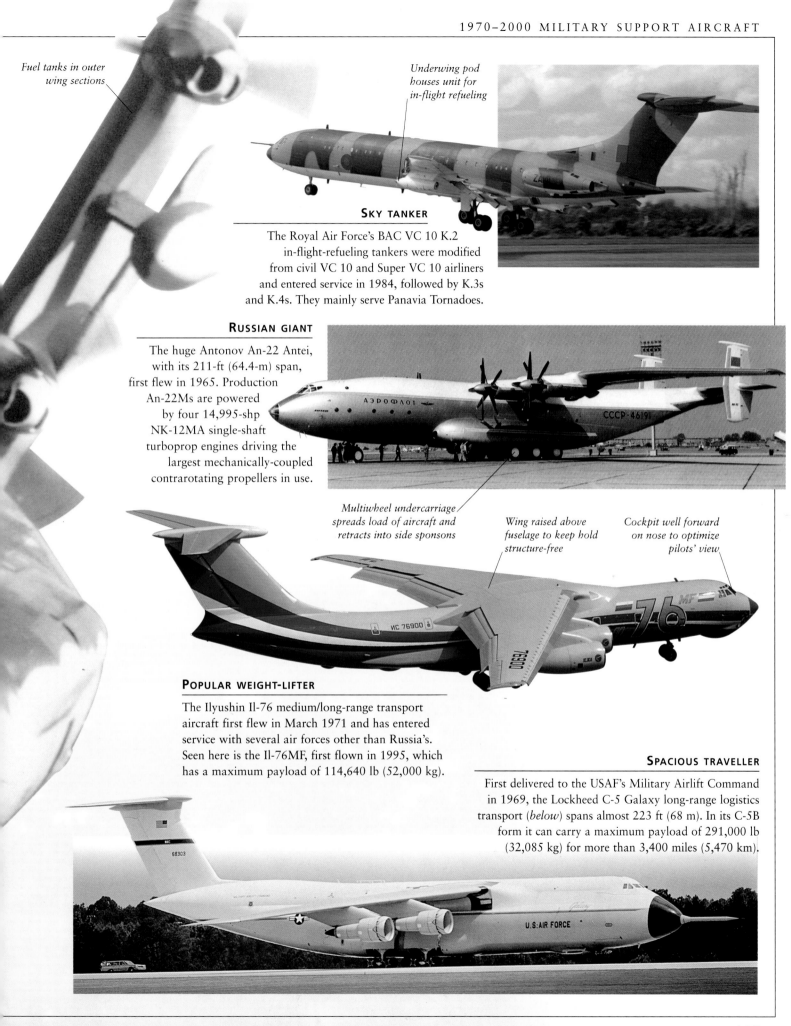

Fuel tanks in outer wing sections

Underwing pod houses unit for in-flight refueling

SKY TANKER

The Royal Air Force's BAC VC 10 K.2 in-flight-refueling tankers were modified from civil VC 10 and Super VC 10 airliners and entered service in 1984, followed by K.3s and K.4s. They mainly serve Panavia Tornadoes.

RUSSIAN GIANT

The huge Antonov An-22 Antei, with its 211-ft (64.4-m) span, first flew in 1965. Production An-22Ms are powered by four 14,995-shp NK-12MA single-shaft turboprop engines driving the largest mechanically-coupled contrarotating propellers in use.

Multiwheel undercarriage spreads load of aircraft and retracts into side sponsons

Wing raised above fuselage to keep hold structure-free

Cockpit well forward on nose to optimize pilots' view

POPULAR WEIGHT-LIFTER

The Ilyushin Il-76 medium/long-range transport aircraft first flew in March 1971 and has entered service with several air forces other than Russia's. Seen here is the Il-76MF, first flown in 1995, which has a maximum payload of 114,640 lb (52,000 kg).

SPACIOUS TRAVELLER

First delivered to the USAF's Military Airlift Command in 1969, the Lockheed C-5 Galaxy long-range logistics transport (*below*) spans almost 223 ft (68 m). In its C-5B form it can carry a maximum payload of 291,000 lb (32,085 kg) for more than 3,400 miles (5,470 km).

1970-2000 LOCKHEED F-117A

AS LONG AGO AS 1975, Lockheed in the US embarked on a program named Have Blue to develop a "stealth" aircraft, employing faceting – the use of critically angled flat surfaces throughout the airframe – to minimize its radar signature. The two prototypes made proved difficult to fly, but showed that the idea was attainable. In 1978 the company began work on five Senior Trend development aircraft, and the first production F-117 Nighthawk fighter/attack aircraft was delivered in 1982. The US Air Force ordered 59 Nighthawks, at a cost of $42.6 million each. Unveiled to the public in 1988, the F-117 played a significant role in Desert Storm, the 1991 war with Iraq.

UPDATED AS REQUIRED

The multifaceted surface of the F-117's peculiar airframe is very apparent in this view. Although initially made almost completely of aluminum alloys, some parts of the aircraft's structure, such as the ruddervators, have been replaced by units made from thermoplastic graphite composites. Systems and equipment have also been progressively updated.

STEALTH AND SPEED

The flat undersurfaces of the F-117's wing are blended into the fuselage, making the whole underside a lifting surface. The exterior is almost entirely covered with matt-black radar-absorbent material. The F-117's configuration gives it a landing speed of 172 mph (227 km/h), so a brake parachute is needed to reduce the length of the landing run.

Engine air intakes covered by grilles to screen compressor face from radar

Main wheels retract forward into fuselage underside

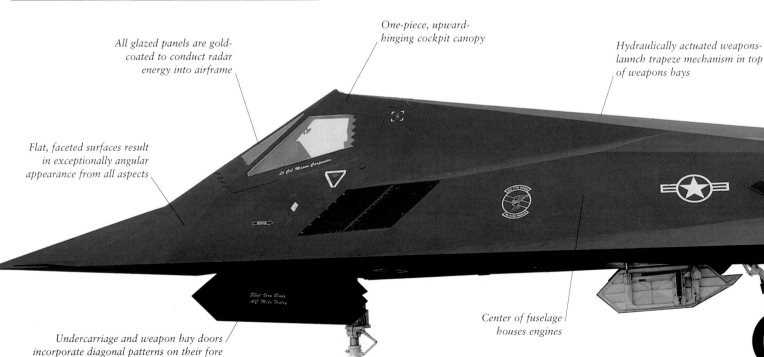

All glazed panels are gold-coated to conduct radar energy into airframe

One-piece, upward-hinging cockpit canopy

Hydraulically actuated weapons-launch trapeze mechanism in top of weapons bays

Flat, faceted surfaces result in exceptionally angular appearance from all aspects

Undercarriage and weapon bay doors incorporate diagonal patterns on their fore and aft edges to dissipate radar energy

Center of fuselage houses engines

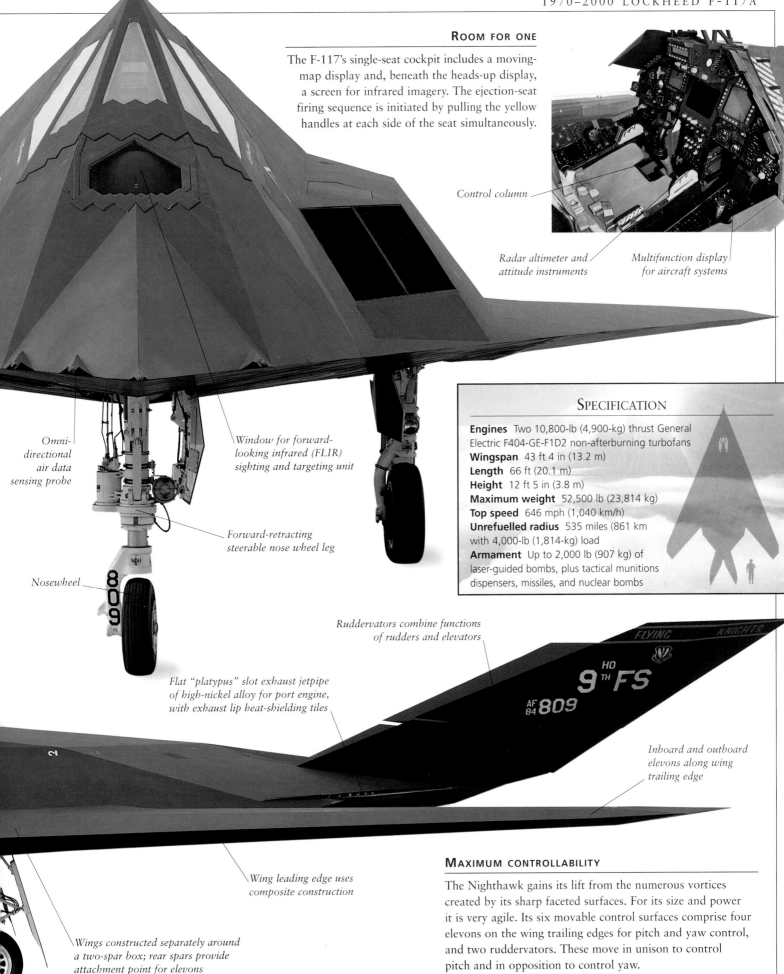

ROOM FOR ONE

The F-117's single-seat cockpit includes a moving-map display and, beneath the heads-up display, a screen for infrared imagery. The ejection-seat firing sequence is initiated by pulling the yellow handles at each side of the seat simultaneously.

Control column

Radar altimeter and attitude instruments

Multifunction display for aircraft systems

Omni-directional air data sensing probe

Window for forward-looking infrared (FLIR) sighting and targeting unit

Forward-retracting steerable nose wheel leg

Nosewheel

SPECIFICATION

Engines Two 10,800-lb (4,900-kg) thrust General Electric F404-GE-F1D2 non-afterburning turbofans
Wingspan 43 ft 4 in (13.2 m)
Length 66 ft (20.1 m)
Height 12 ft 5 in (3.8 m)
Maximum weight 52,500 lb (23,814 kg)
Top speed 646 mph (1,040 km/h)
Unrefuelled radius 535 miles (861 km with 4,000-lb (1,814-kg) load
Armament Up to 2,000 lb (907 kg) of laser-guided bombs, plus tactical munitions dispensers, missiles, and nuclear bombs

Ruddervators combine functions of rudders and elevators

Flat "platypus" slot exhaust jetpipe of high-nickel alloy for port engine, with exhaust lip heat-shielding tiles

FLYING KNIGHTS

9TH HO FS

AF 84 809

Inboard and outboard elevons along wing trailing edge

MAXIMUM CONTROLLABILITY

The Nighthawk gains its lift from the numerous vortices created by its sharp faceted surfaces. For its size and power it is very agile. Its six movable control surfaces comprise four elevons on the wing trailing edges for pitch and yaw control, and two ruddervators. These move in unison to control pitch and in opposition to control yaw.

Wing leading edge uses composite construction

Wings constructed separately around a two-spar box; rear spars provide attachment point for elevons

1970-2000 THE FUTURE OF FLIGHT

THE AIRPLANE'S FUTURE is every bit as incredible as its past. We can seriously contemplate flying from New York to Tokyo in 90 minutes, perhaps in a pilotless airliner, or exploring space in a reusable hypersonic launch vehicle, while cities could be patrolled by unmanned aircraft. However, apart from the technological hurdles that must be overcome, the world's aerospace companies face increasingly formidable investment costs that could cripple development. This means that global partnerships must be formed to share the financial burden, and new levels of manufacturing and engineering efficiency must be achieved.

GOOD FOR BUSINESS

The Vantage business jet under development by VisionAire of Iowa, is unusual in having forward-swept wings. It has undergone major changes including repositioning its engine, changing its fuselage structure and airfoil section, and lowering its wing. Due for delivery at the end of 2002, the Vantage should cruise at around 400 mph (650 km/h).

REMOTE-CONTROL WARFARE

This sinister-looking beast is a Northrop Grumman proposal for an Uninhabited Combat Air Vehicle (UCAV), intended as a low-cost, stealthy, reusable precision-strike weapon system. Operated by a pilot/ mission controller in a command center many miles from the target area, it can loiter over hostile territory to gather target data, deliver precision-guided weapons, and then return to base to refuel and rearm.

Canard control surfaces ahead of wing

BIRD OF PREY

Lockheed Martin/Boeing's F-22 Raptor air-superiority fighter, powered by a pair of Pratt & Whitney F119-100 turbofans, has suffered cuts to its budget as well as in the quantity ordered for the US Air Force. Nonetheless its development testing is proceeding swiftly, and the maker is examining ways to broaden its capabilities. It is set to enter service late in 2005.

Large air intake in front of body

Twin fins and rudders canted outward on either side of engines

Blended fuselage/wing design

Composite material used for wing skins

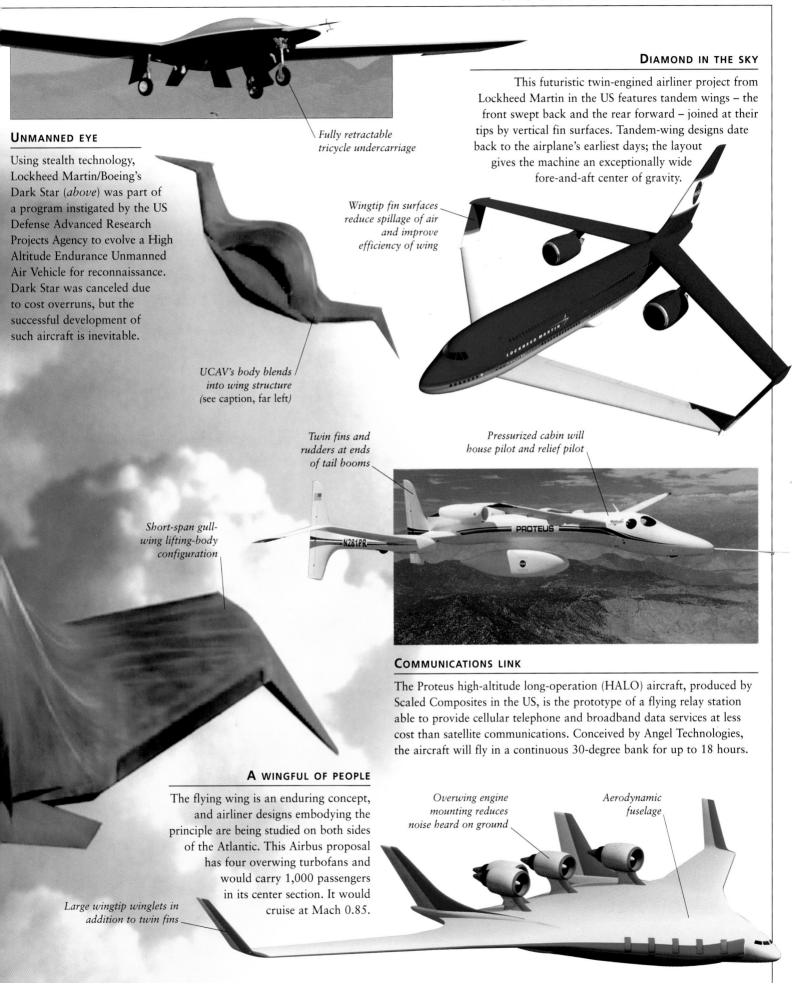

DIAMOND IN THE SKY

This futuristic twin-engined airliner project from Lockheed Martin in the US features tandem wings – the front swept back and the rear forward – joined at their tips by vertical fin surfaces. Tandem-wing designs date back to the airplane's earliest days; the layout gives the machine an exceptionally wide fore-and-aft center of gravity.

Fully retractable tricycle undercarriage

Wingtip fin surfaces reduce spillage of air and improve efficiency of wing

UNMANNED EYE

Using stealth technology, Lockheed Martin/Boeing's Dark Star (*above*) was part of a program instigated by the US Defense Advanced Research Projects Agency to evolve a High Altitude Endurance Unmanned Air Vehicle for reconnaissance. Dark Star was canceled due to cost overruns, but the successful development of such aircraft is inevitable.

UCAV's body blends into wing structure (see caption, far left)

Twin fins and rudders at ends of tail booms

Pressurized cabin will house pilot and relief pilot

Short-span gull-wing lifting-body configuration

COMMUNICATIONS LINK

The Proteus high-altitude long-operation (HALO) aircraft, produced by Scaled Composites in the US, is the prototype of a flying relay station able to provide cellular telephone and broadband data services at less cost than satellite communications. Conceived by Angel Technologies, the aircraft will fly in a continuous 30-degree bank for up to 18 hours.

A WINGFUL OF PEOPLE

The flying wing is an enduring concept, and airliner designs embodying the principle are being studied on both sides of the Atlantic. This Airbus proposal has four overwing turbofans and would carry 1,000 passengers in its center section. It would cruise at Mach 0.85.

Overwing engine mounting reduces noise heard on ground

Aerodynamic fuselage

Large wingtip winglets in addition to twin fins

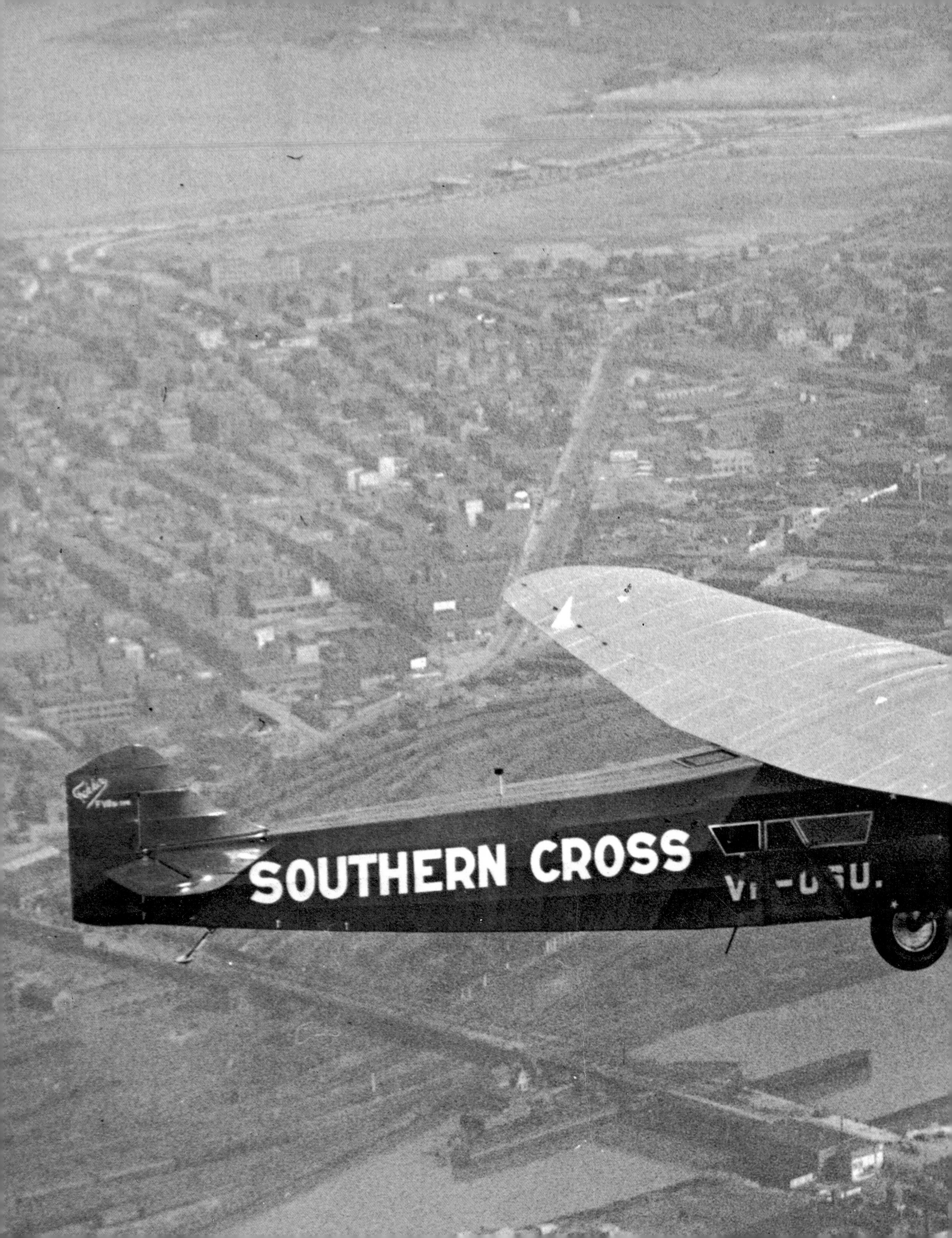
SOUTHERN CROSS

PART THREE

AVIATION INNOVATORS

Great aircraft do not appear by chance. They are the products of great people: pioneers, scientists, designers, manufacturers, and pilots who apply their extraordinary skills in windtunnels, factories, and experimental establishments around the world – and, of course, in the air itself. Their dedication has made flight one of humankind's greatest technical achievements. The following pages contain brief biographies of some of the outstanding contributors to aviation. The list continues to grow.

A

CLÉMENT ADER
1841–1925

Wealthy French electrical engineer Clément Ader made the first piloted powered takeoff in history, at Armainvilliers, France, in October 1890. Ader achieved this feat in his first airplane – the bat-winged,

ADER'S
AVION
III

steam-powered *Éole*, which he built between 1882 and 1890. Although he covered a distance of only 165 ft (50 m), this was enough for the French Army to encourage further experiments. Ader started, and abandoned, work on his *Avion II*, before moving on to the *Avion III*, which employed two steam engines to drive tractor propellers. This project was aborted after two failed tests in front of military witnesses in 1897. Ader's subsequent claims to have flown are not borne out by official reports. Work began on an *Avion IV*, but the French Army lost interest in flying machines in 1898 and ended Ader's contract.

SIR JOHN ALCOCK
1892–1919

Born in Manchester, England, John Alcock is remembered for making the first nonstop transatlantic airplane flight. After qualifying for his pilot's certificate in 1912, he came third in the 1914 London–Manchester race. At the start of World War I Alcock joined the RNAS (Royal Naval Air Service), where he became an instructor. In 1917 he was appointed flight commander, and in September of that year was awarded the DSC

(Distinguished Service Cross) for gallantry. He was later taken prisoner by the Turks after a forced landing during a long-distance bombing raid. After the war Alcock became associated with Vickers Ltd., and it was in a converted Vimy bomber that he and Lt. Arthur Whitten Brown made a nonstop flight from Newfoundland to Ireland, in June 1919. Both men were knighted for their feat. Alcock was killed on December 18, 1919, when his Viking amphibian crashed at Côte d'Evrard in France during an attempted forced landing in fog.

OLEG ANTONOV
1906–1984

Soviet designer Oleg Antonov built his first aircraft, the Golub glider, in 1924. Two years later he became a student at Leningrad Polytechnic Institute. He continued to design gliders and, upon graduation in 1930, joined the new Moscow Glider Factory, where he became chief designer. In 1938, he moved to the Yakovlev design bureau to work on light aircraft, but he was then detached to work on a STOL observation aircraft. Shortly afterwards he was involved in the design of the A-7, one of the first troop-carrying gliders. In 1946 he set up the Antonov design bureau, which went on to produce a family of transport aircraft, including the An-2, An-10, An-12, An-22, An-24, and An-124. One Antonov design, the An-225 Mriya, is the heaviest and most powerful aircraft ever built.

B

GENERAL ITALO BALBO
1896–1940

Italy's most famous interwar pilot, Italo Balbo served with the Alpine troops during World War I and then joined Benito Mussolini's Fascist movement. In 1926, despite knowing nothing about aviation, he was appointed Secretary of State for Air. He quickly learned to fly, and set about reorganizing Italy's air force,

the Regia Aeronautica. In 1933 he led a mass formation of 24 Savoia-Marchetti SM.55X flying boats on a transatlantic round-trip flight from Italy to Chicago, landing on Lake Michigan. As a result the collective noun *balbo* was coined in Italian to describe a large formation of aircraft. Balbo was subsequently appointed governor of Libya. At the outbreak of World War II, he called for Italy to side with Britain, contrary to Mussolini's plans. He continued to lead air patrols over North Africa and was killed when returning from a patrol in 1940, shot down by the antiaircraft guns of his own base.

CAPTAIN FRANK S. BARNWELL
1880–1938

Born in Kent, England, Captain Frank Barnwell was the designer responsible for the outstanding Bristol F.2B Fighter and many other Bristol aircraft from the 1910s to the 1930s. Barnwell served six years as an apprentice with a shipbuilder before joining his brother in a small engineering firm near Stirling, Scotland, where they built several gliders and powered airplanes. In 1911, he joined the British & Colonial Aeroplane Co., later called the Bristol Aeroplane Co., as chief draftsman. From 1913 to 1921, apart from a spell in the RFC (Royal Flying Corps) in 1914–15, he produced a range of designs

including the Scout biplane and the M.1 Bullet monoplane, as well as the outstanding Bristol F.2B. In autumn 1921 Barnwell accepted a technical commission in the RAAF (Royal Australian Air Force), but in 1923 he returned to his old post at Bristol, designing a variety of aircraft that included the Bulldog fighter, the Blenheim bomber, and the Type 138 high-altitude monoplane. In 1938, he designed a light single-seat monoplane for the Civil Air Guard, one of which was built for his own use. On its second flight, on August 2, 1938, it crashed, killing its designer.

JEAN BATTEN

JEAN BATTEN
1909–1982

Multiple world record holder Jean Batten, of Rotorua, New Zealand, sailed to England in 1929, and in December 1932 learned to fly. In May 1934 she established a new women's solo record for an England–Australia flight, traveling the 10,500 miles (16,900 km) from Lympne, Kent, to Darwin in 14 days, 22 hours, 30 minutes, beating Amy Johnson's 1930 record by more than four days. She then flew back from Darwin to Lympne in 17 days, 16 hours, 15 minutes, the first Australia–England solo flight by a woman. In November 1935 she became the first woman to fly solo from England to South America, traveling via South Africa. She claimed world records for both the flight from Lympne to Natal and the South Atlantic crossing. In October 1936, she made the first direct England–New Zealand flight, also breaking the England–Australia solo record. A year later she set a new Australia–England solo record, and became the first person to hold both England–Australia out and back solo records simultaneously.

ALEXANDER GRAHAM BELL
1847–1922

Although better known for his work developing the telephone, in 1907 Bell founded the Aerial Experiment Association (AEA), based in Nova Scotia, Canada, and Hammondsport, New York, to conduct experiments with both gliders and powered airplanes. His team included engineering students F.W. Baldwin and J.D. McCurdy, US Army officer Lt. T.E. Selfridge, and Glenn Curtiss, who provided expertise on gas engines. Four powered airplanes were built and tested in 1908, the most successful being the *June Bug* and the *Silver Dart*; the former won the *Scientific American* trophy for the first public flight in the US, which was made by Curtiss in July 1908. Although the AEA folded in March 1909, Bell continued to experiment with machines using his tetrahedral kite principle.

LAWRENCE DALE BELL
1894–1956

Founder of the aircraft company that bears his name, Lawrence Bell was a mechanic when he joined the Glenn L. Martin company in 1912. He rose to be vice-president and general manager before leaving Martin in January 1925. In 1928, he joined Consolidated at Buffalo, New York, and served as general manager until 1935. He then formed his own company, Bell Aircraft, to build military airplanes. The company produced such famous aircraft as the P-39 Airacobra fighter, the P-59 Airacomet – the USA's first jet aircraft – the X-1 and X-2 rocket-powered high-speed research aircraft, and a large family of helicopters, including the UH-1 "Huey" Iroquois and the V-22 Osprey tiltrotor convertiplane.

GIUSEPPE MARIO BELLANCA
1886–1960

Sicilian-born Giuseppe Bellanca built a two-seat pusher biplane and a monoplane before emigrating from Italy to the US in 1910. The following year he built another aircraft, used it to teach himself to fly, and then opened a flying school at Mineola, Long Island, New York. Bellanca continued to build aircraft while working as a consulting engineer to Wright Aeronautical Corporation in the 1920s, including a machine to demonstrate the company's new air-cooled radial engine. In 1927, with Charles A. Levine, he formed Columbia Aircraft to build distinctive high-wing monoplanes. He founded The Bellanca Aircraft Corporation on December 31, 1927, and production of a wide range of types continued until the late 1980s.

NOEL PEMBERTON BILLING
1881–1948

After making a fortune selling yachts and gunrunning, Noel Pemberton Billing built his first monoplane in 1908. He founded one of Britain's first flying grounds at Fambridge, Essex, in 1909. In September 1913 he won a £500 bet with Frederick Handley Page that he could learn to fly and qualify in a day (he did it before breakfast). He used the money to set up Pemberton-Billing Ltd to build his "Supermarine" flying boats. As an officer in the RNVR (Royal Naval Volunteer Reserve), he was instrumental in the planning of the RNAS (Royal Naval

NOEL PEMBERTON BILLING

Air Service) raid on the Zeppelin sheds at Friedrichshafen, Germany, in November 1914. In 1916 he relinquished his interest in the firm to enter parliament. The company became the Supermarine Aviation Works, achieving fame for its Schneider Trophy seaplanes and its Spitfire fighter.

MARK BIRKIGT
1878–1953

More widely known as a designer of automobiles, Swiss engineer Mark Birkigt is renowned in aviation for designing the V8 engine, which powered such noted World War I aircraft as the British S.E.5a fighter and the French SPAD series. His Hispano-Suiza company, which he established in Barcelona, Spain, in 1904, continued to produce aircraft engines through the interwar years, and also expanded into armaments. Its 20-mm cannon was widely used during and long after World War II. In the 1940s, Hispano-Suiza made large numbers of Rolls-Royce Nene jet engines. In 1968 it was acquired by the French company SNECMA.

RONALD ERIC BISHOP
1903–1989

The designer of the world's first jet airliner, the de Havilland Comet, Ronald Bishop joined the de Havilland Aircraft Company as an apprentice at age 18. At the time of his retirement in 1964, he was deputy managing director and design director. As well as the Comet, he conceived many other civil and military aircraft, most notably the Mosquito, one of the most versatile airplanes of World War II. Other types were the Hornet twin-engined naval fighter, the Vampire jet fighter, the Dove and Heron light commercial transports, and the Sea Vixen naval fighter.

ROBERT BLACKBURN
1885–1955

British engineer Robert Blackburn was working in France in 1908 when Wilbur Wright gave his flying demonstrations there. This inspired him to pursue a career in aviation. His first airplane, a rather heavy monoplane built in 1909, failed to fly, but his Antoinette-type 1911

monoplane launched Blackburn Aeroplanes. The company's name was changed to the Blackburn Aeroplane and Motor Co. Ltd. in 1914. Blackburn's products included a family of interwar spotter aircraft for the Fleet Air Arm, the large Iris and Perth biplane flying boats, the Shark torpedo bomber, the Skua and Roc naval fighters, and the Buccaneer low-level strike aircraft. The famous name eventually disappeared soon after Blackburn Aircraft Ltd joined the Hawker Siddeley Group in 1962.

LOUIS BLÉRIOT
1872–1936

LOUIS BLÉRIOT

French pioneer Louis Blériot secured himself a place in the history books by making the first flight across the English Channel in a powered airplane. Blériot had made his fortune from automobile headlights before entering into aeronautical experiments with the Voisin brothers. In 1906, he put together his own team, producing widely varying designs that he tested himself, crashing frequently. Once the Wright brothers had demonstrated the successful control of an aircraft, Raymond Saulnier produced the Blériot XI monoplane, in which Blériot made his cross-Channel flight on July 25, 1909. The resulting fame of man and machine brought world-wide orders assuring his company's future. Blériot stopped flying later that year, but the Société Blériot Aéronautique thrived in Paris throughout the interwar years.

MARCEL BLOCH
1892–1986

Later to become one of France's foremost aircraft manufacturers, Marcel Bloch was drafted into the Corps of Engineers in 1914 and worked at both the aeronautical laboratory at Chalais-Meudon and the Maurice Farman factory. In 1917, with Henri Potez, he formed SEA (Société d'Études Aéronautiques) to build the SEA.4 two-seat scout. Bloch survived the postwar slump by producing furniture, but in 1930 formed Avions Marcel Bloch to build advanced all-metal civil and military machines. He refused to work for the Nazis after France's defeat in 1940 and was sent to Buchenwald concentration camp, which he survived. In 1945, his family changed its name from Bloch to Dassault, the wartime Resistance code name used by his brother. Marcel then set up Avions Marcel Dassault, which became one of France's greatest aircraft companies.

WILLIAM E. BOEING
1881–1956

After flying in a Curtiss seaplane in 1914, Yale graduate and Seattle timber merchant "Bill" Boeing decided that he could build a better airplane. With US Navy Cdr. G. Conrad Westervelt he created the B&W seaplane. Boeing registered his company, Pacific Aero Products, in July 1916, and renamed it Boeing Airplane Co. in April 1917. During the interwar years, the company built fighters for the US Army and Navy and commercial airliners. Boeing retired in 1934, but his firm went on to produce many outstanding airplanes, including the B-17, B-29, and B-52 bombers, and the 727 and 747 airliners. It was renamed The Boeing Company in 1961.

HAUPTMANN OSWALD BOELCKE
1891–1916

A German pioneer of air fighting, Oswald Boelcke gained his aviator's certificate two weeks after the start of World War I and flew many reconnaissance missions. Awarded the Iron Cross in 1915, he began flying Fokker's new monoplane, equipped with fixed, forward-firing synchronized machine guns, and amassed 40 victories. He developed his own rules of air combat that became known as "Boelcke's Dicta" and were taught to all German airmen. Having advocated the creation of dedicated fighting units, he was recalled from a tour of the Russian front to form a prototype Jagdstaffel ("attack squadron") in 1916. Many German flying aces gained their combat training in this unit under his tutelage. Boelcke was killed on October 28, 1916, when his Albatros biplane was struck by another flown by a comrade.

BOEING (RIGHT) AND WESTERVELT WITH THEIR B&W SEAPLANE

GABRIEL BOREL
[b.–d. unknown]

In 1909, Gabriel Borel and his brother opened a flying school at Mourmelon, France, where two of their pilots, Léon Morane and Raymond Saulnier, built a monoplane known as the Morane-Borel. The airplane gained a good reputation, and between 1910 and 1914 a series of monoplanes, seaplanes, and flying boats emerged from the Borel stable. During World War I they built products for other companies. In 1918 the company was restructured as Société Générale des Constructions Industrielles et Mécaniques. The C.1 and C.2 fighter prototypes were built, but no orders were forthcoming.

AIR MARSHAL SIR WILLIAM SEFTON BRANCKER
1877–1930

Commissioned in the British Royal Artillery in 1896, William Sefton Brancker served in the Boer War and then in India, where a flight in a Bristol Box kite inspired him to learn to fly. During World War I he held several posts, including Director of Air Organization, Commander of the RFC (Royal Flying Corps) in the Middle East, and Major-General in the RAF (Royal Air Force). After the war, Brancker became an active proponent of all forms of civil aviation. He joined Holt Thomas's Aircraft Manufacturing Co., and in 1922 was appointed Britain's Director of Civil Aviation. He died in the 1930 crash of the R.101 airship.

LOUIS BREGUET
1880–1955

The son of wealthy Parisian clockmakers, Louis Breguet turned to aviation in 1907, building a large, unstable helicopter. His first airplane, flown in 1909, led to a series of all-metal biplanes. The Breguet 14 reconnaissance airplane was one of the outstanding aircraft of World War I. After the war he founded the airline Compagnie de Messageries Aériennes, later Air France, while his aircraft company built numerous successful designs, such as the Breguet 19, used for many long-distance

flights. In 1971, control of the company passed to Dassault and the name changed to Avions Marcel Dassault Breguet Aviation. In 1990 it became simply Dassault Aviation.

PAUL W.S. BULMAN
1896–1963

One of Britain's great test pilots, "George" Bulman transferred to the RFC (Royal Flying Corps) from the Royal Artillery in 1915. He served as an RAF (Royal Air Force) test pilot at the Royal Aircraft Establishment, Farnborough, England, from 1919 to 1925. He then became chief test pilot at Hawker Aircraft, where he tested the company's classic range of biplane fighters, light bombers, and, in 1935, the prototype Hurricane fighter. After remaining with Hawker throughout the war, Bulman, by then a director, went into private business in 1945.

WILLIAM SEFTON BRANCKER

COMMANDER RICHARD EVELYN BYRD
1888–1957

Famed for his claim to have made the first airplane flight over the North Pole, Richard Byrd graduated from the US Naval Academy in 1912 and served in administrative roles before joining the pilot training program in World War I. In 1919, he helped plan a transatlantic flight by US Navy Curtiss NC flying boats, and in 1926, with Floyd Bennett, attempted the first airplane flight over the North Pole. Byrd and Bennett's claim to have succeeded earned them the US Congressional Medal of Honor, but it has since transpired that their Fokker Trimotor turned around 150 miles (240 km) short of the Pole. Having failed to beat Lindbergh to Paris, France, in 1927, Byrd turned to Antarctic exploration, making the first flight over the South Pole in 1929.

SIR SYDNEY CAMM
1893–1966

Few British aircraft designers have as many famous airplanes to their credit as Sydney Camm. A skillful builder of flying models in his youth, he joined the Martinsyde company as a woodworker in 1914 and progressed to the drawing office under G.H. Handasyde. Camm moved to Hawker Engineering Co. (later Hawker Aircraft) as a senior draftsman in 1923, and within two years was chief designer. He was appointed to the board in 1935, and at the time of his death was Hawker Siddeley Aviation's director of design. His creations included the Cygnet, Hart, Fury, Hurricane, Sea Fury, Typhoon, Tempest, Sea Hawk, Hunter, and P.1127 Kestrel.

GASTON AND RENÉ CAUDRON
1882–1915, 1884–1959

The Caudron brothers of Picardy, France, built their first airplane in 1908 and in 1910 set up a flying school and a factory, at which they built distinctive twin-boom tractor biplanes. They produced trainers and twin-engined bombers in World War I, and the interwar years saw a variety of designs, including airliners, light aircraft, and successful racing monoplanes. Although they built gliders in 1946, the company failed to revive after World War II.

SIR GEORGE CAYLEY
1773–1857

A baronet from Yorkshire, England, Sir George Cayley is known as "the father of the airplane." About a century before the Wright brothers'

first powered flight he established the basic principles of heavier-than-air flight and founded the science of aerodynamics. He was the first person to divorce the systems of lift and thrust and to conceive the fixed-wing airplane with an independent means of propulsion (1799); the first to build such an aircraft (1809, tested as a glider); the first to use a whirling arm and fly a model glider for aeronautical research (1804); and the first to realize the advantages of streamlining and of cambered air-foils for wings. He also invented the tension wheel (for undercarriages), the caterpillar tractor, and artificial limbs. Cayley flew a full-size triplane glider with a boy aboard in 1849, and sent up his terrified coachman in a monoplane glider four years later. Although unpowered and uncontrolled, these were the first heavier-than-air airplane flights.

CLYDE CESSNA
1880–1954

Raised on a Kansas farm, Clyde Cessna was a natural mechanic who went on to become the founder of one of America's principal light-airplane manufacturers. In 1911, after seeing a flying exhibition, he ordered a Blériot monoplane fuselage and built his own wings. After 13 crashes, Cessna had taught himself to fly, and set himself up as a barnstormer. In 1916–17 he built two more airplanes, but returned to farming until 1925, when he and Walter Beech formed Travel Air. Two years later Cessna left to form Cessna Aircraft. He retired in 1937, passing the company presidency on to his nephew, Dwane Wallace.

SIR ROY CHADWICK
1893–1947

English designer Roy Chadwick was, as a youth, an avid model airplane builder and follower of the pioneers. At the age of 18 he met engineer Alliott Roe and joined him as his personal assistant before moving into the drawing office. A.V. Roe & Co Ltd was formed in 1913, and soon after the outbreak of World War I Chadwick found himself in charge of 100 draughtsmen. He designed the Avro Baby in 1919, and later collaborated with Juan de

la Cierva on Autogiro design. His subsequent designs for Avro included the Avian two-seater, the Tutor trainer for the RAF (Royal Air Force), the Anson, and, most famously of all, the Lancaster bomber. After World War II he designed the Tudor commercial transport. It was in the prototype Tudor II that Chadwick was killed on August 23, 1947, when it crashed shortly after takeoff.

OCTAVE CHANUTE
1832–1910

Paris-born Octave Chanute was taken to New York at the age of six, where he became a wealthy civil engineer, specializing in railroad bridges. He developed a deep interest in aviation, corresponding with all of the leading pioneers. In 1894 he published *Progress in Flying Machines*, an impressive and comprehensive study of the work done worldwide up to that time. In 1896, he began experimenting with multiplane and biplane hang gliders, introducing the Pratt truss bracing system into airplane design. These machines were flown on the shores of Lake Michigan by William Avery and Augustus Herring. From 1900, Chanute was a trusted confidant of

OCTAVE CHANUTE

the Wright brothers, and it was he who, in 1903, took their work to European experimenters through lectures and articles in France.

JUAN DE LA CIERVA
1895–1936

Most famous for his work on the Autogiro rotating-wing aircraft, Juan de la Cierva was born in Murcia, Spain. He became interested in flight at a young age. Model kites and aircraft were followed by two full-

JUAN DE LA CIERVA

size gliders in 1910–11, a powered biplane in 1912, and a monoplane in 1913. In 1919 – by which time he had graduated as a civil engineer – he designed a large trimotor biplane, which crashed on its maiden flight. Determined to devise a safe aircraft, Cierva evolved his Autogiro concept. In 1923 his first successful machine, the C.4, with a fully articulated rotor head, made the first controlled gyroplane flight in history. In 1925 Cierva moved to England and a whole series of Autogiros was produced, many by A.V. Roe. In 1926, the Cierva Autogiro Co. was formed, Autogiros being built under license in France, Germany, Spain, and the US. Cierva was killed in a DC-2 airliner crash at Croydon, England, on December 9, 1936.

COLONEL VIRGINUS E. CLARK
1886–1948

Virginus Clark's brilliance as an engineer was first evident during his training at the US Naval Academy. He subsequently learned to fly and carried out studies in aerodynamics. After being posted to NACA (the National Advisory Committee for Aeronautics) in 1917, he embarked on an intensive study of airfoil sections, developing his own series. Most famous of these is the simple

Clark Y, which gives high lift for low drag and was widely adopted. One of its most notable uses was in Charles Lindbergh's Ryan NYP *Spirit of St. Louis*. Clark also devised an effective drag-reducing cowling for radial engines in the early 1920s. After forming the Clark Aircraft Corporation in the late 1930s he introduced a method of building aircraft by using plastic-impregnated wood, known as Duramold, with remarkable savings in time and cost.

HENRI COANDA
1886–1972

Henri Coanda is best remembered as the discoverer of the "Coanda effect," which is the tendency of air or water to follow a curved surface. Born in Bucharest, Romania, he graduated from the High School of Aeronautics in Paris, France, in 1909 as the first intake's best student. At the second Paris Aero Show in 1910, he exhibited a propellerless biplane with a 50-hp Clerget engine that drove a ducted turbine screw. Although it was totally impractical and never flew, it has often been represented, erroneously, as the first jet aircraft. In 1912, Coanda joined the British & Colonial Aeroplane Company at Bristol, England, for which he designed a distinctive series of conventionally powered biplanes and monoplanes before returning to Romania in 1914.

SIR ALAN COBHAM
1894–1973

British trailblazer Alan Cobham joined the Royal Artillery shortly before World War I, and transferred to the RFC (Royal Flying Corps) in 1917, where he learned to fly. In 1921, after a spell working for a joyriding outfit, he was employed as chief pilot and manager of the de Havilland Aeroplane Hire Service. He made flying tours of Europe and North Africa in 1922; in 1924 he flew Britain's Director of Civil Aviation, Sir Sefton Brancker, to Cape Town and back; and in 1926 he made a return flight to Australia. These flights and others helped establish the routes to be used by Britain's Imperial Airways. In 1932, Cobham launched his National Aviation Day Campaign, a touring air display to foster airmindedness in

the UK. He subsequently pioneered in-flight refuelling techniques. Flight Refuelling Ltd., the company he founded in 1935, was still flourishing at the end of the twentieth century.

JACQUELINE COCHRAN
c.1906–1980

American pilot Jacqueline Cochran was born in Florida. Brought up by poor foster parents she suffered hardship in her youth, but became a well-known beautician and cosmetics tycoon before marrying aviator Floyd Odlum. In 1932, she learned to fly in three weeks, and then began to compete in air races, entering the 1934 MacRobertson race from England to Australia, which she had to abandon in Romania. She won the Bendix Trophy in 1938, flying a Seversky fighter, and in 1939 she became the first woman to make a blind landing. During World War II, Cochran campaigned to establish the WASPs (Women's Airforce Service Pilots). In 1953, in a Canadian-built F-86 Sabre, she became the first woman to break the sound barrier; on the same day, she set a world speed record for women of 652 mph (1,050 km/h).

JACQUELINE COCHRAN

SAMUEL FRANKLIN CODY
1867–1913

SAMUEL FRANKLIN CODY

Born S.F. Cowdery in Iowa, Cody changed his last name in tribute to "Buffalo Bill" Cody, whom he emulated by becoming a skilled horseman, sharpshooter, and lassoist, and running a successful Wild West show. Settling in England in the early 1890s, he developed a man-carrying kite system for the War Office, and was then employed in the building of Britain's first military dirigible, the *Nulli Secundus*. Relying on his intuitive engineering skills, Cody built an airplane for the army, and in this machine – *British Army Aeroplane No. 1* – he made the first sustained and controlled powered flight in Britain on October 16, 1908. After dismissal by the War Office in 1909, he developed his own series of airplanes. Flying these aircraft, he won the British Empire Michelin Cup in 1910, the number one and two Michelin Cups in 1911, and the British Military Trials in 1912. Cody was killed in 1913 when the "Waterplane" he had built for the Circuit of Britain race broke up in flight.

PAUL CORNU
1881–1944

French cycle and car salesman Paul Cornu is remembered for his claim to have built the first manned helicopter to rise vertically under its own power. He began designing and experimenting with model helicopters in

1905. The successful operation of a large model in 1906 encouraged him to build a full-size version. Powered by a 24-hp Antoinette engine, this tandem-twin-rotor device allegedly rose to a height of 1 ft (30 cm), with a man aboard, near Lisieux, France, on November 3, 1907. The claim that this machine had the ability to hover manned or unmanned has since been questioned. Cornu lacked the finances to develop further his ideas on rotary flight.

CAPTAIN DIEUDONNÉ COSTES
1896–1973

After claiming eight victories as a French scout pilot in World War I, and flying on Air Union's cross-Channel services after the war, Dieudonné Costes won international acclaim with a series of record-breaking long-distance flights he made as Louis Breguet's chief pilot. These included flights from Paris to Aswan, Egypt, and to Persia in 1926, and from Paris to Nijnitagilsk, Siberia, in 1927. Later that year he began a circumnavigation of the globe. He flew from Paris to Senegal in West Africa, on to Brazil (making the first direct air crossing of the South Atlantic), down the Atlantic coast of South America, and up the Pacific seaboard to Washington state. The airplane was then shipped to Japan, from where Costes flew back to Paris. In 1930 Costes made the first direct, nonstop Paris-to-New York flight in the Breguet XIX Super TR *Point d'Interrogation*. He then made a 16,387-mile (26,383-km) goodwill tour of the US.

GROUP CAPTAIN JOHN CUNNINGHAM
1917–

John Cunningham was one of the most distinguished British civil and military pilots of the 1940s and 1950s. He joined the de Havilland Aircraft Company's light aircraft development department in 1938. The outbreak of World War II in the following year thwarted plans for him to attempt the light airplane long-distance record. Serving in the RAF (Royal Air Force) during the war, he became the first Briton to shoot down an enemy bomber at night. This feat gained Cunningham a reputation as a nightfighter pilot, and he went on to destroy a total of 20 enemy aircraft.

After the war he was appointed chief test pilot for de Havilland in 1946. His achievements in this role included piloting the maiden flight of the de Havilland Comet jet airliner and, in 1955, circumnavigating the globe in the Comet 3. The 30,000-mile (48,300-km) flight took 56 hours to complete. In 1958 Cunningham was made a director of de Havilland. He later became an executive director of British Aerospace.

GLENN H. CURTISS
1878–1930

Pioneer and innovator Glenn Hammond Curtiss was born in Hammondsport, New York, where he set up a successful bicycle and motorcycle manufacturing business. His ability with engines led to him joining Alexander Graham Bell's AEA (Aerial Experiment Association). In 1908 Curtiss designed the AEA's third airplane, the *June Bug*, in which he made the first public flight in the USA. He then left to set up his own airplane manufacturing company, which produced the world's first practical seaplanes and flying boats. His Curtiss JN "Jenny" trainers were widely used in World War I, and the large Curtiss flying boats were developed into long-range patrol aircraft for the RNAS (Royal Naval Air Service). Curtiss was taken to court by the Wrights

for infringing their patent for airplane control, and eventually lost a lengthy and bitter legal battle.

SIR GEOFFREY DE HAVILLAND
1882–1965

British aircraft designer Geoffrey de Havilland started out in the auto industry before building his first airplane in 1908. Although this machine was a failure, his second airplane was so successful that both it and its creator were taken on by Britain's War Office. He became the designer and test pilot for the Royal Aircraft Factory at Farnborough, England, producing the B.E.1, B.E.2, F.E.2, S.E.1, and B.S.1. In 1914, he joined the Aircraft Manufacturing Company (Airco) in the same role. In 1920, he started his own company, building a variety of civil and military aircraft, most famously the D.H.60 Moth light airplane, the Mosquito, the Vampire, and the Comet.

DE HAVILLAND VAMPIRE

LÉON DELAGRANGE
1873–1910

Born in Orléans, France, Léon Delagrange was a popular sculptor in Paris when his interest in aviation was inspired by Voisin's gliding experiments. In 1907, he bought an airplane from this pioneer and taught himself to fly. Embarking on a tour of Europe, he became the first person to fly in Italy and, at Turin in July 1908, was the first to carry a female passenger, Thérèse Peltier.

A safe, steady pilot, he set several distance records. In December 1909, flying a Blériot monoplane, he made a flight of 124 miles (200 km) in

2 hours 32 minutes. He died on January 4, 1910, when the port wing of his Blériot – in which he had fitted a 50-hp engine instead of its original 25-hp unit – collapsed during a turn at 40 ft (12 m). The machine fell onto a hangar, throwing him out.

ARMAND DEPERDUSSIN
1869–1924

From 1910 to 1913, wealthy French businessman Armand Deperdussin and his design engineer, Louis Béchereau, worked together to produce a family of fast, stylish monoplanes. Flying one of these machines, the aviator Jules Védrines won the Gordon Bennett Trophy race, held in Chicago on September 9, 1912, setting a record speed of 108.2 mph (174 km/h). The following year one of their seaplanes won the first Schneider Trophy contest in April. Another Deperdussin racer defended the Gordon Bennett Trophy title at Reims, France, on September 29, 1913, setting a new speed record at the same time.

Despite these triumphs, and the elegant, molded-plywood, monocoque fuselages of some of the later racing models, orders were thin on the ground. Deperdussin resorted to large-scale embezzlement, for which he was arrested in the closing months of 1913. The company that he had created was taken over by Louis Blériot. After a prolonged investigation Deperdussin was eventually given a suspended sentence. He shot himself in 1924.

JAMES DOOLITTLE WITH A CURTISS RACING SEAPLANE

LIEUTENANT GENERAL JAMES DOOLITTLE
1896–1993

American aviator James Doolittle is probably best remembered for leading his country's first bombing raid on Japan in World War II. Doolittle built a glider in his schooldays, before joining the US Army Signal Corps as a flying cadet in 1917. In 1922, he made the first one-stop flight across the US. A superb test pilot, he was also a stuntman and wing-walker. He won the Schneider Trophy for the US in 1925, flying a Curtiss seaplane, and in 1929 made the first blind flight, relying entirely on instruments. Despite becoming manager of Shell Oil's aviation department in 1930, he continued to fly, setting a world speed record for landplanes in 1931. He returned to active duty in 1940, and in April 1942 masterminded the famous raid on Tokyo by 16 B-25 Mitchell bombers. He later formed the 12th Air Force and commanded the 15th and 8th Air Forces. After the war Doolittle returned to Shell, where he went on to become a company director.

PROFESSOR CLAUDE DORNIER
1884–1969

German aircraft designer Claude Dornier was born in Bavaria and received his engineering education in Munich. In 1910 he was engaged by Count von Zeppelin to check the viability of the count's airship designs. He also designed a series of airplanes for the Zeppelin company during World War I, which included several giant seaplanes and flying boats that were constructed with metal airframes. Some of this work for Zepplin continued after the war but, when aircraft manufacture in Germany was prohibited in 1922, Dornier set up his own works in Switzerland and Italy. There he developed the celebrated Wal and Do X flying boats. World War II saw the arrival of new Dornier military aircraft, such as the Do 17 and 217 bombers and the Do 335 push-pull fighter-bomber. After the war Dornier's civil products included the Do 31 – the world's first V/STOL jet transport – and the Do 228 utility and commuter aircraft.

DONALD WILLS DOUGLAS
1892–1981

Donald Douglas, founder of the eponymous airplane company, was born in Brooklyn, New York, and joined the Connecticut Aircraft Co. in 1915. Later the same year he moved to the Glenn Martin company in California, designing the MB-1 bomber. In 1920, with a large loan from sportsman David Davis, the Davis-Douglas Co. was formed to build an airplane to fly nonstop across the US. When this crashed, Douglas set up his own company and took over a contract to build torpedo bombers for the US Navy. In 1924, two modified versions built for the US Army Air Service, known as DWCs (Douglas World Cruisers), made the first around-the-world flight. The company found great success in the 1930s with the DC-1, DC-2, and DC-3/C-47 Dakota transports. The later DC-4, DC-6, and DC-7 four-engined transports also sold well, and were followed by the DC-8, DC-9, and DC-10 jets. The company merged with McDonnell in 1967.

ARMAND AND HENRI DUFAUX
1883–1941, 1879–1980

The Dufaux brothers of Geneva, Switzerland, were the inventors of the Motosacoche motorcycle, which used a gasoline engine that could be attached to a bicycle. In 1905, they demonstrated a model helicopter in Paris. Its 3-hp twin-cylinder engine drove a pair of two-bladed rotors on lateral outriggers. It lifted 14 lb (6.4 kg) of ballast, but was guided by vertical cables. Their first airplane,

a heavy machine with a 120-hp Dufaux engine, crashed in 1907. The following year they constructed a 100-hp combined helicopter and airplane that was designed to take off vertically and glide horizontally. This was followed by a biplane in which Armand flew the length of Lake Geneva in 1910. Four Dufaux biplanes were built.

FÉLIX DU TEMPLE DE LA CROIX
1823–1890

French naval officer Félix du Temple de la Croix is credited with the first powered, piloted takeoff. In the 1850s, with his brother Louis, he built a model airplane powered first by clockwork and then by steam, which made tentative flights around 1857. In that year Félix patented a full-size aircraft with a swept-forward wing, retractable three-wheeled undercarriage, and boatlike nacelle. In 1874 a full-scale monoplane based on this design, powered by a two-cylinder hot-air engine, was finished at Brest, France. It achieved a powered takeoff – but not a powered flight – when run down an inclined ramp. Two years later the brothers fitted a lightweight steam boiler into the aircraft, but there is no record of the machine being tested in this form.

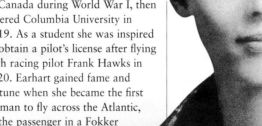

AMELIA EARHART
1898–1937

Born in Kansas, the famous aviator Amelia Earhart worked as a nurse in Canada during World War I, then entered Columbia University in 1919. As a student she was inspired to obtain a pilot's license after flying with racing pilot Frank Hawks in 1920. Earhart gained fame and fortune when she became the first woman to fly across the Atlantic, as the passenger in a Fokker Tri-motor, on June 17–18, 1927. Although she did no piloting during this flight, Earhart soon began to establish her own flying records. Her achievements included becoming the first woman to make a trans-continental round-trip

flight across the US, establishing the world's autogyro altitude record in 1931, and being the first person to fly from Mexico City to New Jersey, and from Hawaii to California. In 1932, flying a Lockheed Vega, she became the first woman to fly an airplane across the Atlantic.

In July 1937, while attempting to fly around the world in a Lockheed Electra, Earhart and her navigator, Fred Noonan, disappeared over the Pacific. The circumstances of their disappearance remain a mystery.

SIR GEORGE EDWARDS
1908–

During an illustrious career, Sir George Edwards established himself as one of Britain's most influential aviation engineers. Upon graduating from London University at the age of 20, he joined Vickers Aviation at Weybridge in England. Under chief designer R.K. Pierson he worked on aircraft such as the Wellington, Warwick, and Windsor bombers. He was promoted to experimental manager in 1940 and became chief designer five years later, leading the development of the VC.1 Viking, the first postwar British transport

aircraft to enter airline service. He was involved in all of the postwar Vickers/BAC (British Aircraft Corporation) designs – the Viscount, Vanguard, Valiant, VC10, and Concorde. Between 1963 and 1975 he served as chairman of BAC.

JACOB CHRISTIAN HANSEN ELLEHAMMER
1871–1946

JACOB ELLEHAMMER

An accomplished Danish inventor, Jacob Ellehammer built his first full-size airplane at Copenhagen in 1905, powering it with a 9-hp three-cylinder engine of his own design. He made unpiloted tethered tests on a circular track on the isle of Lindholme early in 1906, during which the aircraft rose off the ground. Ellehammer then uprated the engine to give 20 hp, and the machine was modified as a "semi-biplane." In this form the aircraft again made tethered flights. After relocating his trials to Copenhagen, Ellehammer built a triplane in which he made some 200 hop-flights in 1907. In 1908, he won a prize of 5,000 marks when he made the first powered hop-flight in Germany in his new tractor biplane. He subsequently built both a seaplane and a monoplane, neither of which was flown. Ellehammer also became interested in helicopters and experimented with a model rotorcraft in 1911.

AMELIA EARHART

ROBERT ESNAULT-PELTERIE
1881–1957

The ever-inventive French engineer Robert Esnault-Pelterie built his first aircraft, a poor copy of a Wright-type glider, in 1904. He quickly followed this with a glider with small wingtip control surfaces that doubled as ailerons (the first to be fitted to a full-size aircraft) and elevators. Both of these machines were unsuccessful. Then, in 1907, came his first powered airplane, the R.E.P.1 monoplane with a 30-hp semi-radial engine of his own design, which made only tentative flights. The R.E.P.2 of 1908 was more successful, and, in a modified form, made many flights in the following year. Esnault-Pelterie eventually evolved more conventional designs, some of which saw service in the early years of World War I, but by this time he had turned his attention to the even greater challenges of rocketry and space travel.

DOKTOR IGO ETRICH
1879–1967

The name of Austrian engineer Igo Etrich will be forever associated with the distinctive Taube ("Dove") monoplanes. These were developed from tailless gliders that Etrich and fellow Austrian Franz Wels began testing in 1904. The birdlike wings were inspired by the seed of the Zanonia palm tree. The first successful machines appeared in 1909, and soon afterward Etrich reached an agreement for Taubes to be built in Germany by the Rumpler Flugzeugwerke. A number of other manufacturers subsequently copied the design. Many Rumpler Taubes saw service as reconnaissance aircraft early in World War I, although by then the design was outdated.

HENRI FABRE
1882–1984

Responsible for designing the first seaplane to take off from water, French engineer Henri Fabre began studying aviation in 1905. After conducting a series of aerodynamic experiments, he designed and built

HENRI FABRE

his first seaplane in 1909, but this never flew. His second seaplane was one of the first airplanes to use the new Gnome seven-cylinder rotary engine, and it made its first flights from water on March 28 and 29, 1910. These historic flights were piloted by Fabre himself, who had never flown before. Although it continued to be modified and flown into 1911, this unconventional tail-first machine had little development potential. As a result, Fabre ran out of money and had to abandon his experiments. He retained an interest in seaplanes, however, and became a successful designer of floats for other manufacturers' airplanes.

SIR RICHARD FAIREY
1887–1957

British aircraft manufacturer Sir Richard Fairey was originally an electrical engineer and a keen model airplane builder. He began his career in aviation in 1911 as shop manager of the Blair-Atholl Syndicate, which built stable tailless airplanes. He then moved to Short Brothers, where he was appointed works manager and chief engineer. In 1915, he set up the Fairey Aviation Company, mostly building Short and Sopwith aircraft under license. After World War I Fairey concentrated on developing his own aircraft. The interwar years saw the appearance of his IIID/F series of military general-purpose airplanes, the Flycatcher naval fighter, and the Fox bomber – an aeroplane that revolutionized aircraft design in Britain. During World War II Fairey's most notable aircraft were the Swordfish, Albacore, and Barracuda torpedo bombers. His postwar products included the Gannet, the Rotodyne compound convertible transport helicopter, and the F.D.2 – the first airplane to exceed 1,000 mph (1,610 km/h).

HENRY AND MAURICE FARMAN
1874–1958, 1877–1964

Influential in the early development of aviation, the Farman brothers were born in France to English parents. Their involvement in flying began when Maurice started ballooning and took Henry aloft. This inspired Henry to buy a Voisin biplane in 1907. After making a number of alterations to improve its performance, he won a prize for the first recorded flight of 492 ft (150 m) later that year, and on January 13, 1908, won 50,000 French francs for the first officially observed 3,281-ft (1-km) closed-circuit flight in Europe. In 1909 Henry won a further 63,000 francs at the Reims meeting in France, and opened his own aircraft factory. The boxkite biplane he produced there became one of the most widely used and copied designs of the era. In 1912 Maurice joined the business and together they founded Avions Henri et Maurice Farman. The company achieved early success with the MF.7 "Longhorn" and MF.11 "Shorthorn" biplanes, and continued to flourish until it was nationalized in 1936. The Farman brothers then retired from the business.

SIR ROY FEDDEN
1885–1973

Born in Bristol, England, Roy Fedden was an important figure in the development of airplane engines. He began his career as an automobile engineer with the Brazil-Straker company in 1906. After persuading his employers to build their own engines, he was appointed chief engineer. During World War I he oversaw the production of Rolls-Royce and Renault engines and was also put in charge of designing a new radial aircraft engine. The Jupiter prototype he developed became the first in a great line of engines.

When Brazil-Straker was absorbed into the Bristol Aeroplane Company in 1920, Fedden was retained as chief engineer and oversaw the development of the Mercury, Hercules, and Centaurus series of engines until 1942. That year he became special technical adviser to Britain's Ministry of Aircraft Production, and led missions to the US, Italy, and Germany. After the war he founded Roy Fedden Ltd., and designed cars and aircraft engines.

ANTON FLETTNER
1885–1961

German innovator Anton Flettner gave his name to a tab he invented that allows a large control surface to be moved using light control-column force. He is best known, however, for his later pioneering work on rotorcraft. After forming Flettner GmbH in 1935 he built the Fl 184 and 185 autogyros, and then developed the Fl 265, a helicopter with two intermeshing, counter-rotating rotors. Six of these machines were built for the German Navy in

FARMAN F.16 BIPLANE (1912)

1939–40. The Fl 265 was followed by the Fl 282 Kolibri. Over 1,000 of these helicopters were ordered, but the factories building them were bombed in 1943: only 24 saw service. After World War II Flettner worked for the US Navy, before founding his own company in New York in 1949.

DOKTOR HEINRICH KARL JOHANN FOCKE
1890–1979

A pioneer of rotorcraft in Germany, Heinrich Focke served as a pilot in World War I. In 1924 he founded the Focke-Wulf company with Georg Wulf, initially building commercial transports and training aircraft. After the arrival of designer Kurt Tank in 1931 the company made a chain of successful airplanes, but Focke pursued his interest in rotorcraft, building Cierva C.19 and C.30 Autogiros. When the Nazis dismissed him from his company in 1936 he started an offshoot, Focke-Achgelis, where he built the Fa 61 helicopter. Employing twin lateral rotors, it made its first free flight in June 1936. Focke's World War II helicopter, the Fa 223 Drache, was ordered into production, but most of those built were destroyed by bombing.

ANTHONY HERMAN GERARD FOKKER
1890–1939

Renowned for designing Germany's most successful World War I fighter aircraft, Anthony Fokker was the son of a wealthy Dutch plantation

owner. He was attracted to aviation by Wilbur Wright's flights in France in 1908, but he had to wait until he completed his military service in 1910 before he could build his own airplane, abetted by Franz von Daum. By the end of that year he was making short hop-flights, and in May 1911 he gained his pilot's rating. Fokker then designed a succession of Spin ("Spider") monoplanes and set up the Fokker Aeroplanbau at Johannisthal, near Berlin, to build them. The company supplied Germany with more than 40 types of aircraft during World War I, including the Eindecker monoplane and the agile Dr.1 triplane. After the war Fokker moved the business to the Netherlands, where it continued to thrive, constructing transport monoplanes and military aircraft.

HENRY PHILLIP FOLLAND
1889–1954

After ten years in the British automobile industry, Henry Folland began a distinguished career as an airplane designer under Geoffrey de Havilland at the Royal Aircraft Factory, Farnborough, England, in 1912. When de Havilland left in 1914, Folland took over leadership of the design team and was responsible

ANTHONY FOKKER

for producing the renowned S.E.5 fighter. He joined the Gloucestershire Aircraft Company (later Gloster) in 1920, where he designed a series of racing seaplanes for the Schneider Trophy contests, as well as a range of fighters including the Gauntlet, Gamecock, and Gladiator. In 1937 he left to start his own company, Folland Aircraft. During World War II the company undertook sub-contract work and after the war it produced the Gnat jet fighter/trainer. Folland retired in 1951.

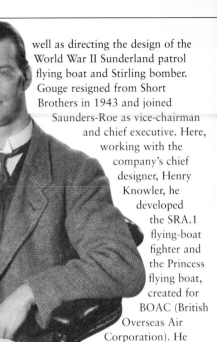

HENRY PHILLIP FOLLAND

G

SIR ARTHUR GOUGE
1890–1969

Arthur Gouge is remembered for developing classic British seaplanes and flying boats. He joined Short Brothers at Rochester, England, as a mechanic in 1915, working on the Type 184 seaplane. He was then put in charge of a team that developed some of Britain's first all-metal aircraft. He was appointed chief designer in 1926, at a time when Short Brothers was producing great flying boats such as the Singapore and the Calcutta. Responsible for all of the company's aircraft design between 1926 and 1943, Gouge oversaw the production of the majestic Empire Class mono-planes for Imperial Airways as

well as directing the design of the World War II Sunderland patrol flying boat and Stirling bomber. Gouge resigned from Short Brothers in 1943 and joined Saunders-Roe as vice-chairman and chief executive. Here, working with the company's chief designer, Henry Knowler, he developed the SRA.1 flying-boat fighter and the Princess flying boat, created for BOAC (British Overseas Air Corporation). He retired in 1959.

HANS GRADE
1879–1946

Hans Grade is remembered as the first native German to fly. He founded a motorcycle factory in his twenties, before acquiring his first airplane, a primitive Ellehammer-inspired 35-hp tractor triplane, in 1908. He tested this machine at Magdeburg, Germany, in the winter of 1908–09. Its best flight covered a distance of 1,312 ft (400 m) on February 18, 1909. Later that year, Grade also successfully flew a high-wing tractor monoplane. He established the Hans Grade Flieger-werke in 1911 to build high-wing aircraft, and used some of these to train pilots at the Grade flying school. The factory was sold to Aviatik after the start of World War I.

CLAUDE GRAHAME-WHITE
1879–1959

British pilot and entrepreneur Claude Grahame-White visited the Blériot factory while he was in France for the 1909 Reims meeting, ordered an airplane, and taught himself to fly. After briefly running a flying school in France, he opened one at Brooklands in England, and then established the London Aerodrome at Hendon. In 1910, he gained prominence by his dogged race with French pilot Louis Paulhan to win the *Daily Mail*'s £10,000 prize for the first flight from London to Manchester. Although he lost the race, he made the first point-to-point night flight in England. In World War I he joined the RNAS (Royal Naval Air Service), taking part in a raid on German bases in Belgium in 1915. Graham-White resigned his commission soon afterwards to concentrate on building aircraft, and his company produced a series of original designs up to 1919. After the war he dealt in real estate.

DANIEL GUGGENHEIM
1856–1930

Philadelphia-born industrialist and philanthropist Daniel Guggenheim became a benefactor of aviation in the 1920s. His son Harry, a US naval aviator, persuaded him to endow New York University's aerodynamics program with $500,000 in 1923. Three years later he established the Daniel Guggenheim Fund for the Promotion of Aeronautics, to which he eventually donated $3 million. The fund helped to develop instrument flying, aviation safety, and rocketry. Among the events it financed was the Guggenheim Safe Aircraft Competition, held in the late 1920s.

MIKHAIL GURYEVICH
1893–1976

Mikhail Guryevich was cofounder of the design bureau responsible for producing the Soviet Union's highly successful series of MiG fighters. Born near Kursk, Russia, he studied aeronautics at Kharkov University, l'Académie de l'Aéronautique in Paris, and Kharkov Technical Institute, finally graduating in 1923. He worked for the Soviet Union's Central Construction Bureau before joining the Richard design bureau in 1928. He was appointed deputy chief of the Kochyerigin bureau in 1931, where he led the design of the TSh-3 armored attack monoplane. Between 1936 and 1938 Guryevich worked at Douglas in the United States on the DC-3 program. He then returned to the Soviet Union and joined an experimental design section (OKO) headed by Artyem Mikoyan to work on the Kh high-altitude interceptor. In 1942, the OKO became the Mikoyan and Guryevich (MiG) design bureau, which produced a string of fighters during and after World War II. Guryevich retired in 1964.

LAWRENCE HARGRAVE
1850–1915

Famed for developing the box-kite, Hargrave was born in England but brought up in Australia, where he trained as an engineer-draftsman. In 1883, while working at Sydney Observatory, Hargrave came into an inheritance that allowed him to devote his energies to aviation and other scientific experiments. He went on to test a large number of model ornithopters – aircraft propelled by flapping wings – and airplanes powered by rubber and compressed air. In 1889 he designed and built a radial rotary engine that enabled one of his models to fly 128 ft (39 m) in eight seconds on January 2, 1891. He also conducted experiments with curved surfaces, and, most notably, built a boxkite glider that lifted him 16 ft (5 m) off the ground in 1894. Hargrave never succeeded in building a person-carrying airplane, but he shared the results of his experiments with other pioneers, who used the box-kite principle in early airplane design.

HARRY GEORGE HAWKER
1889–1921

Harry Hawker was born in Victoria, Australia. He was fascinated by engineering from a young age, and ran away from school to work with automobiles. He was inspired to become a pilot after seeing the famous escapologist Harry Houdini fly. Traveling with two friends to England, in 1912 he gained employment with

HARRY HAWKER

Sopwith Aviation at Brooklands and learned to fly. He proved a natural pilot, and became the company's demonstration and test pilot. In the years before and during World War I he made many notable flights and tested countless Sopwith prototypes, as well as making some valuable contributions to their design. In 1919, Hawker and Lt. Cdr. Mackenzie Grieve tried to win the £10,000 *Daily Mail* prize for a nonstop transatlantic flight in a Sopwith Atlantic, but failed when they were forced to ditch in the ocean. Fortunately they were rescued by a tramp steamer. Hawker remained undaunted and took up motor racing as well as test flying. He was killed on July 12, 1921, during a practice flight for the Aerial Derby, when the Nieuport Goshawk biplane he was flying crashed. The company that built the Hurricane fighter during World War II was named after him – Hawker Aircraft.

EDWARD H. HEINEMANN
1908–1991

Born in Michigan, Edward Heinemann was inspired to design airplanes by the 1926 around-the-world flight of the Douglas World Cruisers. He joined Douglas as a draftsman and, after a period working for Northrop, returned there to lead the design of a number of famous airplanes, including the SBD Dauntless dive-bomber, the A-20 Havoc attack bomber, the D-558-1 Skystreak world speed record breaker, the D-558-2 Sky-rocket (the first airplane to attain Mach 2), and the A-4 Skyhawk attack bomber, which became known as "Heinemann's Hot Rod."

HARRY HAWKER

ERNST HEINKEL
1888–1958

Best remembered for the military aircraft he designed for Germany in World War II, Ernst Heinkel built his first airplane, a boxkite biplane, in 1911. He subsequently worked for LVG and Albatros before moving to Hansa-Brandenburg, where he designed a series of seaplanes. In 1922, encouraged by orders from Sweden for his designs, Heinkel set up his own company, which made a range of single-engined trainers, military aircraft, seaplanes, and flying boats over the next ten years. In 1935 he formed Ernst Heinkel AG. The company's famous World War II military aircraft included the He 111 bomber, the He 178 (the world's first turbojet-powered airplane), and the He 280 twin-jet fighter. After the war the company name changed to Heinkel, prior to its absorption by VFW in 1964.

CLAUDE GRAHAME-WHITE (RIGHT) AND PASSENGER

WILLIAM SAMUEL HENSON
1812–1888

Engineer and inventor William Henson was born in Nottingham, England. He began experimenting with gliding models in 1840, and in 1842 patented a steam-powered monoplane exhibiting many features of the powered aircraft developed 60 years later. When he formed the Aerial Steam Transit Company in 1843, numerous fanciful impressions of his "Aerial Steam Carriage" in flight were published. A large-scale model of this airplane, built with the help of John Stringfellow, was tested in 1847, but proved incapable of sustained flight. Discouraged, Henson gave up the project and emigrated to America, leaving Stringfellow to carry on his work.

HERBERT JOHN LOUIS HINKLER
1892–1933

Australian pilot "Bert" Hinkler was born in Bundaberg, Queensland. He

BERT HINKLER

served in Britain's RNAS (Royal Naval Air Service) from 1914 until the end of World War I, emerging as a distinguished pilot. After the war he became a test pilot for Avro in England, and in 1920 flew an Avro Baby biplane nonstop from London to Turin in northern Italy. In 1921, in the same machine, Hinkler made a nonstop 800-mile (1,280-km) flight up the east coast of Australia from Sydney to his native Bundaberg. In 1927 he achieved the longest nonstop flight by a light aeroplane up to that time, flying from Croydon, England, to Riga, Latvia, a distance of 1,200 miles (1,920 km), in the prototype Avian. Early in 1928 he made a solo England–Australia flight in 15½ days, and he followed this in 1931 with the first solo flight across the South Atlantic. Two years later Hinkler was killed in a crash in the Alps while attempting to better the England–Australia record.

JIRO HORIKOSHI
1903–1982

The designer of some of Japan's most notable fighter planes of the 1930s and 1940s, Jiro Horikoshi studied engineering at Tokyo University's Department of Aeronautics. In 1927 he joined the Mitsubishi Internal Combustion Engine Co. (later the Nagoya Manufacturing Plant of Mitsubishi Heavy Industries). Here he worked as chief designer on the unsuccessful Prototype 7 carrier-based fighter in 1932, and on the all-metal Prototype 9 land-based fighter in 1934. Adopted for service as the Type 96, it played a significant part in Japan's war with China from 1937. Horikoshi's most famous design was the Prototype 12. Begun in 1937, it became the Mitsubishi A6M Reisen. As Navy Type 0, or Zero, it was one of the outstanding fighters of World War II. The J2M Raiden, its successor, was used to defend Japan against bombing raids toward the end of the war.

REIMAR AND WALTER HORTEN
1915–1993, 1913–

Creators of a celebrated series of gliders and airplanes, German brothers Reimar and Walter Horten built their first

tailless, wooden, prone-piloted glider in 1931. Four examples of their second design, the Ho II of 1934, were built, one of which was fitted with an engine in 1935. After a spell of military training the Hortens resumed their work in 1938 and, with official backing, built the Ho III and Ho IV gliders. The powered Ho V of the World War II period used bonded plastic in its structure. The Ho VII was also a powered machine, while another of their designs, the Ho IX twin-jet tailless fighter, flew briefly before the war's end. After the war Walter Horten contributed to the reestablishment of the Luftwaffe in Germany, while his brother emigrated to Argentina, designing the Instituto Aerotecnico's I.A.38 tailless transport.

HOWARD ROBARD HUGHES
1905–1976

Eccentric and extravagant American millionaire Howard Hughes learned to fly in 1927. He quickly gained a commercial pilot's license and found out all he could about airplanes. After racing a modified Boeing fighter in 1934, he founded the Hughes Aircraft Company to build the H-1 racer, in which he set a new world landplane speed record of 352.3 mph (563.7 km/h) in 1935. He also set a new US transcontinental record in January 1936, flying a Northrop Gamma, and beat this the following year in the modified H-1. In 1938, flying a Lockheed 14 Super Electra, Hughes flew around the world in just over 91 hours, another new record. During World War II Hughes directed his energies toward developing the gigantic

H-4 Hercules flying boat, the world's largest airplane, and the XF-11 photoreconnaissance aircraft. He narrowly escaped death in 1946 when the XF-11 he was piloting on a test flight crashed. The H-4 flew only once, under Hughes's piloting, on November 2, 1947. After this Hughes flew only infrequently.

SERGEI VLADIMIROVICH ILYUSHIN
1894–1977

Born in the Vologda district of Russia, Sergei Ilyushin began his career in aviation in 1916 as a mechanic on Il'ya Mouramets bombers. He joined the army and qualified as a pilot in 1917, then entered the Zhukovskii Air Force Academy in 1922. He graduated as a designer in 1926 and was appointed to the scientific and technical committee of the Soviet Air Force administration. Ilyushin moved to the Central Aerodynamics and Hydrodynamics Institute in 1932, becoming deputy to Andrei Tupolev at the department of experimental airplane construction. He was later put in charge of the long-range bomber brigade in the Central Construction Bureau. Apart from a brief spell as director of the chief administration of the Soviet aviation industry, Ilyushin stayed at this bureau, which was named after him, until 1976. Its most famous product was the Il-2/Il-10 attack aircraft, built in greater numbers than any other airplane in history.

HUGHES H-4 HERCULES, NICKNAMED "SPRUCE GOOSE"

AMY JOHNSON

J

AMY JOHNSON
1903–1941

Born in Hull, England, Amy Johnson was working as a stenographer when she joined the London Aeroplane Club in 1928. She became the first licensed female ground mechanic in England, and qualified as a pilot in July 1929. The following year she made a remarkable solo flight from England to Australia in 19½ days, flying a de Havilland D.H.60 Moth. In July 1933 she flew across the Atlantic with her husband, Scottish pilot Jim Mollison, in a D.H.84 Dragon. The next year the couple flew a D.H.88 Comet racer in the MacRobertson England–Australia race, setting record times for the flights between England and Iraq and England and India, but they later had to retire from the race. They divorced in 1937. Johnson joined the Air Transport Auxiliary in World War II and was drowned when the Airspeed Oxford she was ferrying ditched in the Thames estuary in January 1941.

CLARENCE LEONARD JOHNSON
1910–1990

American aircraft designer "Kelly" Johnson was responsible for many outstanding aeroplanes during more than 40 years at Lockheed. Awarded a degree in aeronautical engineering by the University of Michigan in 1932, he joined Lockheed in the

following year. By 1938 he was chief research engineer. Among the 40 aircraft he designed for the company were the P-38 Lightning fighter, the Constellation airliner, the P-80 Shooting Star jet fighter, the F-104 Starfighter, and the U-2, YF-12A, and SR-71 high-altitude reconnaissance aircraft. Johnson retired in 1975.

PROFESSOR HUGO JUNKERS
1859–1935

HUGO JUNKERS

Born in Düsseldorf, Germany, and trained as an engineer, future aircraft manufacturer Hugo Junkers founded his first company in 1895, and in 1897 was appointed professor of thermodynamics at Aachen High School. In 1910 he patented an all-metal, all-wing airplane – the twin

engines, crew, and passengers were to be housed within the wings. He built the first Junkers all-metal airplane, using steel, in 1915, and the first light-alloy machine the following year. In 1919 he founded the Junkers Flugzeugwerke where, using experience gained with his military designs in World War I, he produced a series of all-metal airliners with distinctive corrugated skinning, including the renowned Ju 52/3m trimotor. Junkers also inaugurated an internal German air service, in 1921. Junkers' company built the Ju 87 Stuka dive-bomber, perhaps its most famous airplane, after his retirement in 1932.

K

ALEXANDER KARTVELI
1896–1974

Aircraft designer Alexander Kartveli was born in Russia but studied engineering at l'École Supérieure d'Aéronautique in Paris, France. He returned to Russia, but fled in the wake of the 1917 revolution. After working for Blériot and Fokker, he finally settled with Seversky in the US in 1934. He became chief engineer of newly formed Republic Aircraft in 1939, a post he held

until 1960. Here he led the design of Seversky's P-35 advanced monoplane fighter and its successors, the P-43 and the Republic P-47 Thunderbolt. After World War II he headed the design of several successful jet fighters, such as the F-84 Thunderjet and the F-105 Thunderchief.

SIR CHARLES KINGSFORD SMITH
1897–1935

Born in Brisbane, Australia, Charles Kingsford Smith began his flying career as a pilot in the RFC (Royal Flying Corps) during World War I. After the war he joined Western Australian Airways. In 1928 he made the first flight across the Pacific, from the US to Australia, in the Fokker F.VIIb-3m *Southern Cross*. He also made the first non-stop flight across Australia, and the first Australia–New Zealand flight. In 1929 he formed Australian National Airways. The following year he flew solo in an Avro Avian from England to Darwin in a record 10½ days. In 1934 he made the first single-engined transpacific flight, from Australia to the US, in a Lockheed Altair. During an England–Australia flight in 1935 his Altair disappeared off Burma; Kingsford Smith and his companion were never found.

CHARLES KINGSFORD SMITH (SECOND FROM RIGHT)

FREDERIK KOOLHOVEN
1886–1946

Dutch engineer "Frits" Koolhoven learnt to fly at the Hanriot school in France, and won his pilot's brevet in 1910. In 1912 "Kully" joined the Deperdussin company as a designer under Louis Béchereau. He was chief engineer at the company's British offshoot when Deperdussin collapsed in 1913. He then moved to Armstrong Whitworth's new aircraft department, where as chief designer he developed the F.K.3 and F.K.8 reconnaissance aircraft. In 1917 he joined British Aerial Transport, designing several military and civil aircraft. After BAT's closure in 1920 he returned to the Netherlands as designer for the Nationale Vliegtuig-industrie until 1926, when he became a freelance consultant. In 1934 he formed his own company, Koolhoven Vliegtuigen, which produced a wide range of aircraft until it was destroyed by bombing in 1940.

DOCTOR FREDERICK WILLIAM LANCHESTER
1868–1946

British engineer and inventor Dr. Frederick Lanchester is probably best remembered for his role in the development of the automobile – he built the first British motor car in 1895. But Lanchester was also a pioneer of aeronautics. He tested numerous model gliders in the 1890s and established the concepts that formed the basis of the modern theory of lift and drag as early as 1894. His theories were beyond the comprehension of most of his contemporaries, but received wider recognition when they appeared in his two volumes on *Aerial Flight*, published in 1907 and 1908. From 1909 to 1920 he was a member of the British government's Advisory Committee for Aeronautics.

SAMUEL PIERPONT LANGLEY
1834–1906

Born in Roxbury, Massachusetts, astronomer Samuel P. Langley was one of the America's foremost aviation pioneers. He first became interested in aeronautics while he was working at the Allegheny Observatory in Pennsylvania, and built a whirling arm to test airfoils. In 1887 he became Secretary of the Smithsonian Institution in Washington, D.C., where he continued his experiments, constructing more than 100 rubber-powered models, and then building much larger models powered by steam engines. His "Aerodromes" Nos. 5 and 6 made outstanding flights in 1896, and the government granted him $50,000 to develop a manned airplane. Sadly, the two catapult launches his machine made from a houseboat on the Potomac river in 1903 were disastrous failures. Public ridicule and the government's loss of interest in his projects hastened Langley's death.

SAMUEL P. LANGLEY

SYEMYEN ALEKSEYEVICH LAVOCHKIN
1900–1960

Responsible for developing some of the Soviet Union's best World War II fighters, Syemyen Lavochkin was born in Smolensk, Russia. He entered Moscow Technical High School in 1920 to study engineering, and later specialized in aviation. After working at the Central Construction Bureau and the Bureau of Special Design, he became a senior engineer at the Chief Administration of the Aviation Industry in the early 1930s. Here Lavochkin became convinced that plastic-impregnated birch laminates could be used in airframes, to save steel and light alloys. In 1938 he set up a bureau with V.P. Gorbunov and M.I. Gudkov to build fighters. The LAGG La-5 and its derivatives proved highly effective during World War II. In the postwar jet era the bureau was unable to compete with its rivals, and was disbanded in 1960.

JEAN-MARIE LE BRIS
1808–1872

A courageous and ingenious retired French sea captain, Jean-Marie Le Bris tested two full-size gliders based on the albatross. In his first glider he made one short glide from a towed launch at Trefeuntec (c.1857), but broke his leg while attempting a second, untowed launch in a quarry. The second machine, which was tested near Brest in 1868 with ballast instead of a human pilot, also flew before crashing. Le Bris, who was killed in a brawl in 1872, had an inspirational influence on the later French aviation pioneers.

LEONARDO DA VINCI
1452–1519

A universal genius, Leonardo was the first man of science to investigate the problems of flight. Most of his aircraft designs were of flapping-wing machines (ornithopters) that copied the perceived actions of birds and bats, but he also devised a helicopter and a parachute (though not the first). His ideas on flight were constantly hampered by two misconceptions: firstly that man's skill and muscle-power could enable him to imitate the birds, and secondly that birds propelled themselves by beating their wings downward and backward. His most productive aeronautical period was 1482–99, when he designed a range of ornithopters with prone or standing pilots, and even an early hangglider. Sadly, because his manuscripts were inaccessible until the late nineteenth century, his work had no direct influence upon the early development of aviation.

LÉON LEVAVASSEUR
1863–1921

One of France's outstanding early aircraft designers, Léon Levavasseur studied art before his fascination with new technology prompted him to become an engineer. He built his first airplane, with government sponsorship, at Puteaux, Paris, in 1903. The aircraft was a failure, but its 80-hp engine – also designed by Levavasseur and named Antoinette after his partner's daughter – was highly advanced. In 1905 he made 8- and 16-cylinder versions of up to 100 hp. In May 1906, with Capt Ferdinand Ferber, he founded the Société Antoinette, which built a range of Levavasseur-designed monoplanes at its Puteaux factory.

OTTO LILIENTHAL
1848–1896

Prussian mechanical engineer Otto Lilienthal had a profound influence on the development of flight. He first experimented with ornithopters (flapping-wing machines) and in 1889 published his classic book *Bird Flight as the Basis of Aviation*. He then turned to fixed-wing hang gliders, flying his first in 1891. From then until 1896 he built 12 gliders, including both monoplanes and biplanes, the most successful of which was his No. 11 "standard" monoplane of 1894. This became the first aircraft to be built in quantity, since at least eight were made for other experimenters around the world. Lilienthal made more than 1,000 flights. On August 9, 1896, while flying near Stölln, Germany, his glider stalled and crashed; he died from his injuries the following day.

OTTO LILIENTHAL

CHARLES AUGUSTUS LINDBERGH
1902–1974

American pilot Charles Lindbergh was the first man to fly solo non-stop across the Atlantic. The son of a Minnesota congressman, he went to engineering college but, finding it boring, left in 1922 to learn to fly. After two years with as a barnstormer he joined the US Army Air Corps, and in 1926 became an airmail pilot. During this time he twice had to bail out of an airplane during bad weather. He then set his sights on the $25,000 Orteig prize for the first nonstop flight from New York to Paris. Backed by businessmen from St. Louis, Missouri, he had a mono-plane, *The Spirit of St. Louis*, built by Ryan, and on May 20–21, 1927, accomplished the Paris flight solo, winning worldwide fame. Despite the kidnap and murder of their infant son in 1932, he and his wife, Anne Morrow, continued to pioneer air routes. His campaign to keep the US out of World War II later harmed his reputation, but he returned to favor through active participation in the war effort after the Japanese attack on Pearl Harbor. Postwar he worked as a technical adviser to the airline Pan Am.

CHARLES LINDBERGH

ALLAN HAINES LOCKHEED
1889–1969

Born with the last name Loughhead, this American aircraft manufacturer adopted Lockheed as a corporate name in 1926 before legally taking it as his own name in 1934. Allan Loughhead was working as a car mechanic in Chicago in 1910 when he taught himself to fly in a Curtiss belonging to his employer. He then started building his own airplanes. On returning to his native California in 1913, he formed the Alco Hydro-Aeroplane Co. with his brother Malcolm. This company built only one flying machine. In 1916 the brothers formed Loughhead Aircraft, which struggled on until 1921. In 1926 Allan Loughhead

PROFESSOR ALEXANDER MARTIN LIPPISCH
1894–1976

Professor Alexander Lippisch began his career in Germany in the 1920s designing sailplanes. He first gained recognition for his research into tailless aircraft and rocket propulsion, which he began around 1928. After working for the German Sailplane Research Institute, Lippisch joined Messerschmitt in 1939, and was largely responsible for the Me 163 Komet rocket-propelled bomber interceptor used by the Luftwaffe in World War II. He then began investigating supersonic delta wings, and after the war continued his researches in the US. Before his death Lippisch worked on the Rhein Flugzeugbau X-113AM surface skimmer.

relaunched the firm with the help of designer John Northrop as the Lockheed Aircraft Co., building Northrop's handsome streamlined Vega monoplane. In 1932 Lockheed was sold to an investment group and went on to become one of the US's leading aircraft manufacturers. Lockheed's own businesses did not fare so well: Loughhead Brothers Aircraft Corp, founded in 1930, failed, as did Alcor, founded in 1937.

GROVER CLEVELAND LOENING
1888–1976

American aircraft manufacturer Grover Loening was born in the German port of Bremen, where his father was US Consul General. He graduated from Columbia University in 1908 with the first US master's degree in aeronautical science. In 1911 he joined the Queen Aircraft Corp of New York, moving in 1913 to manage Orville Wright's Dayton plant. After holding senior posts in the US Army Aviation Section, he founded the Loening Aeronautical Corp in 1917, building landplanes and amphibians. When the company merged with Curtiss-Wright in 1928 he left to start the Grover Loening Aircraft Co, which built small naval and civil amphibians until 1936. During World War II he advised the US government on aviation matters.

SIR HIRAM STEVENS MAXIM
1840–1916

Best known for the machine gun that bears his name, Hiram Maxim was born in Maine, but settled in England in 1881. In 1888 his

confidence and mechanical skills led backers to put up £20,000 over five years towards developing an airplane. In 1890 he began the construction of a massive biplane test-rig at Baldwyn's Park in Kent. Powered by two 180-hp Maxim steam engines turning propellers 17 ft 10 in (5.5 m) in diameter, it had an untried and inadequate control system. When it was tested on July 31, 1894, the biplane lifted from its running rails but fouled the upper restraining rails. It was badly damaged, and after this was used only for demonstration runs. A brief association with British pioneer Percy Pilcher in 1896–97 came to naught, and Maxim's final attempt to build an airplane in 1910 resulted in an impractical and unflown biplane.

JAMES SMITH McDONNELL
1899–1980

James McDonnell, the founder of one of America's most successful aircraft corporations, was born in Denver, Colorado. He graduated from Princeton University in 1921 and gained a degree in aeronautical engineering at the Massachusetts Institute of Technology in 1925, by which time he had won his wings with the Army Air Service. He worked for numerous US aircraft companies, eventually becoming chief project engineer of landplanes with the Glenn L. Martin Co. In 1938 he resigned and formed the McDonnell Aircraft Corp. This expanded greatly in the course of World War II and subsequently built a series of highly successful military jet aircraft, including the world's first carrier-borne jet fighter, the FH-1 Phantom. In 1967 the company merged with Douglas Aircraft to create the McDonnell Douglas Corp.

McDONNELL FH-1 PHANTOM

PROFESSOR WILLY EMIL MESSERSCHMITT
1898–1978

Famous German aircraft designer Willy Messerschmitt was born in Frankfurt-am-Main, and built his first full-size gliders with an architect friend in 1913. Exempted from military service during World War I due to poor health, he attended the Munich Institute of Technology and after the war founded his own aircraft company in 1923. Three years later he set up an arrangement under which the aircraft he designed were built by BFW (Bayerische Flugzeug-werke). True success came with the Bf 108 cabin monoplane and the Bf 109 fighter, which went on to become one of the greatest fighters of World War II. BFW was renamed in 1938 as Messerschmitt AG, and produced the Me 262 jet fighter toward the end of the war. After the war Messerschmitt went to Argentina, but he returned to Germany in the 1950s. In 1965 he purchased the Junkers organization, which became MBB (Messerschmitt-Bölkow-Blohm) in 1969.

WILLY MESSERCHMITT

ARTYEM IVANOVICH MIKOYAN
1905–1970

Armenian-born Soviet aircraft designer Artyem Mikoyan entered the Frunze Military Academy after joining the Red Army and moved to the Zhukovskii Air Force Academy in 1930. After graduating he joined Nikolai Polikarpov's brigade to work on the I-153 fighter, before being chosen to lead an experimental design section (OKO) in 1939. With Mikhail Guryevich, he worked on the Kh high-altitude interceptor, and then on a series of World War II fighters, designated MiG for Mikoyan and Guryevich. After the war Mikoyan produced jet fighters, notably the MiG-15, -17, -19, and -21. He was head of the bureau until his death.

MIKHAIL LEONTYEVICH MIL
1909–1970

A leading pioneer of rotary-wing flight in the Soviet Union, Mikhail Mil was born in Siberia. After graduating from the Novochyerkassk Aviation Institute in 1931 he joined Aleksandr Izakson's brigade at the Central Aero- and Hydrodynamic Institute (CAHI), where he worked as chief designer of the A-15 autogyro rotating-wing aircraft. In 1936 he became deputy chief designer to Nikolai Kamov, and during World War II flew Kamov-developed A-7 autogyros at the front. Mil was appointed head of CAHI's rotating-wing laboratory in 1945, but left two years later to form his own design bureau. The helicopters it produced included the Mi-1, Mi-4, and Mi-10, and the V-12, the largest helicopter ever.

REGINALD JOSEPH MITCHELL
1895–1937

Designer of Britain's most famous World War II fighter, the Spitfire, Reginald Mitchell was born in Stoke-on-Trent, England. He served a five-year apprenticeship with a locomotive engineering firm before joining the Supermarine Aviation Works at Southampton in 1917. Within two years he was appointed chief designer, developing a line of successful flying boats and seaplanes. Mitchell's S.5 and S.6 seaplanes ultimately won the Schneider Trophy for Britain. When Vickers acquired Supermarine in 1928, it was largely to gain Mitchell's skills. His masterpiece, the Spitfire, first flew in 1936. Adopted by the RAF (Royal Air Force), it proved to be a potent fighter, serving throughout World War II.

JAMES ALLAN MOLLISON
1905–1959

Born in Scotland and educated at Glasgow Academy, "Jim" Mollison took a commission in the RAF (Royal Air Force) in 1923, and underwent an advanced pilot's course at the Central Flying School in 1927. Transferred to the RAF Reserve in 1928, he became an instructor at the Australian Aero Club in Adelaide, and then worked with Kingsford Smith at Australian National Airways. In 1931, flying a Moth, Mollison set a record for a solo Australia–England flight. Changing to a cabin Puss Moth, he then set an England–Cape Town record in 1932, and later that year was the first to fly the Atlantic solo from east to west. In 1933, after marrying Amy Johnson, he made a solo flight over the South Atlantic, and also flew across the Atlantic with his wife. In 1936, flying solo from Newfoundland to Croydon, England, he set a new transatlantic record of 13 hours 17 minutes. During World War II he served in the Air Transport Auxiliary.

J.A. MOLLISON

LÉON AND ROBERT CHARLES MORANE
1885–1918, 1886–1968

The Morane brothers played an important role in the development of France's aviation industry. After working as a manager for Louis Blériot, in 1911 Léon Morane set up an aircraft company with his brother Robert, designer Raymond Saulnier, and Gabriel Borel. The Morane-Borel-Saulnier company built two monoplanes before Borel left in October 1911. Renamed Morane-Saulnier, the company went on to produce a successful family of monoplanes and biplanes, some of which saw service in World War I. After Léon's death in 1918 the company concentrated on parasol-winged, radial-engined fighters and trainers, and in the late 1930s produced the MS.405 and 406 fighters. After World War II the company built light aircraft. It was taken over by Potez in 1963.

R.J. MITCHELL (CENTER FRONT) WITH 1927 SCHNEIDER TROPHY GROUP

ALEKSANDR FEDOROVICH MOZHAISKII
1825–1890

Born in the St. Petersburg region, Russian aviation pioneer Alexsandr Mozhaiskii trained as a naval cadet, although he also had an education in engineering. He served in the Baltic, the Sea of Japan, and the Crimea, and finished his naval service as a captain in 1873. He was given a civil post in the Ukraine, where he pursued an interest in bird flight and kite flying. After his return to St. Petersburg in 1876 he began constructing a large monoplane powered by two English-designed and -built steam engines. In the summer of 1884, at Krasnoe Selo near St. Petersburg, the monoplane was launched down a ramp with a mechanic at the helm, but it crashed after a short hop. Work on a modified version was discontinued in 1887.

ÉDOUARD DE NIEUPORT
1875–1911

Born in French Algiers and trained as an engineer, Édouard de Nieuport (originally Niéport) set up a business making spark plugs and magnetos. After supplying electrical equipment for Henry Farman's Voisin biplane, in 1908 he founded his first aircraft company, building a monoplane. The company failed, but in 1910 he set up a successor, SA des Etablissements Nieuport, at Issy, Paris, to make fast monoplanes. In September 1911 he set a world speed record in one of these planes. Later that month he was killed during a demonstration flight, but his company went on to build some of France's best World War I fighters under the leadership of Henri Deutsche de la Meurthe.

JOHN DUDLEY NORTH
1893–1968

British aircraft engineer and designer John North was originally a marine engineering apprentice, but his apprenticeship was transferred to the Aeronautical Syndicate and, when that firm failed, to the Grahame-White company, where he rose to be chief engineer. He designed a number of airplanes for Grahame-White between 1912 and 1915, and then became superintendent of the Austin Motor Co.'s aviation department. At the end of 1917 he joined Boulton & Paul in Norwich as chief engineer and designer. Among the many aircraft he was involved with at Boulton & Paul were the Sidestrand and Overstrand bombers, the R101 airship, and the Defiant two-seat fighter. By the time North retired in 1954 he was the company's managing director and chairman.

JOHN KNUDSEN NORTHROP
1895–1981

American aircraft manufacturer "Jack" Northrop was born in New Jersey. He began his aviation career with the Loughhead brothers in 1916, and then moved in 1923 to Douglas, where he worked on the World Cruiser design. Three years later he was back with Allan Loughhead, becoming a cofounder of the Lockheed Aircraft Company. Northrop designed the Lockheed Vega monoplane with Gerry Vultee, but in 1927 he left to form the Avion Corp to explore all-metal aircraft structures. In 1932, with Donald Douglas, he formed the Northrop Corp, which produced a series of high-speed all-metal monoplanes. The corporation became the El Segundo division of Douglas in 1937, but Northrop continued to make a significant contribution in devising new construction methods. In 1939 Northrop formed his own independent company, Northrop Aircraft, where he remained as a director until 1952 and designed the XB-35 flying-wing bomber.

DR HANS VON OHAIN
1911–1998

Born in Dessau, Germany, Hans von Ohain studied at the University of Göttingen, where he conceived of a propulsion system for aircraft based on the turbojet. His work came to the attention of Ernst Heinkel who provided finance and facilities for further research, and then in 1936 employed him and his assistant, Max Hahn. The first demonstration engine was running by September 1937, and on August 27, 1939, the Heinkel He 178, powered by an HeS 3b engine, became the first airplane to fly solely under turbojet power. Von Ohain went on to develop the new 011 jet engine with BMW and Junkers, but the project was abandoned at the war's end. Postwar he went to the US as a researcher at Wright-Patterson Air Force Base. In 1963 he became chief scientist at the aerospace research laboratories there, and in 1975 he was appointed chief scientist of the base's Aero Propulsion Laboratory.

SIR FREDERICK HANDLEY PAGE
1885–1962

Often referred to simply as "HP," prominent aircraft manufacturer Frederick Handley Page was born in Cheltenham, England, and trained as an electrical engineer at Finsbury

SIR FREDERICK HANDLEY PAGE

Technical College, London. In 1906 he became chief product designer for a large electrical manufacturing company, but his true love was aviation. He experimented with models and worked with José Wiess on his tailless airplanes before setting up his own aircraft company in 1909. His first really successful airplane, the Type E of 1911, was followed by the famous O/400 and V/1500 giant bombers of World War I. In the interwar years the company designed a series of airliners and bombers, and then produced the Hampden and Halifax bombers during World War II. After the war Handley Page continued to produce notable designs, such as the Hastings transport and the Victor jet bomber, but HP's refusal to merge his company precipitated its collapse in 1970.

JOHN KNUDSEN NORTHROP'S
XB-35 FLYING-WING BOMBER

POTEZ 25

PERCY SINCLAIR PILCHER
1867–1899

British pioneer Percy Pilcher was born in Bath, England, and served in the Royal Navy from 1880 to 1887. He then found work in the shipbuilding industry and as an assistant lecturer at Glasgow University, during which time he became fascinated by the pioneering flights of Otto Lilienthal. In 1895 Pilcher built his first hang-glider, the Bat, which was moderately successful. He quickly followed this by building the Beetle, the Gull, and then the Hawk, which was flown at Eynsford in Kent after Pilcher joined Hiram Maxim there in 1896. He continued flying the Hawk (usually under tow) in 1897; but in 1898, influenced by Octave Chanute's multiplane glider, he designed a triplane into which he planned to install a small gasoline engine. However, shortly after this machine was completed, and before it was flown, the Hawk collapsed while Pilcher was demonstrating it on September 30, 1899. He died of his injuries two days later.

RHEINHOLD PLATZ
1886–1966

Born in Brandenburg, Germany, Reinhold Platz played a key role in the success of the Fokker airplane company. Platz learnt the technique of autogenous welding in a Berlin oxygen factory in 1904, and taught the skill in many European factories before joining Fokker Aeroplanbau in 1912. He persuaded Anthony Fokker to adopt a steel-tube fuselage structure that combined strength and lightness with ease of construction. The two men developed a close working relationship that produced Fokker's outstanding range of World War I fighters. For much of the war Platz was in charge of the workshop, tasked with making and testing the aircraft parts. Promoted to designer in 1916, he remained with Fokker until 1931, and was instrumental in developing Fokker's interwar monoplane airliners.

NIKOLAI NIKOLAYEVICH POLIKARPOV
1892–1944

The creator of almost all Soviet fighter, trainer, and reconnaissance aircraft built up to 1941, Nikolai Polikarpov graduated from St. Petersburg Polytechnic Institute as an aeronautical engineer in 1916. He worked on Il'ya Mouramets aircraft until 1918, when he joined the former Duks plant as chief engineer. In 1926 he became director of the department of experimental aircraft construction at State Aviation Factory 25. In 1929 Stalin accused him of sabotaging the Soviet aviation program. Arrested along with his entire design team, he created the I-5 fighter in the prison design office at State Aviation Factory 39. Released in 1933, Polikarpov was the chief landplane designer for the Central Construction Bureau before forming his own design bureau in 1937. Aircraft produced by Polikarpov's bureau included the I-16 monoplane fighter and the NB bomber. The bureau was closed after his death.

WILEY POST
1898–1935

The first man to fly solo around the world, Wiley Post was born in Texas, and learned mechanics at school in Kansas. While working in an oilfield he lost an eye in a drilling accident and used the insurance money to buy an airplane. After learning to fly, Post became the personal pilot of F.C. Hall, a rich oilman, who in 1931 offered to back an attempt on an around-the-world flight. Flying Hall's Lockheed Vega *Winnie Mae*, Post set off on June 23 that year with navigator Harold Gatty and completed the circumnavigation in 8 days, 15 hours, 51 minutes. Post capped this in 1933 by making the flight solo in the same airplane in less time. The next year he began experimenting with pressure suits and supercharged engines to attain high-altitude flight. Post was killed in an air crash in Alaska while flying to Russia with humorist Will Rogers in 1935.

HENRY CHARLES ALEXANDRE POTEZ
1891–1981

Born in Meaulte, France, Henry Potez designed his first airplane in 1911 after graduating from the École Supérieure d'Aéronautique.

Serving as a technical assistant to French aviation officers during World War I, he met Marcel Bloch, the future founder of Avions Marcel Dassault. Potez and Bloch designed and marketed an improved propeller, and in 1916 formed SEA (Société d'Études Aéronautiques) to build aircraft. The company's finances collapsed in 1919, but Potez then formed Aéroplanes Henry Potez, which built many successful designs, including the Potez 25 military two-seater. The firm was nationalized in 1936 and became part of Société Nationale de Constructions Aéronautiques du Nord, with Potez as head of the group. In 1953 he founded the Société des Avions et Moteurs Henry Potez, which was taken over by Sud-Aviation in 1967.

WILEY POST WITH LOCKHEED VEGA *WINNIE MAE*

ZYGMUNT PULAWSKI
1901–1931

Born in Lublin, Poland, Zygmunt Pulawski designed his first aircraft, the S.L.3 glider, while studying at the Warsaw Technical University. He also entered a design for a two-seat army-support biplane in the 1924 Polish War Ministry combat aircraft design competition, and tied for fourth place. This enabled Pulawski, upon graduation in 1925, to further his technical education in France, where he worked for Louis Breguet. Returning to Poland, he passed through the Polish military pilots school and in 1928 joined the new Panstwowe Zaklady Lotnicze (PZL – "State Aviation Factory"). His first design for PZL, the P.1 interceptor monoplane, had a highly original wing design and was very advanced for its time. Subsequent developments of this aircraft produced a successful series of fighters that culminated in the highly maneuverable P-11s, with which the Polish Air Force valiantly faced the German Luftwaffe in 1939. Pulawski never lived to see this. He died on March 21, 1931, while testing a light amphibious aircraft he had designed – the aircraft suffered a control malfunction and crashed.

R

SIR ALLIOTT VERDON ROE
1877–1958

Born in Manchester, England, the aircraft manufacturer Alliott Roe was the founder of Avro. He began his career as an apprentice to the Lancashire and Yorkshire Railway Locomotive Works. After studying marine engineering at King's College, London, he worked as an engineer for the British and South African Royal Mail Co. and in the automobile industry before seizing the chance to work on an ambitious "Gyropter" for G.L.O. Davidson in 1906. An enthusiastic builder of

model aircraft, in 1907 Roe began building a full-size biplane based on one of his models. This machine achieved brief tentative hops when tested at Brooklands, but it was not until 1910 that Roe began to make significant flights, in a triplane of his own design. Later that year he formed A.V. Roe & Co., soon renamed Avro. With the appearance of the Type 504 in 1913, which was used both as a bomber and a trainer during World War I, the business flourished, eventually growing into one of Britain's greatest aircraft manufacturers. When Armstrong Siddeley acquired a controlling interest in Avro in 1928, Roe bought into S.E. Saunders, which became Saunders-Roe and was noted for its flying-boat designs. He remained its president until his death in 1958.

ADOLF KARL ROHRBACH
1889–1939

A pioneer of all-metal aircraft, German designer Adolf Rohrbach earned a diploma in shipbuilding at Darmstadt Technical University and worked for the Blohm & Voss

SIR ALLIOTT VERDON ROE

shipyard in Hamburg before he became involved in aviation. In 1914 he joined the Zeppelin works at Friedrichshafen, where he met Claude Dornier and worked on large seaplanes. In 1917 he was transferred to Zeppelin's Staaken plant as a designer, and in 1919 he succeeded Prof. Alexander Baumann as chief designer. In this role he was responsible for producing the remarkable E.4/20 four-engined all-metal monoplane airliner. After receiving a doctorate in 1921, Rohrbach founded the Rohrbach Metallflugzeugbau in 1922. In order to overcome the restrictions on the construction of aircraft in Germany imposed by the Treaty of Versailles, he also set up Rohrbach Metall-Aeroplan Co A/S in Copenhagen, Denmark. These companies produced a range of Rohrbach's landplanes and flying boats up until 1934, when Weser took the company over. Rohrbach was retained as technical director.

S

ALBERTO SANTOS-DUMONT
1873–1932

A pioneer of both airships and airplanes, Alberto Santos-Dumont was born in Brazil but conducted his experiments in France. Inspired by gas balloons during a family visit to Paris in 1891, he took up ballooning himself in 1897 and embarked on dirigible construction, building no fewer than 12 lighter-than-air flying machines by 1907. During this period he won the 100,000-franc Deutsch prize in 1901 by flying his No. 6 airship from the Paris suburb of St. Cloud to circle the Eiffel Tower. In 1905 he also began designing heavier-than-air powered airplanes. On November 12, 1906, in his No. 14*bis*, a cumbersome canard (tail-first) biplane, he made the first powered flights in Europe. His most successful aircraft were a pair of diminutive high-wing monoplanes, the No. 19 and its development, the No. 20 *Demoiselle* – the world's first light airplanes. In 1910, at the age of 37, Santos-Dumont developed multiple sclerosis

ALBERTO SANTOS-DUMONT

and was forced to give up flying. Depressed by the development of airplanes as a weapon of war in Europe, he returned to Brazil and had nothing further to do with aviation. He killed himself in 1932.

RAYMOND SAULNIER
1881–1964

One of France's most distinguished aircraft designers, Raymond Saulnier graduated as an engineer from the École Centrale in Paris in 1905 and was then drafted into the artillery. Following this military service and a trip to Brazil, he joined the Blériot company as an engineer in 1908. Here he worked on several aircraft designs, including the original Blériot XI monoplane in which Louis Blériot carried out his epoch-making cross-Channel flight in 1909. That same year he left Blériot, formed the Société des Aéroplanes Saulnier, and designed and built a monoplane of his own. His company went bankrupt in 1910. After a brief association with Gabriel Borel, he formed Morane-Saulnier with the Morane brothers in 1911. This company established its reputation with a series of high-performance Saulnier-designed monoplanes, which served in World War I.

LOUIS AND LAURENT SEGUIN
1869–1918, 1883–1944

The Seguin brothers' involvement in engine design began in 1895, when Louis Seguin founded an engine manufacturing business in Paris, France. Ten years later, when his half-brother, Laurent, joined him, they reorganized the company to build small automobile engines, naming it the Société des Moteurs Gnôme. That year, Laurent told Louis that they should design a "rotative motor for the developing field of aviation." Although similar rotary engines, in which radially disposed cylinders revolved around a stationary crankshaft, had been used in cars and motorcycles, they had never been applied to a full-size aircraft. The Seguins' first rotative engines were built in 1908, and seven-cylinder 50-hp Gnomes for airplanes went into production the following year. These engines were extremely successful as they had exceptional power-to-weight ratios for their time and did not need radiators. They continued to be developed throughout World War I.

ALEXANDER PROKOFIEFF DE SEVERSKY
1894–1974

A company founder and promoter of air power, Alexander Seversky was born into a wealthy Russian family in Tbilisi, Georgia. He graduated from the Imperial Russian Naval Academy in 1914, and then studied engineering at the Military School of Aeronautics in Sebastopol. In 1915 he joined the Baltic Sea Naval Air Service, and lost a leg after he was forced to ditch his damaged aircraft

and its bombs exploded. He returned to the front within a year, flying with an artificial leg, and rose to the rank of commander. In 1917 he was sent to the US as vice-chairman of the Russian Naval Aviation Commission. The Russian Revolution made him decide to stay in America. In 1921 he developed a new bombsight, and used the $50,000 that the American government paid for the patent rights to set up the Seversky Aero Corp (which later became Republic Aviation). As president and general manager he oversaw the production of the P-35 fighter, which later evolved into the P-47 Thunderbolt. Published in 1942, Seversky's book *Victory Through Air Power* proved a bestseller, and in 1945 he was appointed special consultant to the American Secretary of War.

HORACE LEONARD, ALBERT EUSTACE, AND HUGH OSWALD SHORT
1872–1917, 1875–1932, 1883–1969

British manufacturers of a string of successful aircraft, the Short brothers' interest in aviation began in 1897 when Eustace and Oswald bought a balloon and learned to fly it. By 1900 the two brothers were constructing balloons at a factory in Paris, France, belonging to Édouard Surcouf. They then returned to England and set up their own balloon factory. In 1908 the third brother, Horace, joined the business and together they embarked on airplane construction. In 1909 the Short brothers were contracted to build six Wright biplanes under license. By the outbreak of World War I their company had become well established and was building

its own designs. In particular, Short Brothers gained a reputation for marine airplanes, the most notable of these being the Type 184 seaplane of 1915–18 and the Empire flying boats built for Imperial Airways in the late 1930s. The Short Brothers company still survived at the end of the twentieth century under the umbrella of Bombardier of Canada.

IGOR IVANOVICH SIKORSKY
1889–1972

An important pioneer of rotary flight, Igor Sikorsky was born in Kiev, Ukraine, then part of the Russian Empire. After graduating from Kiev Polytechnical Institute, he built his first helicopters in 1908 and 1910, but their failure led him to turn to airplanes. His S-6 of 1911–12 won the first prize in a competition sponsored by the Russian armed forces and he was made designer at the new aviation department of the Russo-Baltic Wagon Works. In 1911 Sikorsky conceived a large four-engined airplane, the *Bolshoi Baltiiskiy*, which first flew in 1913 and sired the Il'ya Mouramets bombers of World War I. After the Bolsheviks took power in Russia in the 1917 revolution, Sikorsky emigrated to the US, where he founded the Sikorsky Aero Engineering Corp in 1923. After building several successful amphibians and flying boats, in 1939 he reverted to designing helicopters, eventually achieving practical flights in his VS-300, from which a great family of helicopters evolved. Sikorsky retired in 1957 but remained an engineering consultant to the company until his death.

SIR THOMAS OCTAVE MURDOCH SOPWITH
1888–1989

SIR THOMAS SOPWITH

British pilot and company founder "Tom" Sopwith was born in London. Trained as a civil engineer, he took up ballooning in 1906 and in 1910 taught himself to fly airplanes. By the end of that year he had set new British distance and duration records in a Howard Wright biplane. After establishing his reputation as a top sporting pilot, he set up the Sopwith Flying School at Brooklands in 1912. He then embarked on aircraft design and construction, founding the Sopwith Aviation Company, which produced its first airplane in 1913. A victory by a Sopwith Tabloid in the 1914 Schneider Trophy contest was followed by the production of a string of famous World War I fighters, such as the 1½ Strutter, Pup, and Camel. After the war the company went into voluntary liquidation. Sopwith then formed the H.G. Hawker Engineering Co., renamed Hawker Aircraft Ltd in 1933, by which time Sopwith was joint managing director. When the company became Hawker Siddeley Aircraft in 1935, he was in overall control. He retired as chairman in 1963, but retained the honorary position of president.

IGOR IVANOVICH SIKORSKY FLYING HIS VS-300

SUKHOI SU-24 VARIABLE-GEOMETRY FIGHTER

DR. ELMER AND LAWRENCE BURST SPERRY
1860–1930, 1892–1923

In 1913 American engineer Elmer Sperry developed a gyroscopic stabilizer for aircraft. In the same year, his son Lawrence took a job at the Curtiss flying school and was the project engineer for the installation of his father's gyro-stabilization system there. In 1914 he demonstrated the system in Paris, France, by flying a Curtiss flying boat hands-off. The success of these trials prompted his

LAWRENCE SPERRY

father to carry on with his work. Elmer Sperry subsequently invented the directional gyro, gyro horizon, and drift indicator. His son also won a reputation as a designer. During World War I he devised a retractable undercarriage and a flying bomb. He then went on to develop the Messenger biplane after the war. During a European sales tour in 1923 he ditched in the English Channel; although the plane was recovered, he was never found.

WILLIAM BUSHNELL STOUT
1880–1956

Born in Illinois, "Bill" Stout studied engineering at the University of Minnesota. He became aviation editor of the *Chicago Tribune* in 1912 and then founded the magazine *Aerial Age*. He was a consultant to the US Aircraft Production Board during World War I, and after the war his Stout Engineering Laboratories constructed the *Batwing*, a cantilever monoplane. Stout then developed a twin-engined, all-metal monoplane for the US Navy and wrote to 100 businessmen asking each of them to contribute $1,000 to help him set up the Stout Metal Airplane Co. Among those who contributed was Henry Ford, who bought the company in 1925. Stout left the company before the first Ford Tri-Motor monoplanes appeared in 1928, but he resurrected the Stout Engineering Laboratories in 1929, producing the Sky Car monoplane.

JOHN STRINGFELLOW
1799–1883

Born near Sheffield, England, John Stringfellow became involved with William Henson's aeronautical experiments in the 1840s. Relying on his manufacturing experience as a lacemaker, he designed and built ingenious light steam engines for Henson's large model airplanes, one of which was tested near Chard, Somerset, in 1847. Although the model failed to fly, Stringfellow carried on the work after Henson's departure for America. He built and tested an improved Henson-type monoplane in 1848, and a triplane model in 1868 – neither of which managed to achieve sustained powered flight. The triplane's engine, however, won a £100 prize as "the lightest steam engine in proportion to its power" at the 1868 Aeronautical Exhibition held in London's Crystal Palace.

PAVEL OSIPOVICH SUKHOI
1898–1975

Responsible for designing a range of notable Soviet aircraft, Pavel Sukhoi was born in Belorussia and studied at Moscow University and Moscow Higher Technical School. After the 1917 Russian Revolution he served in the Red Army, then joined the Central Aero- and Hydrodynamic Institute in 1920. There he worked as a junior designer under Andrei Tupolev before leading the team that designed the ANT-5 fighter. In 1932 he became head of Brigade 3 of the

Department of Experimental Aeroplane Construction, where he developed several ANT types. He then led design at the Factory for Experimental Construction from 1936. Sukhoi opened his own bureau in 1939, which developed a range of fighters and record-breaking long-distance aircraft. The bureau was closed by Stalin in 1949, but Sukhoi reopened it in 1953 when Stalin died. A line of successful jet fighters ensued, including the variable-geometry Su-24.

KURT WALDEMAR TANK
1898–1983

Aircraft designer Kurt Tank was born in Bromberg-Schwedenhöhe, Germany. He left school at 17 to fight in World War I, and after the war he worked at the Ohrenstein & Koppel locomotive works. He then studied electrical engineering at Berlin Technical High School, where he was a founder of the Akaflieg, the Berlin Academicals Flying Group, which designed, built, and flew gliders. In 1924 he joined Rohrbach as a designer, and learnt to fly the following year. At the end of 1929 he left to work with Willy Messerschmitt at BFW, but stayed for only 18 months before joining the Focke-Wulf Fluzeugbau in Bremen. There he was appointed technical director in 1933. Notable Tank designs included the Fw 200

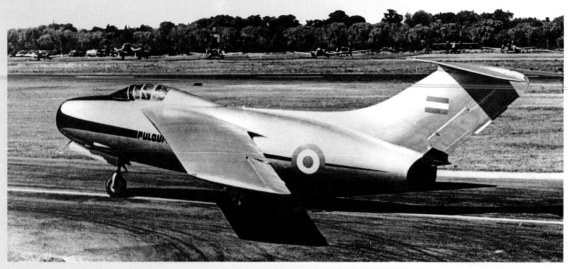

PULQÚI II JET FIGHTER DESIGNED BY KURT TANK

Condor and the Fw 190, one of the great fighters of World War II. By 1942 Tank was head of Focke-Wulf. Postwar he emigrated to Argentina, where he designed the Pulqúi II jet fighter, first flown in 1950. In the mid-1950s he went to India and led design of the Hindustan Aeronautics HF-24 Marut supersonic fighter.

JUAN TERRY TRIPPE
1899–1981

Juan Trippe, the founder of Pan Am, was born in New Jersey. He left Yale University in 1917 to become a bomber pilot in the US Navy, but returned there after World War I and graduated in 1922. After a number of forays into the airline business he became head of AVCO (Aviation Corporation of America), competing on the Key West–Havana route. He won an exclusive contract from the Cuban government to carry mail, and set up Pan American Airways (later Pan Am) as AVCO's operating subsidiary in 1927. He was Pan Am's president until 1968. The airline's rapid growth was largely due to Trippe's leadership and to his adroit business practices.

ANDREI NIKOLAYEVICH
TUPOLEV
1888–1972

Soviet designer Andrei Tupolev was born at Pustomanzov, near Kalinin, Russia. In 1908 he went to Moscow Higher Technical School, where he studied engineering under Nikolai Zhukovskii. In 1911 he was arrested for revolutionary activities, but he resumed his studies in 1914 and became an engineer at the Duks factory the following year. In 1918 he was a cofounder of the Central Aero- and Hydrodynamics Institute. He headed the 1922 state committee on metal aircraft construction, and in 1924 formed the Department of Aviation, Hydroaviation and Experimental Construction. In 1931 he was appointed chief engineer of the Chief Administration of the Aviation Industry. Arrested in 1937, during the Stalinist purges, Tupolev worked as a designer in "special prisons" until his release in 1943. From 1944 he managed the Soviet copy of the Boeing B-29, and after World War II his bureau produced a long line of military and civil aircraft that continues today.

ALFRED VICTOR VERVILLE
1890–1970

In 1914, after seeing a Curtiss pilot give a daredevil display, Detroit-born French-Canadian "Fred" Verville left the Hudson Motor Company and joined Curtiss at Hammondsport, New York. There he contributed to early designs including the famous Jenny trainer. Returning to Detroit, he worked for the Fisher Body Co., but after the US entered World War I he was loaned to the US Air Service Engineering Division at McCook Field, Ohio, as a designer. The Bureau of Aircraft Production then assigned him to the Lockhart Mission, which was sent to France to study Allied fighter programs. Impressed by the work of SPAD designer Louis Béchereau, Verville returned to McCook Field and designed the VCP (Verville Chasse Plane), from which evolved the VCP-R racer, winner of the 1920 Pulitzer Race. In 1922 he followed up with the R-3 monoplane, an aircraft with a low, cantilever wing and retractable undercarriage, which won the 1924 Pulitzer Race. In 1925 the Buhl-Verville Aircraft Co. was formed, producing the Airster and CW-3 commercial aircraft. In 1927 he set up Verville Aircraft, but this company went into liquidation in 1932. Verville then returned to government service.

GABRIEL AND CHARLES
VOISIN
1880–1973, 1888–1912

An architectural student turned engineer, Gabriel Voisin was born in Lyons, France. His involvement in aviation began with an interest in kites. In 1904, inspired by a lecture given by French pioneer Ferdnand Ferber, who had experimented with crude Wright-type gliders, he learned to fly. He piloted French aviation patron Ernest Archdeacon's glider and then became the engineer in Archdeacon's firm, Le Syndicat de l'Aéronautique. In 1906, with his brother Charles, he set up Les Frères Voisin at Billancourt, Paris, the world's first true airplane factory. The first powered Voisin biplanes were cumbersome box-kites with no lateral control, but the company went on to develop a family of pusher biplanes. After Charles Voisin died in a car crash in 1912, Gabriel set up Aéroplanes G. Voisin. During World War I the company delivered some 10,000 aircraft, mostly sturdy but primitive pushers. The company's last aircraft was the BN4 night bomber of 1920; Gabriel Voisin then concentrated on automobile manufacture.

RICHARD TRAVIS WHITCOMB
1921–

Born in Illinois, American inventor Richard Whitcomb graduated from Worcester Polytechnic Institute, Massachusetts, in 1943. He was then engaged by NACA (National Advisory Committee for Aeronautics) to work at its Langley Laboratory on problems relating to supersonic flight. In 1954 he was awarded the Collier Trophy for his discovery and verification of the area rule of aerodynamic flow, which enabled Convair's suitably modified F-102 to become the US Air Force's first operational supersonic aircraft. He followed this in the 1960s with the development of NASA's supercritical wing, which enabled airplanes to cruise faster at a given power setting or to carry a heavier payload at the same speed. He also invented the eponymous winglets that, attached

A PAN AM BOEING 727 (SEE JUAN TRIPPE)

to wingtips, unwind the main wingtip vortices, decreasing the drag of the wing by about 14 percent.

AIR COMMODORE SIR FRANK WHITTLE
1907–1996

Frank Whittle was a pioneer of jet aircraft. Born in Coventry, England, he joined the RAF (Royal Air Force) as an apprentice in 1923. In 1926 he won a cadetship at the RAF College, Cranwell, and trained as a pilot. Two years later he wrote a thesis on the possibilities of rocket propulsion and gas-turbine-driven propellers. Whittle pursued his flying career in the RAF, eventually becoming a test pilot, while in his spare time he conceived a gas-turbine engine that produced a propelling jet. Although Britain's Air Ministry rejected the idea, he patented it. In 1934 Whittle went to Cambridge University, taking a first in Mechanical Sciences, and in 1936 the Power Jets company was set up to develop his engine. Despite financial difficulties and official indifference the WU engine was run in 1939. It was fitted to the Gloster E.28/39, which became the first jet airplane to fly in Britain when it made its maiden flight at Cranwell on May 15, 1941. Whittle left Power Jets when it was nationalized in 1944, and in 1946 became technical adviser on engine production and design at the Air Ministry. He left the RAF in 1948, and emigrated to the US in 1976.

ORVILLE WRIGHT (IN WRIGHT BIPLANE) AND WILBUR WRIGHT

WILBUR AND ORVILLE WRIGHT
1867–1912, 1871–1948

Inspired by the pioneering flights of Otto Lilienthal, the Wright brothers, who were bicycle makers, embarked on aviation experiments in 1899. Working as designers, scientists, engineers, builders, and test pilots, they carried out glider flights and windtunnel tests to develop the world's first truly successful airplane, the *Flyer*. It made the first powered, sustained, and controlled flights at Kitty Hawk, North Carolina, on December 17, 1903. They improved upon this design with the *Flyer III*, built in 1905, which was the first powered airplane that was fully controllable and capable of making repeated prolonged flights. Wilbur's flight demonstrations in France in 1908 revolutionized European aviation, but marketing the invention proved even harder than creating it, and lengthy courtroom patent battles interfered with further developments. After Wilbur died of typhoid in 1912, Orville sold his manufacturing and patent rights in 1915, but went on advising and experimenting.

ALEKSANDR SERGEYEVICH YAKOVLEV
1906–1989

The noted Soviet aircraft designer Aleksandr Yakovlev first built his own gliders in the early 1920s, and then got a job in the Zhukovskii Air Force Academy workshops. In 1931 he joined Nikolai Polikarpov's bureau as an engineering supervisor, but was expelled when one of his designs suffered flutter and had to be force-landed. In 1934 Yakovlev set up his own bureau. During World War II the factory built 37,000 fighters, and in 1940 Yakovlev was made Deputy Commissar of the Aviation Industry. Postwar his bureau produced a wide variety of aircraft, including tactical jets, helicopters, and jet transports.

GENERAL CHARLES ELWOOD YEAGER
1923–

One of the world's great test pilots, "Chuck" Yeager was born in West Virginia, graduated from high school in 1941, and enlisted in the US Army Air Corps. Assigned to the Eighth Air Force's 357th Fighter Group, flying P-51 Mustangs, he claimed 13 German aircraft from 1943, including an Me 262 jet. In 1945 he became a test pilot at Wright Field, Dayton, Ohio; and two years later he volunteered for the supersonic aircraft project at Rogers Dry Lake, California, flying the rocket-propelled air-launched Bell XS-1. On October 14, 1947, Yeager became the first person to exceed the speed of sound, attaining Mach 1.06. In 1953 he set another speed record in the X1-A, reaching Mach 2.44. His subsequent Air Force career included commanding a school for training astronauts and leading 405th Fighter Wing in the Vietnam War. Yeager retired from the Air Force, as a general, in 1975. He became a flight consultant at Edwards Air Force Base.

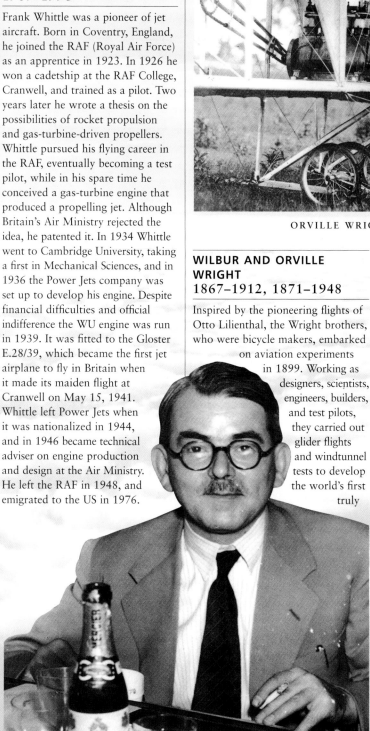

AIR COMMODORE SIR FRANK WHITTLE

GLOSSARY

AERODYNAMICS The physics of the movement of objects through air or gas.

AERONAUT The pilot of a lighter-than-air aircraft, especially a balloon.

AFTERBURNER Device that injects additional fuel into the specially designed jetpipe of a turbojet to provide augmented thrust. Also called reheat.

AILERON Control surface attached to wingtip trailing edge (or between wingtips on some early biplanes) to provide control in roll around the aircraft's longitudinal axis.

AIR BRAKE A surface that can be extended into the airflow under manual or hydraulic power to reduce an airplane's forward speed.

AIRFOIL A solid body such as a wing, rotor, or propeller, designed to move through air and produce lift or thrust.

AIRFOIL SECTION The outline of a section through an airfoil.

AIRFRAME The assembled structure of an aircraft, including system components forming an integral part of structure and influencing strength, integrity, or shape.

ALCLAD Trade name of rust-resistant aluminum/duralumin alloy.

ALLIES The nations united against the German and Austro-Hungarian forces in World War I, and against the Axis forces in World War II.

ALL-MOVING TAIL PLANE A variable-incidence tail plane that serves as the primary control surface in pitch; an alternative to separate elevators.

ALTIMETER Instrument for measuring an aircraft's altitude.

AMPHIBIAN An aircraft capable of operating from land and water, and of transferring from one to the other.

AMRAAM Advanced medium-range air-to-air missile.

ANGLE OF ATTACK The angle at which a wing meets the local undisturbed airflow. Not to be confused with angle of incidence.

ANGLE OF INCIDENCE The fore-and-aft angle at which a wing or tailplane is attached to the fuselage, in relation to the aircraft's horizontal axis. Not to be confused with angle of attack.

ANHEDRAL The downward slope of a wing or tail plane from root to tip.

ARRESTER HOOK A strong hook attached to some land-based and all carrier-based combat airplanes to engage an arrester wire and thus shorten the landing run.

ARTIFICIAL HORIZON See **GYRO HORIZON.**

ASPECT RATIO The ratio of the span of a wing divided by its mean chord. A high-aspect-ratio wing is long and narrow; a low-aspect-ratio wing is short and deep.

ASTRODOME A transparent dome in an airplane fuselage through which a navigator can navigate by the stars, using a sextant.

ATTITUDE An aircraft's flying position at a given time.

AUTOGYRO A rotorcraft propelled by a horizontal thrust system such as a propeller and lifted by an unpowered rotor free to spin under the action of the air flowing through its disc from below.

AUTOMATIC PILOT/AUTOPILOT Airborne electronic system that automatically stabilizes an aircraft about its three axes, restores it to its original flightpath after a disturbance, and, in its modern form, can be preset to make the aircraft follow a desired trajectory.

AUXILIARY POWER UNIT (APU) An airborne power generation system, other than propulsion or lift engines, used to generate power for airborne systems such as electrics, hydraulics, air conditioning, avionics, main-engine starting, pressurization, etc.

AVIATOR Pre-World War II term for the pilot of a heavier-than-air aircraft.

BALLONET Flexible gas-tight compartment inside an airship envelope that can be inflated to compensate for variation in the volume of lifting gas to maintain pressure.

BIPLANE A fixed-wing aircraft having two superimposed wings.

BOOMS Braced structural members extending forward or aft of wings to carry foreplanes or tail surfaces.

BOWDEN CABLE A form of control with a cable sliding within an outer sleeve.

BOXKITE A form of kite having two or more superimposed surfaces joined by side curtains; also applied to early biplanes with a similar structure.

BOX SPAR A spar consisting of front and rear webs connected by upper and lower booms or sheets, forming a strong box structure to which the wing leading- and trailing-edge structures are attached.

BUBBLE CANOPY A clear, teardrop-shaped cockpit cover. Its minimal framework allows the pilot an unobscured all-around view.

BULKHEAD A major transverse structural member in a fuselage or hull; used to separate compartments or pressurized and nonpressurized sections, for example.

BUNGEE Elastic cord comprising many strands of rubber in a braided sheath.

CABANE A structure of braced struts used to support a load above a fuselage or wing.

CAMBER The curvature of an airfoil section.

CAMERA GUN A gun-shaped camera used to train pilots and gunners in weaponry and air combat.

CANARD A tail-first airplane, or the foreplane attached to such a machine.

CANTILEVER WING A wing whose structure does not require external struts or bracing wires; rigidly attached at one end only.

CAR A passenger- or engine-carrying nacelle suspended beneath an airship.

CARBURETOR An apparatus for mixing air with fuel vapor for combustion in internal combustion engines.

CASTOR, TO To swivel around the supporting leg (i.e., of a wheel).

CENTERBODY Streamlined body in the center of circular or semicircular supersonic intake.

CENTER-SECTION Central portion of fuselage or wing structure.

CHAFF Radar-reflective particulate matter sized to match known or suspected wavelengths being used by the enemy, and released by an aircraft to confuse detection systems.

CHINE 1. On a flying-boat hull or seaplane float, the extreme side member running approximately parallel to the keel. 2. In supersonic aircraft, a sharp edge forming the lateral extremity of the fuselage and merging into the wing.

CLEAN Term used to denote the lack of drag-inducing attachments or projections on a wing or fuselage.

COAXIAL Rotating around a common axis.

COCKPIT A space occupied by a pilot and/or other occupants, such as a gunner. Usually restricted to smaller aircraft.

COLLECTOR RING A tubular ring connecting the exhaust ports of the cylinders of a radial engine. Used to collect the exhaust gases and channel them into a common exhaust pipe.

COMPRESSOR The assembly at the front of a turbojet engine that compresses the air entering the intake.

CONSTANT-SPEED PROPELLER A propeller having a control system, incorporating a governor and feedback, that automatically adjusts the pitch to maintain a selected number of revolutions per minute.

CONTRAROTATING Rotating in opposite directions on the same axis.

CONVERTIPLANE An aircraft capable of flight in at least two distinct modes, for example vertical flight supported by a rotor and forward flight supported by a wing, and of converting between the two.

COUNTER-ROTATING Rotating in opposite directions on separate axes in the same plane.

COWL(ING) Covering over engine or other parts of aircraft, often using hinged or removable panels.

CRESCENT WING Wing planform shape resembling waxing or waning moon.

CROSS-BRACED Held rigid by wires anchored at the extremities of the structural frame and crossing at its center.

DEICING Means of removing ice accretions from the leading edges of flying surfaces. Mechanical system uses inflatable rubber "boots," which can be pulsated, causing the ice to crack and break away. There are also thermal and chemical systems.

DELTA WING A wing having a triangular planform; after the similarly shaped Greek character.

DIHEDRAL Angling of wings or tail planes upward from root to tip when seen from head on, to achieve lateral stability.

DIRECT-INJECTION ENGINE An engine in which the fuel is injected directly into each cylinder.

DIRIGIBLE An airship. Originally a dirigible balloon, the word meaning capable of being guided.

DOPE Liquid, usually having a nitro-cellulose or cellulose-acetate base, applied to fabric to tauten it, strengthen it, and make it airtight.

DOUBLE-DELTA WING A delta wing having two angles of sweepback to its leading edge.

DOUBLE-SURFACED WING Wing having covering on upper and lower surfaces.

DRAG The retarding force acting on aircraft structure while in flight.

DRIFT INDICATOR An instrument indicating an aircraft's angle of drift, i.e., the lateral component of its motion due to crosswind.

DROOPING AILERONS Ailerons that droop when flaps are lowered, to increase lift but preserve lateral control.

DURALUMIN Wrought alloy of aluminum with small percentages of copper, magnesium, and manganese. Sometimes abbreviated to dural.

EFIS Electronic flight instrumentation system. Provides primary flight and navigation information on color cathode-ray tubes.

ELEVATOR Movable control surface to govern aircraft in pitch (i.e., up and down).

ELEVONS Wing control surfaces, especially on tailless aircraft, with functions of elevators and ailerons.

ENVELOPE In an airship, the vessel containing the lifting gas.

FAIRING A light superstructure used to streamline any projections or junctions in the airframe structure and thereby reduce drag. Anything thus covered is said to be "faired."

FENCE A vertical surface across the upper surface of a wing, from front to rear, to direct airflow over the wing.

FIBRELAM Trade name of a pre-cured composite sandwich material used for airliner floors and other areas of large commercial aircraft.

FILLET A fairing leading along a fuselage from fin or tailplane, or at the trailing edge of a wing root.

FIN A vertical or inclined airfoil, usually at the rear or on a wingtip, to increase directional stability.

FIREWALL A fire-resistant bulkhead employed behind an engine to present a barrier and prevent an engine fire from spreading into the airframe.

FLAME DAMPER Shroud or extension to an exhaust pipe to prevent visual detection at night.

FLAP Movable surface forming part of leading or trailing edge of an airfoil and able to hinge downward or move rearward on tracks to alter the wing's camber, cross-section, and area to enhance low-speed lift and drag and thereby reduce approach and landing speeds.

FLIGHTDECK The area occupied by the flight crew on a large aircraft.

FLOTATION BAGS Inflatable bags housed in an airframe or attached to it to enable it to float on water.

FLUTTER The dangerous high-frequency oscillation of a structure owing to the interaction of aerodynamic and aero-elastic forces. If allowed to develop it can tear an airframe apart.

FLY-BY-WIRE A flight control system that uses electrical signaling instead of mechanical control linkages.

FLYING BOAT An airplane with a watertight hull enabling it to operate from water.

FLYING WING An airplane consisting almost entirely of wing, with little or no fuselage.

FOREPLANE A horizontal airfoil mounted on the nose or forward fuselage of an airplane to improve takeoff and low-speed handling. It can be fixed or retractable, nonmoving, or adjustable, and can have slats, flaps, or elevators.

FORMER Light secondary structure added to the airframe before covering to improve its external shape.

FORWARD-LOOKING INFRARED (FLIR) Infrared vision enhancement and aiming system for low-light and night operations.

FUG BOOTS Fleece-lined leather thigh boots worn by World War I pilots, so-called because of the "fuggy" atmosphere that built up inside them.

FULLY FEATHERING PROPELLER A propeller with blades that can be turned with their edges facing into the line of flight in the event of engine failure, thereby reducing their drag to an absolute minimum and preventing the engine from suffering possible further damage owing to the propeller "windmilling."

FUSELAGE Main body of an airplane.

"G" Gravity.

GEODETICS Basketwork-like metal framework system devised by Dr. Barnes Wallis of Vickers that did not need a stress-bearing covering.

GILLS Adjustable hinged flaps at the rear of engine cowlings, used to control the flow of cooling air.

GLASS COCKPIT A cockpit featuring electronics displays using screens in place of traditional instruments.

GONDOLA The car of an airship.

GREAT CIRCLE DISTANCE Distance between two points on the Earth's surface, measured along a line whose plane passes through the Earth's center.

GROUND ANGLE The angle that the longitudinal axis of an airplane's fuselage makes with the ground when the machine is parked.

GULL WING A wing with pronounced dihedral from the root, changing to little dihedral or even anhedral to the tip.

GYRO HORIZON Primary cockpit flight instrument that indicates the aircraft's attitude in relation to the horizon ahead. Also called artificial horizon.

HANGARAGE 1. Housing of airplanes in hangars. 2. The fee charged for the provision of such facilities.

HEAD-UP DISPLAY (HUD) An electronic and optical system in which information concerning the aircraft's performance, attitude, and combat status is projected into the pilot's line of sight, thereby avoiding the need for him to look down into the cockpit.

HIGH WING Wing mounted high on the fuselage.

HORN A lever arm attached to a control surface, to which the control cables from the cockpit are attached.

HORN BALANCE A balance area on a control surface, projecting forward of the surface's hinge line.

HOT-AIR ENGINE A piston engine that runs on hot air.

HULL 1. The fuselage of a flying boat. 2. the gas-carrying body of a rigid airship.

HYPERSONIC Having a Mach number exceeding 5.

INLINE ENGINE An engine in which the cylinders are in either a single fore-and-aft row or in several such rows, as in a V or W configuration.

INTEGRAL FUEL TANK Tank included as part of aircraft structure, and coated with sealant.

INTERMESHING ROTORS Helicopter rotors having independent axes but whose planes of rotation overlap. They therefore have to be mechanically synchronized to prevent the blades from colliding.

INTERPLANE STRUTS In a multiplane, the external vertical struts linking the main spars of each wing unit.

INTERRUPTER GEAR A device that interrupts the firing of a rigidly mounted machine gun to prevent it from firing as the aircraft's propeller blade passes in front of the gun barrel.

JET Commonly used to describe a turbojet-propelled aircraft, but applicable to an aircraft propelled by any form of reaction-propulsion unit, such as a rocket.

KREUGER FLAP Leading-edge flap forming part of wing undersurface, hinged to swing down and forward to give a bluff leading edge to a high-speed wing.

LANDING LIGHT A light, usually in the aircraft nose or wing leading edge, used to assist the pilot when landing at night or in poor visibility.

LANDPLANE An airplane designed or equipped to operate from land.

LATERAL CONTROL Control in the rolling plane.

LEADING EDGE The front edge of a wing, rotor, tail, or other airfoil.

LEADING-EDGE ROOT EXTENSIONS (LERX) Extensions projecting forward of the wing root leading edge, which increase a combat airplane's maneuver lift and improve handling.

LIQUID-COOLED Generally, any engine cooled by liquid, including water, but usually restricted to cooling by a water/alcohol or glycol mix.

LONGERON Principal longitudinal structural members of a fuselage or hull structure.

LOOK-DOWN SHOOT-DOWN The ability to destroy low-level hostile aircraft from high altitude against land or clutter background that interferes with many radars.

LOW WING A wing mounted low on the fuselage.

MACH NUMBER The ratio of true air-speed to the speed of sound in the surrounding air. This varies with altitude, density, and temperature.

MEDIUM BOMBER A category of bomber that was unfortunately defined quite differently by different air forces, either using bomb load or range as the criterion. The type was so developed during 1920–50 that the numerical values became meaningless.

MID-WING A wing mounted midway up the fuselage.

MONOCOQUE A three-dimensional structure, such as a fuselage, with all its strength in its skin and the underlying frames and stringers, and with no interior structure or bracing.

MONOPLANE A fixed-wing airplane having a single wing.

MOVING-MAP DISPLAY A cockpit display in which a topographical, radar, infrared, target, or other form of map is projected optically on screen with the aircraft's position fixed.

NACA National Advisory Committee for Aeronautics (US; renamed NASA in 1958).

NACA COWLING A special drag-reducing annular cowling for radial engines.

NACELLE A fabric, wood, or metal enclosure, usually streamlined, that contains crew, engines, gun positions, or any other drag-inducing parts of an aircraft.

NASA National Aeronautics and Space Administration (US).

NATO North Atlantic Treaty Organization.

NEGATIVE "G" Subject to acceleration in the vertical plane in the opposite-to-normal sense usually imposed by gravity, or "g," as in an aircraft in sustained inverted flight, or in a pushover from a steep climb into a steep dive. The wings are bent downward.

NON-RIGID An airship in which the envelope's shape is maintained by the pressure of the gas and air ballonets within.

ORNITHOPTER An airplane propelled by wings that flap or oscillate.

PARASOL WING A wing held above the fuselage on a pylon and/or struts.

PARK-BENCH AILERONS Ailerons mounted on struts above the wing trailing edge; so called because they resemble small park benches.

PITCH 1. Movement in the vertical plane. 2. The distance a propeller would advance through the air in one revolution.

PITOT PROBE A probe on the nose or wing of an airplane that incorporates a pitot tube.

PITOT TUBE An open-ended tube facing into the line of flight which records airspeed on a cockpit instrument by means of air pressure.

PLANFORM An object's shape when viewed from above.

PLANING BOTTOM Faired smooth surface on the underside of a float or flying-boat hull.

PLEXIGLAS Trade name of a family of acrylic-acid resin plastics, especially transparent, used for blown moldings such as cockpit panels and canopies and gun blisters.

POD Nacelle to house an engine, either on the fuselage or on the wing of an airplane; hence "podded."

PORT 1. The left side of an aircraft, looking forward from the rear. 2. An opening or aperture, such as those provided for guns.

POWERED CONTROLS A system in which aircraft controls are power-operated.

POWERPLANT The permanently installed prime movers responsible for propulsion, including propellers and drive mechanism where applicable.

PRATT TRUSS A system of cross-bracing used in civil engineering, notably in bridges, which was applied to gliders by Octave Chanute and became the standard bracing system for biplanes and multiplanes.

PRESSURE SUIT An all-enclosing garment worn by pilots and aircrew of unpressurized aircraft, which keeps the wearer's body under suitable pressure to maintain the bodily functions.

PRESSURIZED Applied to a cabin or cockpit in which the pressure is maintained at or above a selected level regardless of how high the aircraft might ascend, for the comfort of its occupants.

PROPELLER A rotating hub with helical radial blades which provide thrust to drive an aircraft.

PUSHER An airplane in which the propeller is positioned at the rear of the fuselage or nacelle(s), and therefore is seen to "push" the aircraft rather than "pull" it. See also **TRACTOR**.

PYLON 1. A pyramidal structure of two or more posts used as an anchorage for bracing or control wires. 2. A faired strut used to carry engines or weapons externally.

RADIAL ENGINE An engine in which the cylinders are disposed radially around the crankshaft.

RADOME Aerodynamic protective covering over radar or other antenna, usually with mechanical scanning. Contraction of "radar dome."

RAFWIRES Streamline-section flying wires of drawn steel, used to brace biplane and multiplane wings. Developed by Royal Aircraft Factory in England, hence the name.

RAMJET A jet engine similar to a turbojet but with no mechanical compressor or turbine. Compression of the incoming air is accomplished entirely by the vehicle's speed through the atmosphere. The vehicle cannot start from rest, but needs to be accelerated to the ramjet's operating speed by other means, such as assisted takeoff aboard another aircraft.

RAMP DOORS Movable doors inside the engine intake ramps of jet aircraft that control air flow to the engines.

REACTION CONTROL VALVES Small nozzles at the extremities of VTOL aircraft, supplied with hot, high-pressure air bled from a jet engine and used to control the aircraft's attitude and trajectory at low airspeeds.

REFLECTOR GUNSIGHT A gunsight in which the aiming marks are projected as bright points on a glass screen through which the pilot or other weapon-aimer views the target.

REVERSIBLE-PITCH PROPELLER A propeller whose pitch can be reversed once on the ground to help slow an aircraft down.

RIB Primary structural member of a wing, usually running fore and aft and joining leading and trailing edges, and maintaining correct wing profile.

RIGID An airship in which an internal framework gives the hull its shape.

ROTARY ENGINE An internal combustion engine in which the crankshaft remains stationary and the crankcase and cylinders rotate about it, thereby cooling themselves and doing away with the need for a flywheel and water radiator. The propeller is attached or geared to the crankcase.

ROTATING-WING AIRCRAFT Aircraft in which lift is derived from rotary lifting surfaces.

ROTOR A system of rotating airfoils ("blades") whose primary purpose is to provide lift.

ROTORCRAFT A generic term for all aircraft that derive their lift from rotors, including helicopters and autogyros.

ROTORHEAD The hub of a rotorcraft, to which rotor blades are attached.

RUDDER Movable control surface effecting control in yaw.

RUDDERVATORS Movable flight-control surfaces combining the functions of rudders and elevators.

SAILWING 1. A limp fabric wing, used on some hang gliders, that adopts a lifting profile only in a suitable relative wind. 2. An aircraft having such a wing.

SCARFF RING Standard British cockpit mounting for hand-aimed machine gun(s), 1916–30s, using ring-mounted elevating U-shaped frame. Named after its inventor.

SCOUT World War I term for a single-seat fighter aircraft.

SEAPLANE An airplane with floats to enable it to operate from water.

SEMI-MONOCOQUE A structure in which the loads are carried partly by the frame and stringers and partly by the skin.

SEMI-RIGID An airship with a rigid keel to help maintain the envelope's form and support the loads.

SERVO-TAB An auxiliary movable surface added to a control surface to reduce the pilot workload required to move the main surface.

SHIPBOARD FIGHTER A fighter airplane operated from a capital ship; either an aircraft carrier, or a cruiser or other vessel with a catapult launching system.

SHOULDER WING A wing mounted between the high- and mid-wing positions on the fuselage.

SHP Shaft horsepower. Horsepower measured at an engine output shaft.

SIDCOT SUIT A warm one-piece flying suit invented by British pilot Sidney Cotton, later widely adopted.

SIDE-CURTAINS Fixed vertical surfaces between the wings of early biplanes and triplanes.

SIDESLIP The tendency for an airplane to slide inward in an incorrectly balanced turn. Also a deliberately induced maneuver to lose height without a significant loss of airspeed.

SINGLE-SURFACE WING A wing having only one surface, either above or below ribs. Generally, most wings are double-surfaced.

SINGLE-ACTING Control surfaces that operate in one direction only. Single-acting ailerons move only downward when the pilot operates the control, and are otherwise held level by the airflow over the wing or by bungee or spring restrainers.

SINK RATE The rate of descent of an unpowered lifting body, especially a glider, in free fall.

SKIDS Runners used instead of, or in addition to, wheels in an airplane undercarriage. Sometimes added to wingtips to prevent damage.

SLAT Movable portion of a wing leading edge that is recessed against the main surface in cruising flight, but lifts away at high angles of attack either by aerodynamic force or hydraulically, moving forward and down to create a slot between itself and the wing. Can also be a fixed portion of an airfoil.

SLOT A gap between the main airfoil and a slat, through which the airflow accelerates at high angles of attack to prevent breakaway and loss of lift.

SPAR(S) Main spanwise structural member(s) of a wing, which carries the ribs and other secondary structural components to which the covering is attached.

SPATS Teardrop-shaped streamline fairings around the wheels of non-retractable undercarriages.

SPINNER A domed, streamlined fairing covering the hub of a propeller.

SPLITTER PLATE A plate positioned between the fuselage and the air intake of a jet engine, to smooth the flow of air into the engine.

SPOILERS Hinged or otherwise movable surfaces on the upper rear surface of a wing which reduce lift when open and usually increase drag.

SPONSON 1. A projection from the hull of a flying boat, taking the form of a short, buoyant, thick wing to provide stability on the water instead of wingtip floats. 2. The external fuselage undercarriage housings on transport aircraft.

SPREADER BAR A rigid member linking main undercarriage legs.

STAGGER Relative positioning of multiplane wings, so that the upper wings are either further forward or behind the lower wings (called "backstagger," or "negative stagger," in the latter case).

STALL The point at which the airflow breaks away from an airfoil and lift is lost due to the change in the angle of the surface to the airflow. Can also happen to compressor blades of a gas turbine engine, causing loss of thrust.

STARBOARD The right side of an aircraft, looking forward from the rear.

STRAKE A long, streamlined shallow surface aligned with the airflow.

STRESSED SKIN A form of semi-monocoque structure in which the skin (usually metal) makes an important contribution to the stiffness of the structure and bears a significant proportion of the flight loads.

STRUT 1. A rigid bracing member forming part of a structural framework; between the longerons in a fuselage, for example, or between the upper and lower wings of a biplane. 2. The leg of an undercarriage.

SUPERCHARGER A compressor driven by a crankshaft, step-up gears, or an exhaust turbine, which increases the density of the air or mixture supplied to the cylinders of an internal combustion engine, especially to boost power at high altitudes.

SUPERCRITICAL WING A special NASA-designed wing that enables airplanes to cruise faster at a given power setting or to carry a heavier payload at the same speed.

SUPERSONIC Faster than the speed of sound.

SURGE Gross breakdown of airflow through the compressor of a turbojet engine.

SWEEP, SWEEPBACK The angling back of an airplane's flying surfaces from root to tip.

SWING-WING Applied to an airplane whose wing may be pivoted fore and aft in flight to vary the angle of sweep according to velocity. Also called variable-geometry.

TACHOMETER Instrument for indicating speed of a rotating shaft, such as an engine crankshaft.

TAIL PLANE A fixed auxiliary surface at rear of fuselage providing stability in pitch, and to which the elevators are often attached.

TESTBED A mounting, either on the ground or on an aircraft itself, upon which an item is mounted for testing. An aircraft so used is sometimes referred to as a "flying testbed."

TETRAHEDRAL KITES Kites composed of numerous small tetrahedrons (triangular pyramids) with two sides acting as lifting surfaces and the others open, joined in a variety of combinations.

THERMAL-IMAGING A system that measures and electronically records thermal radiation emitted by objects, usually on infrared wavelengths, and produces displays or printouts.

THRUST VECTORING Controlling an airplane's trajectory by rotating the axis of the propulsive thrust, usually by means of swivelling nozzles on a jet engine.

TILT-ROTOR An aircraft with rotors that allow it to take off vertically and may then be swiveled through 90 degrees to power it in forward flight.

TORQUE Twisting movement caused by a rotating unit such as a propeller, rotor, or rotary engine.

TORSION BOX The main structural basis of a wing, consisting of the front and rear spars joined by strong upper and lower skins.

TOW MISSILE Tube-launched, optically tracked, wire-guided missile.

TRACK The distance between the wheels or trucks of the main undercarriage, measured center-to-center.

TRACK-WHILE-SCAN A radar/electronic countermeasures scan produced by two simultaneous scans in two planes, usually one vertically and one horizontally, allowing a target to be accurately tracked.

TRACTOR An airplane in which the propeller is positioned at the front of the fuselage or nacelle(s), and is seen to work in "traction," pulling the aircraft along. Hence tractor engine. See also **PUSHER**.

TRAILING EDGE Rear edge of airfoil.

TRAINER Any aircraft used to train pilots or aircrew.

TRANSONIC In the region of transition from subsonic to supersonic flight.

TRIM TAB A small hinged portion in the trailing edge of a flight control surface whose setting is adjustable, used to hold the main surface in the desired neutral position for trimmed flight.

TRIPLANE An airplane having three superimposed wings.

TROUSERS Streamline fairings around the legs and wheels of nonretractable undercarriages.

TRUCK Undercarriage with two or more wheel pairs.

TURBOJET The simplest form of gas turbine. Comprising a compressor, combustion chamber, and turbine, the last taking off just sufficient energy to drive the compressor. Most of the energy remains in the gas, which is expelled at high velocity through a nozzle to propel the aircraft.

TURBOPROP A gas turbine engine with extra turbine power geared down to drive a propeller. Originally called a propeller-turbine.

TURBOSHAFT A gas turbine engine for delivering shaft power.

TWIN-BOOM Applied to an airplane with its tail surfaces carried on two booms projecting aft from the wings.

VARIABLE-GEOMETRY See **SWING-WING**.

VARIABLE-GEOMETRY INTAKE/INLET An intake/inlet for a jet engine, with ramps, doors, and other devices to control/regulate incoming air flow.

VECTORED THRUST Propulsive thrust whose axis can be rotated to control the aircraft's trajectory.

WARREN GIRDER A truss structure in which upper and lower spars are joined by symmetrical diagonal members arranged in a zig-zag pattern when seen from the front.

WIDEBODY Commercial transport aircraft with an internal cabin width sufficient for passenger seating to be divided into three multiseat ranks.

WINDTUNNEL A device in which a fluid such as air is driven through a duct to flow past an object under test to assess its aerodynamics or behavior.

WINGLETS Upturned wingtip or added auxiliary airfoils above and/or below a wingtip which increase the wing's efficiency in cruising flight by reducing the tip vortices and recovering the energy lost therein.

WING WARPING The lateral control of an airplane by torsion of the outer trailing edges of its wings, instead of by ailerons; the effect is the same.

WIRE-BRACED Applied to any structure which uses tensioned wire bracing to maintain its rigidity, such as a simple wooden-girder fuselage, a two-spar wing panel, or the superimposed wings of a biplane.

YAW Rotation of an aircraft around its vertical axis.

INDEX

Page numbers in *italics* refer to illustrations unaccompanied by text.

QR

S

ACKNOWLEDGMENTS

AUTHOR'S ACKNOWLEDGMENTS

I would like to thank the following for their assistance and cooperation in the preparation of this volume: Michael Oakey, Tony Harmsworth, and Lydia Matharu of *Aeroplane Monthly*; Michel Ledet of *Avions* Magazine; Bill Gunston; Kim Hearn of the *Flight* Collection; Alex Imrie; Carol Reed and Debra Warburton of *Flight International*; Richard Simpson of the RAF Museum; Alex Revell; and the staff of TPR Photographic Laboratories Ltd. Finally, and most importantly, I thank my copilot, Marilyn Bellidori, for her amazing and often sorely tested tolerance of my obsession with things aeronautical, and for her unhesitating assistance whenever things seemed to be entering into an irrecoverable flat spin.

Additional photography by Mark Hamilton, Dave King, Mike Dunning, Peter Chadwick, Peter Anderson, Martin Cameron, James Stevenson, and Dave Rudkin.

PUBLISHER'S ACKNOWLEDGMENTS

Dorling Kindersley would like to thank:
Peter Adams, Mary Lindsay, and Nicola Munro for editorial assistance; Emma Ashby, Christine Lacey, and Adam Powers for design assistance; Melanie Simmonds for picture library research; Tyrone O'Dea and Simon Pentelow for photography assistance; Christopher Gordon for administration; Hilary Bird for the index. Also, a special thanks to Philip Jarrett for access to his extensive library of photographs.

PICTURE CREDITS

The publishers would also like to thank the following for their help with photography:

Vern Blade and Robert Pepper at Holloman Air Force Base, New Mexico; Tracy Curtiss-Taylor at the Fighter Collection, Duxford Air Field; Steve Maxham, Director of the US Army Aviation Museum, Fort Rucker, Alabama; Katie McGuigan and Tom Coe at Qantas; Sean Penn and the staff at the Royal Air Force Museum, Hendon; Elly Sallingboe; Russell C. Sneddon and Dolly for all their help at the Air Force Armament Museum, Eglin Air Base, Fort Walton Beach, Florida; Mike Stapley; Chris Thornton at *Flight International* magazine.

Dorling Kindersley would also like to thank the following for their kind permission to reproduce their photographs:

a=above; *b*=below; *c*=center; *l*=left; *r*=right; *t*=top

Aviation Picture Library: Austin Brown 2*tr*, 31*cr*, 34*tr*, 39*b*, 40*br*, 41*br*, 42*cl*, 86*br*, 94*tr*, 94*cl*, 97*tr*, 97*bl*, 103*cra*, 103*bl*, 104*tr*, 104*cr*, 105*tr*, 105*c*, 108–9, 115*tr*, 118–19, 119*cb*, 122*b*, 123*bc*, 127*crb*, 127*t*, 130*cl*, 131*tl*, 131*cr*, 132*br*, 164*bl*, 164*bl*; John Stroud Collection 88*tr*; Stephen Piercey 101*c*, 101*br*; Derek Cattani 130–1*c*; **Aviation Images:** Mark Wagner 1, 17*tc*, 105*br*, 126*cl*, 127*br*, 137*cr*, 138*cl*; **Defence Picture Library:** 123*crb*; **Paolo Franzini:** 76*b*; **Imperial War Museum:** 39, 78; **Lockheed Martin:** 139*tr*; **Photo Link:** Mike Vines 59*tl*; **Popperfoto:** 54–5*t*; Reuters 124*tr*; **Quadrant Picture Library:** 140*tr*, 140–1, 141*tl*, 141*br*; NASA 141*cr*; **RAF Official © Crown Copyright Reserved:** 115*cl*, 122–3; **Skyscan:** Colin Smedley 118–19; Peter W Richardson 55*br*; **Society of British Aerospace Companies Ltd:** 120; **TRH Pictures:** 86–7, 112*t*; Northrop 133*cr*; Tim Senior 86*bl*, 132*bl*. Jacket: **Aviation Images Mark Wagner** (back below); © 1986 **Mark Meyer** (spine); **Dan Patterson** (front). All other photographs: Philip Jarrett.

FRONT JACKET IMAGE: NORTH AMERICAN MUSTANG F-6D, PHOTORECONNAISSANCE VERSION OF P-51D